Ninja Foodi

Cookbook For Beginners

1200

Days of Easy, Healthy, Step-by-Step Recipes For Your Ninja Foodi, an Experience For all Beginners and Advanced Users

Manjin Oil

CONTENTS

Beef, Pork & Lamb 28

Poultry 46

Vegan & Vegetable 78

Snacks, Appetizers & Sides 94

Desserts 109

INDEX 125

INTRODUCTION

YOU, READING THIS BOOK, ARE THE REASON I DO WHAT I DO. I WANT to transform the way you cook and make it easier for you to cook a delicious meal for you and your family. I want you to be proud to put dinner on the table!

You are the reason we develop thousands of foolproof recipes that will make you fall in love with cooking. We test every recipe so you have confidence when it is time to cook. Whether you are whipping up a quick breakfast so you can get the kids out the door and off to school, prepping a healthy and nutritious lunch so you can skip the café, or making a delicious dinner so the family can spend time together around the table—my team and I have you covered.

The Ninja Foodi combines the speed of a pressure cooker with the quick crisping action of an air fryer to give you TenderCrisp™ Technology. By harnessing pressurized steam to quickly cook and tenderize ingredients, then using the revolutionary crisping lid for a crispy finish, you can make quick, delicious meals from real food. Oh, and did I mention there is only one pot to clean?

Perhaps you have already experienced the revolution that is the Ninja Foodi Pressure Cooker.

Perhaps you are part of the Ninja Foodi Family on social media, sharing your creations and looking for more ways to use your Foodi Pressure Cooker and unlock its full potential.

Perhaps you just purchased a Ninja Foodi Pressure Cooker or received one as a gift and you're not sure where to start.

This book is for you! The Big Ninja Foodi Pressure Cooker Cookbook is the ultimate, official cookbook from the Ninja Test Kitchen, packed to the brim with our tips, tricks, and techniques for making the most of the pressure cooker that crisps.

Scale It Up, Scale It Down

All of the recipes throughout this cookbook were developed using the original Ninja Foodi Pressure Cooker, which has a 6.5-quart cooking pot. But never fear: Most of the recipes throughout the book will work with all of the Ninja Foodi models. Follow my recommendations for how to modify the recipes based on the Foodi you have.

Scale it up! If you have the Ninja Foodi Deluxe Pressure Cooker, you can easily modify the recipes throughout this book—plus you can scale the recipes up to feed more people! The Foodi Deluxe has an 8-quart cooking pot and the Deluxe Reversible Rack for two times the protein capacity. Note that some of the recipes may require a bit more cook time or an extra shake of the Cook & Crisp Basket. For best results, check progress throughout cooking, and shake the basket frequently. As a good rule of thumb, you can scale up Pressure recipes like soups, stews, and chilies by as much as 50 percent when using the Foodi Deluxe. You can also fit 50 percent more in the Cook & Crisp Basket.

Scale it down! The Ninja Foodi Compact Pressure Cooker is, as the name suggests, compact. So it is perfect for one to two people. Because of the smaller size, some recipes may require a bit less cook time or fewer shakes of the Cook & Crisp Basket. For best results, check progress throughout cooking. As a good rule of thumb, you can scale down Pressure recipes like soups, stews, and chilies by as much as 50 percent when using the Foodi Compact. And for recipes that call for the basket, you will fit about 50 percent fewer ingredients. Also note that the Foodi Compact Pressure Cooker does not come with a Reversible Rack, so you will need to make some 360 Meals in two steps. If you are following a recipe that calls for broiling, choose Air Crisp on the highest temperature setting instead.

Pressure Lid

Use the pressure lid to turn the Ninja Foodi into the ultimate pressure cooker, cooking and tenderizing food faster than you ever thought possible. Turn the valve from the seal to the vent position to steam your favorite fish and veggies or slow cook your favorite stew.

Crisping Lid

The crisping lid adapts the fan and temperature so that you can Air Crisp, Bake/Roast, Broil, and Dehydrate. Use the crisping lid after pressure cooking for the ultimate Tender Crisp meal or use it on its own for the ultimate Air Crisping experience. On some Ninja Foodi Pressure Cooker models, the crisping lid goes as low as 100°F so that you can dehydrate fruits, veggies, and meat for yummy snacks with no added sugars.

Cooking Pot

The Ninja Foodi's cooking pot was specifically designed with an extra wide diameter so that you can sauté vegetables and sear meat without crowding the pot. Go from searing and sautéing to pressure or slow cooking all in the same pot. Since it is covered in a ceramic coating, the cooking pot can handle whatever you want to cook in it. A word of caution: Be sure to use silicone or wooden utensils so as not to scratch the pot.

Cook & Crisp Basket

The Cook & Crisp Basket is designed to make sure that each bite comes out perfectly golden brown and crispy. Use the Cook & Crisp Basket to Air Crisp crunchy French fries and crispy chicken wings or to dehydrate mangos, apples, and beets. You can use the Cook & Crisp Basket when making TenderCrisp recipes, like finger-licking barbecue or a whole roasted chicken. Like the cooking pot, the Cook & Crisp Basket is ceramic coated for easy cleanup so be sure to use silicone or wooden utensils.

Reversible Rack

In the lower position, the Reversible Rack allows you to steam veggies and fish quickly and easily. In the higher position, you can broil steaks for a crisp crust or cheesy bread to perfectly golden brown, or you can cook a full meal—protein, starch, and a vegetable—in one pot.

FOODI PRESSURE COOKER FUNCTIONS

Now that you are acquainted with the Ninja Foodi Pressure Cooker and its parts, let's dive into the nine unique cooking functions and take a look at what you can use them to make.

Pressure

The Ninja Foodi is a far cry from your grandmother's pressure cooker, but the science behind it is the same—pressurized steam infuses moisture into ingredients and quickly cooks them from the inside out. Pressure cooking is ideal for tenderizing tough cuts of meat, quickly cooking rice, and everything in between. To get started, choose between low and high pressure, set the cook time, make sure the valve is in the SEAL position, and voila! Perfect for Carrot Cake Oats, Loaded Potato Soup, or Creamy Tuscan Chicken Pasta.

Steam

Steam is the perfect setting for cooking fresh veggies or fish. Simply add water to the cooking pot and place the Reversible Rack in the lower position. Place your food on top of the rack and secure the lid. If you are using the Ninja Foodi Compact Pressure Cooker, use the Cook & Crisp Basket instead of the Reversible Rack.

Slow Cook

Contrary to pressure cooking, which is used to quickly cook meats, soups, and stews, the slow cooking feature builds flavor by braising food low and slow. If you prefer the convenience of tossing your ingredients into a pot in the morning and coming home to a fully cooked meal, then slow cooking will be your go-to. The Ninja Foodi is equipped with both low and high slow cook settings. Check out this Slow Cooked Chicken in White Wine and Garlic or use your favorite slow cooker recipe.

Sear/Sauté

Use your Ninja Foodi just as you would your stove, alternating between low, medium low, medium, medium high, and high. Easily go from a gentle simmer to a screaming-hot sear. Use this function as a first step before pressure cooking or slow cooking to unlock more flavor from your aromatic ingredients like onions and garlic.

Air Crisp

Air Crisp is our version of air fry. With Air Crisp you can achieve that crispy, crunchy, golden brown texture we all crave—without all the fat and oil. Use this feature in conjunction with the Cook & Crisp Basket to cook your favorite frozen foods: French fries, onion rings, chicken nuggets, and more. Be sure to shake the basket at least once or twice to ensure the crispiest, most even results, and don't be afraid to sneak a peek under the crisping lid so that you can remove your food when it is crisped to your liking. Try the Ham, Egg, and Cheese Breakfast Pockets, Rosemary Hush Puppies, or Fried Oreos, all crisped to perfection!

Bake/Roast

The Ninja Foodi Pressure Cooker also works as a mini convection oven, cooking your favorite baked dishes and roasted meats in less time than your oven. Use the bake/roast function to make Curried Chickpea and Roasted Tomato Shakshuka or Italian Pasta Potpie.

Broil

Broil reaches the hottest temperature of all of the crisping lid settings. Use Broil to add a crispy, cheesy finish to baked pasta dishes or reverse sear your favorite steak for a restaurant-style crisp crust. With Broil, you are cooking your food directly under very high heat, so be sure to open the lid to sneak a peek frequently so that your food is crisped to your liking and not overdone. If you are using the Ninja Foodi Compact Pressure Cooker, it does not have Broil. Instead, choose Air Crisp on the highest temperature setting.

Dehydrate

Dehydrators can be expensive and take up space in the kitchen. These single-function appliances are usually relegated to the basement after a few uses, but if your Foodi Pressure Cooker has this feature, you can dehydrate fruits, vegetables, meats, herbs, and more without adding another appliance to your collection. Try making the Sweet Potato and Beetroot Chips for a healthy homemade snack.

Yogurt

Yogurt is the newest feature added to the Foodi™ Pressure Cooker. Now you can make homemade yogurt easily with just a few simple ingredients. No need for guesswork here. If you do not have the yogurt feature on your Foodi Pressure Cooker model, there are a number of hacks you can follow to make yogurt in the original Foodi Pressure Cooker

Breakfast

French Dip Sandwiches

Servings: 8
Cooking Time: 1 Hr 35 Min
Ingredients:

- 2 ½ pounds beef roast /1125g
- 2 tbsp olive oil /30ml
- 1 onion; chopped
- 4 garlic cloves; sliced
- ½ cup dry red wine /125ml
- 2 cups beef broth stock /500ml
- 1 tsp dried oregano /5g
- 16 slices Fontina cheese
- 8 split hoagie rolls

Directions:

1. Generously apply pepper and salt to the beef for seasoning. Warm oil on Sear/Sauté and brown the beef for 2 to 3 minutes per side. Set aside on a plate.
2. Add onions and cook for 3 minutes, until translucent. Mix in garlic and cook for one a minute until soft.
3. To the Foodi, add red wine to deglaze. Scrape the cooking surface to remove any browned sections of the food using a wooden spoon's flat edge; mix in beef broth and take back the juices and beef to your pressure cooker. Over the meat, scatter some oregano.
4. Seal the pressure lid, choose Pressure, set to High, and set the timer to 50 minutes; press Start. Release pressure naturally for around 10 minutes. Transfer the beef to a cutting board and slice.
5. Roll the sliced beef and add a topping of onions. Each sandwich should be topped with 2 slices fontina cheese.
6. Place the sandwiches in the pot, close the crisping lid and select Air Crisp. Adjust the temperature to 360°F or 183°C and the time to 3 minutes. Press Start. When cooking is complete, the cheese should be cheese melt.

Crustless Quiche

Servings: 2
Cooking Time: 40 Min
Ingredients:

- 4 eggs
- ¼ cup chopped kalamata olives /32.5g
- ¼ cup chopped onion /32.5g
- ½ cup milk /125ml
- ½ cup chopped tomatoes /65g
- 1 cup crumbled feta cheese /130g
- 1 tbsp chopped basil /15g
- 1 tbsp chopped oregano /15g
- 2 tbsp olive oil /30ml
- Salt and pepper to taste

Directions:

1. Brush a pie pan with the olive oil. Beat the eggs along with the milk, salt, and pepper. Stir in all of the remaining Ingredients.
2. Pour the egg mixture into the pan. Close the crisping lid and cook for 30 minutes on Air Crisp mode at 340 °F or 172°C. Leave to cool before serving.

Sausage & Egg Stuffed Peppers

Servings: 4
Cooking Time: 6 Hours
Ingredients:

- ½ lb. breakfast sausage
- 4 bell peppers
- ½ cup water
- 6 eggs
- ½ cup cheddar Jack cheese, grated
- 4 oz. green chilies, diced
- ¼ tsp salt
- 1/8 tsp pepper
- 2 tbsp. green onion, diced

Directions:

1. Set cooker to sauté on med-high heat.
2. Add sausage and cook, breaking up with spatula, until no longer pink. Transfer to a bowl and drain off the grease.
3. Cut the tops off the peppers and remove the seeds and ribs. Place in the cooking pot and pour the water around them.
4. In a medium bowl, whisk eggs until smooth. Stir in cheese, chilies, salt, and pepper until combined. Fill the peppers with the egg mixture.
5. Secure the lid and set to slow cooker function on high. Set the timer for 4 hours.
6. Casserole is done when the eggs are set, if not done when the timer goes off, cook another 1-2 hours. Garnish with green onions and serve.

Nutrition Info:

- Calories 364,Total Fat 22g,Total Carbs 15g,Protein 27g,Sodium 874mg.

Cinnamon Crumb Donuts

Servings: 6

Cooking Time: 10 Minutes

Ingredients:

- Butter flavored cooking spray
- ¼ cup Stevia, granulated
- 1 cup + 3 ½ tbsp. flour, divided
- ¼ tsp cinnamon
- ¼ cup butter, cut in cubes
- ½ cup Stevia brown sugar, packed
- ½ tsp salt
- 1 tsp baking powder
- ½ cup sour cream
- 2 ½ tbsp. butter, melted
- 1 egg, room temperature
- ½ cup Stevia confectioners' sugar
- ½ tbsp. milk
- ½ tsp vanilla

Directions:

1. Select air fryer function and heat cooker to 350°F. Spray a 6 mold donut pan with cooking spray.
2. In a small bowl, combine ¼ cup granulated Stevia, 3 ½ tablespoons flour, and ¼ teaspoon cinnamon.
3. With a pastry cutter, or fork, cut in the cold butter until mixture resembles coarse crumbs. Cover and chill until ready to use.
4. In a large bowl, stir together 1 cup flour, the Stevia brown sugar, salt, and baking powder.
5. In a separate bowl, whisk together sour cream, melted butter, and egg. Stir into dry ingredients just until combined.
6. Spoon dough into prepared pan. Sprinkle chilled crumb topping evenly over the tops.
7. Place the pan in the cooker and secure the tender-crisp lid. Cook 10-11 minutes or donuts pass the toothpick test. Cool in the pan 10 minutes then transfer to a wire rack.
8. In a small bowl, whisk together Stevia powdered sugar substitute, milk, and vanilla. Drizzle donuts with glaze and serve.

Nutrition Info:

- Calories 250,Total Fat 18g,Total Carbs 21g,Protein 4g,Sodium 366mg.

Maple Giant Pancake

Servings: 6

Cooking Time: 30 Min

Ingredients:

- 3 cups flour /390g
- ⅓ cup olive oil /84ml
- ⅓ cup sparkling water /84ml
- ¾ cup sugar /98g
- 5 eggs
- 2 tbsp maple syrup /30ml
- ⅓ tsp salt /1.67g
- 1 ½ tsp baking soda /7.5g
- A dollop of whipped cream to serve

Directions:

1. Start by pouring the flour, sugar, eggs, olive oil, sparkling water, salt, and baking soda into a food processor and blend until smooth. Pour the batter into the Ninja Foodi and let it sit in there for 15 minutes. Close the lid and secure the pressure valve.
2. Select the Pressure mode on Low pressure for 10 minutes. Press Start/Stop.
3. Once the timer goes off, press Start/Stop, quick-release the pressure valve to let out any steam and open the lid.
4. Gently run a spatula around the pancake to let loose any sticking. Once ready, slide the pancake onto a serving plate and drizzle with maple syrup. Top with the whipped cream to serve

Double Berry Dutch Baby

Servings: 6

Cooking Time: 25 Minutes

Ingredients:

- 1 tbsp. butter, melted
- 2 eggs
- ½ cup skim milk
- 1 tsp vanilla
- ½ cup flour
- ¼ tsp cinnamon
- 1/8 tsp salt
- 2 tbsp. sugar
- 2 tsp cornstarch
- 1/3 cup water
- ½ cup strawberries, sliced
- ½ cup blueberries

Directions:

1. Select air fryer function and heat cooker to 400°F. Pour melted butter in an 8-inch round pan and swirl to coat bottom.
2. In a medium bowl, whisk together eggs, milk, and vanilla.
3. In a small bowl, combine flour, cinnamon, and salt. Whisk into egg mixture until smooth. Pour into prepared pan.
4. Place in the cooker and secure the tender-crisp lid. Bake 18-20 minutes until golden brown and set in the center.
5. Remove pancake from the cooker and set to sauté on medium heat.
6. Add sugar, cornstarch, and water to the cooking pot and stir until smooth.
7. Stir in both berries and bring to a boil. Cook about 5 minutes, stirring frequently, until berries have softened and mixture has thickened. Spoon into pancake, slice and serve.

Nutrition Info:

- Calories 125,Total Fat 4g,Total Carbs 17g,Protein 4g,Sodium 100mg.

Baked Eggs In Mushrooms

Servings: 4

Cooking Time: 15 Minutes

Ingredients:

- 4 large Portobello mushrooms, rinse & remove stems
- 4 eggs
- 1 ½ tbsp. extra virgin olive oil
- ½ tsp salt, divided
- ½ tsp black pepper, divided

Directions:

1. Set to bake function on 450°F.
2. Rub mushrooms with oil and half the salt and pepper. Place on a small baking sheet, cap side down.
3. Carefully crack an egg into each mushroom and season with remaining salt and pepper.
4. Place sheet in the cooker and secure the tender-crisp lid. Bake 12-15 minutes, or until whites of the eggs are cooked through. Serve immediately.

Nutrition Info:

- Calories 122,Total Fat 10g,Total Carbs 2g,Protein 7g,Sodium 363mg.

Cinnamon Bun Oatmeal

Servings:6

Cooking Time: 26 Minutes

Ingredients:

- 1 cup gluten-free steel-cut oats
- 3½ cups water
- ¼ teaspoon sea salt
- 1 teaspoon nutmeg
- 2 teaspoons cinnamon, divided
- ½ cup all-purpose flour
- ½ cup rolled oats
- ⅔ cup brown sugar
- ⅓ cup cold unsalted butter, cut into pieces
- 2 tablespoons granulated sugar
- ¾ cup raisins
- 2 ounces cream cheese, at room temperature
- 2 tablespoons confectioners' sugar
- 1 teaspoon whole milk

Directions:

1. Place the steel-cut oats, water, salt, nutmeg, and 1 teaspoon of cinnamon in the pot. Assemble pressure lid, making sure the pressure release valve is in the SEAL position.
2. Select PRESSURE and set to HI. Set time to 11 minutes. Select START/STOP to begin.
3. In a medium bowl, combine the flour, rolled oats, brown sugar, butter, remaining 1 teaspoon of cinnamon, and granulated sugar until a crumble forms.
4. When pressure cooking is complete, allow pressure to naturally release for 5 minutes. After 5 minutes, quick release any remaining pressure by moving the pressure release valve to the VENT position. Carefully remove lid when unit has finished releasing pressure.
5. Stir the raisins into the oatmeal. Cover and let sit 5 minutes to thicken.
6. Evenly spread the crumble topping over the oatmeal. Close crisping lid.
7. Select AIR CRISP, set temperature to 400°F, and set time to 10 minutes. Select START/STOP to begin.
8. In a small bowl, whisk together the cream cheese, confectioners' sugar, and milk. Add more milk or sugar, as needed, to reach your desired consistency.
9. When crumble topping is browned, cooking is complete. Open lid and serve the oatmeal in individual bowls topped with a swirl of cream cheese topping.

Nutrition Info:

- Calories: 454,Total Fat: 16g,Sodium: 117mg,Carbohydrates: 73g,Protein: 8g.

Strawberry Muffins

Servings: 12

Cooking Time: 25 Minutes

Ingredients:

- 1 ¼ cups white whole wheat flour
- 1/3 cup oats
- ½ tsp cinnamon
- ½ tsp baking soda
- 1 tsp baking powder
- ½ tsp salt
- 2/3 cup Stevia
- 3/4 cup Greek yogurt
- 1 egg
- 1/3 cup coconut oil, melted
- 1 cup strawberries, chopped

Directions:

1. Set to air fryer function on 375°F. Line 2 6-cup muffin tins with paper liners.
2. In a large bowl, combine dry ingredients.
3. In a medium bowl, whisk together yogurt, egg, and oil. Stir in berries and add to dry ingredients. Stir just until combined.
4. Fill prepared muffin tins 2/3 full. Place pans, one at a time, in the cooker and secure the tender-crisp lid. Bake 25 minutes, or until muffins pass the toothpick test. Repeat.
5. Let cool in the pan 10 minutes, then transfer to wire rack to cool completely.

Nutrition Info:

- Calories 131,Total Fat 8g,Total Carbs 27g,Protein 4g,Sodium 163mg.

Breakfast Souffles

Servings: 6
Cooking Time: 20 Minutes
Ingredients:

- 1 lb. thick cut bacon, chopped
- 8 oz. pork sausage links, chopped
- Nonstick cooking spray
- 5 eggs, separated
- 1/3 cup heavy cream
- ½ cup cheddar cheese, grated
- ½ tsp salt
- ¼ tsp thyme

Directions:

1. Set cooker to sauté function on med-high.
2. Add the bacon and cook until almost crisp. Transfer to a paper towel lined plate.
3. Add the sausage and cook until done. Transfer to a separate paper towel lined plate.
4. Drain off fat and set cooker to air fry setting. Preheat to 350°F.
5. Spray 6 ramekins with cooking spray.
6. In a large bowl, beat egg whites until stiff peaks form.
7. In a medium bowl, whisk the yolks, cream, cheese, and seasonings together. Stir in the meats and mix well.
8. Gently fold the yolk mixture into the egg whites. Spoon the mixture into the prepared ramekins.
9. Place the rack in the cooker and place the ramekins on top. Secure the tender-crisp lid and bake 20 minutes, or until the soufflés have puffed up. Serve immediately.

Nutrition Info:

- Calories 565,Total Fat 50g,Total Carbs 2g,Protein 24g,Sodium 1134mg.

Peaches & Brown Sugar Oatmeal

Servings: 8
Cooking Time: 8 Hours
Ingredients:

- Nonstick cooking spray
- 2 cups steel cut oats
- 8 cups water
- 1 tsp cinnamon
- ½ cup brown sugar
- 1 tsp vanilla
- 1 cup peaches, cubed

Directions:

1. Spray cooking pot with cooking spray.
2. Add the oats, water, cinnamon, sugar, and vanilla to the pot, stir to combine.
3. Secure the lid and select slow cooker function on low. Set timer for 8 hours.
4. Stir in peaches and serve.

Nutrition Info:

- Calories 231,Total Fat 3g,Total Carbs 46g,Protein 7g,Sodium 7mg.

Quinoa Protein Bake

Servings: 4
Cooking Time: 30 Minutes
Ingredients:

- Nonstick cooking spray
- 1 cup white quinoa, cooked
- 3 egg whites, lightly beaten
- ½ tsp salt
- ¼ cup red bell pepper, chopped
- ¼ cup spinach, chopped
- ½ cup mozzarella cheese, grated

Directions:

1. Spray the cooking pot with cooking spray.
2. In a large bowl, combine all ingredients thoroughly. Pour into pot.
3. Add the tender-crisp lid and select air fry on 350°F. Bake 25-30 minutes until lightly browned on top and eggs are completely set.
4. Let cool a few minutes before serving.

Nutrition Info:

- Calories 191,Total Fat 3g,Total Carbs 28g,Protein 13g,Sodium 441mg.

Sweet Potatoes & Fried Eggs

Servings: 4
Cooking Time:x
Ingredients:

- 2 large sweet potatoes, peel & cut in 1-inch cubes
- 1 tbsp. apple cider vinegar
- 1 ½ tsp salt, divided
- 3 tbsp. extra virgin olive oil, divided
- 1 cup red onion, chopped
- 1 cup green bell pepper, chopped
- 2 cloves garlic, diced fine
- ½ tsp pepper
- ½ tsp cumin
- ½ tsp paprika
- 4 eggs
- 2 tbsp. cilantro, chopped

Directions:

1. Add potatoes, vinegar, and one teaspoon salt to the cooking pot. Add just enough water to cover potatoes.
2. Secure the lid and set to pressure cooking on high. Set timer for 5 minutes. When timer goes off, use quick release to remove the lid. Potatoes should be slightly soft. Drain and set aside.
3. Add one tablespoon oil to the cooking pot and set to sauté function on medium heat. When oil is hot, add onions and bell pepper, cook about 5 minutes or until tender. Add

garlic and cook 1 minute more. Transfer to a bowl and keep warm.

4. Add remaining oil to the pot. When hot, add potatoes, remaining salt, pepper, cumin, and paprika and decrease heat to medium-low. Cook, stirring occasionally, until potatoes are nicely browned on the outside and tender.
5. Stir in the onion mixture and create 4 "wells" in the mixture. Crack an egg in each one.
6. Secure the tender-crisp lid and set to air fryer function on 350°F. Bake until whites are set. Sprinkle with cilantro and serve.

Nutrition Info:

- Calories 239,Total Fat 15g,Total Carbs 18g,Protein 8g,Sodium 982mg.

Cranberry Vanilla Oatmeal

Servings: 6

Cooking Time: 8 Hours

Ingredients:

- Nonstick cooking spray
- 1 ½ cups steel cut oats
- 4 ½ cups water
- 1 ½ tsp cinnamon
- 2 ½ tsp vanilla
- 1 ½ cups cranberries, dried

Directions:

1. Spray the cooking pot with cooking spray.
2. Add the oats, water, cinnamon, and vanilla and stir to combine.
3. Secure the lid and set to slow cooker on low heat. Set timer for 8 hours.
4. When timer goes off stir in cranberries and serve.

Nutrition Info:

- Calories 250,Total Fat 3g,Total Carbs 51g,Protein 7g,Sodium 2mg.

Sweet Potato Hash And Eggs

Servings:6

Cooking Time: 35 Minutes

Ingredients:

- 3 pounds sweet potatoes, diced
- 2 cups water
- 2 tablespoons unsalted butter
- 1 yellow onion, diced
- 3 garlic cloves, minced
- 1 red bell pepper, diced
- 1 green bell pepper, diced
- 1 bunch scallions, sliced
- 2 teaspoons smoked paprika
- Kosher salt
- Freshly ground black pepper
- 6 brown eggs

Directions:

1. Place the sweet potatoes in the Cook & Crisp Basket. Pour the water in pot and insert basket. Assemble the pressure lid, making sure the pressure release valve is in the SEAL position.
2. Select PRESSURE and set to HI. Set timer for 2 minutes. Select START/STOP to begin.
3. When pressure cooking is complete, quick release the pressure by turning the pressure release valve to the VENT position. Carefully remove lid when the unit has finished releasing pressure.
4. Remove basket with sweet potatoes. Pour out any remaining water from the pot.
5. Select SEAR/SAUTÉ and set to MED. Let preheat for 3 minutes.
6. Add the butter, onion, garlic, and bell peppers. Cook for 5 minutes. Add the sweet potatoes, scallions, and paprika and stir. Cook for 5 minutes, stirring occasionally. Season with salt and pepper. Crack the eggs on top of the hash, equally spaced apart. Close crisping lid.
7. Select AIR CRISP, set temperature to 325°F, and set time to 10 minutes. Select START/STOP to begin.
8. When cooking is complete, open lid and serve immediately.

Nutrition Info:

- Calories: 376,Total Fat: 13g,Sodium: 304mg,Carbohydrates: 51g,Protein: 16g.

Pepperoni Omelets

Servings: 4

Cooking Time: 5 Minutes

Ingredients:

- 4 tablespoons heavy cream
- 15 pepperoni slices
- 2 tablespoons butter
- Black pepper and salt to taste
- 6 whole eggs

Directions:

1. Take a suitable and whisk in eggs, cream, pepperoni slices, salt, and pepper.
2. Set your Ninja Foodi to "Sauté" mode and add butter and egg mix.
3. Sauté for 3 minutes, flip.
4. Lock and secure the Ninja Foodi's lid and Air Crisp for 2 minutes at 350 °F.
5. Transfer to a serving plate and enjoy.

Nutrition Info:

- Calories: 141; Fat: 11g; Carbohydrates: 0.6g; Protein: 9g

Bacon And Gruyère Egg Bites

Servings:6

Cooking Time: 26 Minutes

Ingredients:

- 5 slices bacon, cut into ½-inch pieces
- 5 eggs
- 1 teaspoon kosher salt
- ¼ cup sour cream
- 1 cup shredded Gruyère cheese, divided
- Cooking spray
- 1 cup water
- 1 teaspoon chopped parsley, for garnish

Directions:

1. Select SEAR/SAUTÉ and set temperature to HI. Select START/STOP and let preheat for 5 minutes.
2. Add the bacon and cook, stirring frequently, about 5 minutes, or until the fat is rendered and bacon starts to brown. Transfer the bacon to a paper towel-lined plate to drain. Wipe the pot clean of any remaining fat.
3. In a medium bowl, whisk together the eggs, salt, and sour cream until well combined. Fold in ¾ cup of cheese and the bacon.
4. Spray egg molds or Ninja Silicone Mold with the cooking spray. Ladle the egg mixture into each mold, filling them halfway.
5. Pour the water in the pot. Carefully place the egg molds in the pot. Assemble pressure lid, making sure the pressure release valve is in the SEAL position.
6. Select PRESSURE and set to LO. Set time to 10 minutes. Select START/STOP to begin.
7. When pressure cooking is complete, natural release the pressure for 6 minutes, then quick release the remaining pressure by moving the pressure release valve to the VENT position.
8. Carefully remove the lid. Using mitts or a towel, carefully remove egg molds. Top with the remaining ¼ cup of cheese, then place the mold back into the pot. Close the crisping lid.
9. Select AIR CRISP, set temperature to 390°F, and set time to 5 minutes. Select START/STOP to begin.
10. Once cooking is complete, carefully remove the egg molds and set aside to cool for 5 minutes. Using a spoon, carefully remove the egg bites from the molds. Top with chopped parsley and serve immediately.

Nutrition Info:

- Calories: 230,Total Fat: 18g,Sodium: 557mg,Carbohydrates: 2g,Protein: 16g.

Soft-boiled Eggs

Servings: 4

Cooking Time: 15 Min

Ingredients:

- 4 large eggs
- 1 cups water /250ml
- Salt and ground black pepper, to taste.

Directions:

1. To the pressure cooker pot, add water and place a reversible rack. Carefully place eggs on it. Seal the pressure lid, choose Pressure, set to High, and set the timer to 3 minutes. Press Start.
2. When cooking is complete, do a quick pressure release. Allow cooling completely in an ice bath. Peel the eggs and season with salt and pepper before serving.

Sweet Potato, Sausage, And Rosemary Quiche

Servings:6

Cooking Time: 38 Minutes

Ingredients:

- 6 eggs
- ¼ cup sour cream
- ½ pound ground Italian sausage
- 1 tablespoon fresh rosemary, chopped
- 2 medium sweet potatoes, cut into ½-inch cubes
- 2 teaspoons kosher salt
- ½ teaspoon freshly ground black pepper
- 1 store-bought refrigerated pie crust

Directions:

1. In a medium bowl, whisk together the eggs and sour cream until well combined. Set aside.
2. Select SEAR/SAUTÉ and set to HI. Select START/STOP to begin. Let preheat for 5 minutes.
3. Add the sausage and rosemary and cook, stirring frequently, for about 5 minutes. Add the sweet potatoes, salt, and pepper and cook, stirring frequently, for about 5 minutes. Transfer this mixture to a bowl.
4. Place the pie crust in the pan, using your fingers to gently push onto the bottom and sides of the pan. Place pan with pie crust on the Reversible Rack, making sure it is in the lower position. Place rack with pan in pot. Close crisping lid.
5. Select BAKE/ROAST, set temperature to 400°F, and set time to 8 minutes. Select START/STOP to begin.
6. Stir the sausage and sweet potatoes in to the egg mixture.
7. When cooking is complete, open lid and pour the egg mixture into the browned crust. Close crisping lid.
8. Select BAKE/ROAST, set temperature to 360°F, and set time to 15 minutes. Select START/STOP to begin.
9. When cooking is complete, carefully remove pan from pot. Let cool for 10 minutes before removing from pan.

Nutrition Info:

- Calories: 344,Total Fat: 22g,Sodium: 743mg,Carbohydrates: 22g,Protein: 14g.

Ricotta Raspberry Breakfast Cake

Servings: 12
Cooking Time: 40 Minutes

Ingredients:

- Nonstick cooking spray
- 1 ¼ cups oat flour
- ½ tsp xanthan gum
- ¼ cup cornstarch
- ¼ tsp baking soda
- 1 ½ tsp baking powder
- ½ tsp salt
- ½ cup sugar
- 4 tbsp. butter, unsalted, soft
- 1 cup ricotta cheese, room temperature
- 3 eggs, room temperature, beaten
- 1 tsp vanilla
- 1 cup fresh raspberries

Directions:

1. Set to bake function on 350°F. Lightly spray an 8-inch round baking pan with cooking spray.
2. In a large bowl, combine dry ingredients.
3. Make a well in the center and add butter, ricotta, eggs, and vanilla and mix just until combined.
4. Gently fold in half the berries, being careful not to crush them.
5. Pour batter into prepared pan and sprinkle remaining berries on the top. Add the tender-crisp lid and bake 40 minutes, or until a light brown and only a few moist crumbs show on a toothpick when inserted in the center.
6. Let cool in the pan 10 minutes then transfer to a wire rack to cool completely before serving.

Nutrition Info:

- Calories 170,Total Fat 8g,Total Carbs 20g,Protein 6g,Sodium 164mg.

Bacon & Egg Poppers

Servings: 6
Cooking Time: 25 Minutes

Ingredients:

- 12 slices bacon
- 4 jalapeno peppers
- 3 oz. cream cheese, soft
- 8 eggs
- ½ tsp garlic powder
- ½ tsp onion powder
- Salt & pepper, to taste
- Nonstick cooking spray
- ½ cup cheddar cheese, grated

Directions:

1. Select air fryer function and heat cooker to 375°F.
2. Heat a skillet over med-high heat and cook bacon until almost crisp but still pliable. Remove to paper towels to drain and reserve bacon fat for later.
3. Remove the seeds from 3 of the jalapenos and chop them. With the remaining jalapeno, slice into rings.
4. In a large bowl, beat together cream cheese, 1 tablespoon bacon fat, chopped jalapenos, eggs, and seasonings.
5. Spray 2 6-cup muffin tins with cooking spray. Place one slice bacon around the edges of each cup.
6. Pour egg mixture into cups, filling ¾ full then top with cheddar cheese and a jalapeno ring.
7. Place muffin pan, one at a time, in the cooker, secure the tender-crisp lid and bake 20-25 minutes, or until eggs are cooked. Repeat with other pan and serve immediately.

Nutrition Info:

- Calories 399,Total Fat 34g,Total Carbs 3g,Protein 19g,Sodium 666mg.

Paprika Hard-boiled Eggs

Servings: 3
Cooking Time: 25 Min

Ingredients:

- 6 eggs
- 1 cup water /250ml
- 1 tsp sweet paprika /5g
- Salt and ground black pepper, to taste

Directions:

1. In the Foodi, add water and place a reversible rack on top. Lay your eggs on the rack. Seal the pressure lid, choose Pressure, set to High, and set the timer to 5 minutes. Press Start.
2. Once ready, do a natural release for 10 minutes. Transfer the eggs to ice cold water to cool completely. When cooled, peel and slice. Season with salt and pepper. Sprinkle with sweet paprika before serving.

Grilled Broccoli

Servings: 4
Cooking Time: 10 Minutes.

Ingredients:

- 2 heads broccoli, cut into florets
- 4 tablespoons soy sauce
- 2 tablespoons canola oil
- 4 tablespoons balsamic vinegar
- 2 teaspoons choc zero maple syrup
- Sesame seeds, to garnish
- Red pepper flakes, to garnish

Directions:

1. In a mixing bowl, add the soy sauce, balsamic vinegar, oil, and maple syrup. Whisk well and add the broccoli; toss well.
2. Take Ninja Foodi Grill, set it over your kitchen platform, and open the Ninja Foodi's lid.

3. Set the grill grate and close the Ninja Foodi's lid.
4. Press "GRILL" and select the "MAX" grill function. Adjust the timer to 10 minutes and then press the "Start/Stop" button to initiate preheating.
5. After you hear a beep, open the Ninja Foodi's lid.
6. Set the broccoli over the grill grate.
7. Close the Ninja Foodi's lid and allow it to cook until the timer reads zero.
8. Divide into serving plates.
9. Serve warm with red pepper flakes and sesame seeds on top.

Nutrition Info:

- Calories: 141; Fat: 7g; Carbohydrates: 14g; Protein: 4.5g

Peanut Butter Banana Baked Oatmeal

Servings: 8
Cooking Time: 20 Minutes

Ingredients:

- Nonstick cooking spray
- 1 ½ cups oats
- 1/3 cup sugar
- ¾ cup almond milk, unsweetened
- 2 tbsp. coconut oil, melted
- 1 egg
- ½ cup peanut butter, no sugar added
- 1 tsp baking powder
- 1 tsp vanilla
- 1 banana, sliced

Directions:

1. Select bake function and heat to 350°F. Spray an 8-inch baking pan with cooking spray.
2. In a large bowl, combine all ingredients, except bananas, and mix until thoroughly combined. Pour into prepared pan in an even layer.
3. Layer the banana slices on the top and place in the cooker. Secure the tender-crisp lid and bake 20 minutes or until edges start to brown.
4. Carefully remove the pan from the cooker and let cool 10 minutes before slicing and serving.

Nutrition Info:

- Calories 304,Total Fat 13g,Total Carbs 39g,Protein 11g,Sodium 118mg.

Hearty Breakfast Skillet

Servings: 4
Cooking Time: 35 Minutes

Ingredients:

- ¼ cup walnuts
- 2 tbsp. olive oil
- ½ cup onion, chopped
- 4 cups Brussel sprouts, halved
- 2 cups baby Bella mushrooms, chopped
- ¼ tsp salt
- ¼ tsp pepper
- 1 clove garlic, diced fine
- 3 tbsp. chicken broth, low sodium
- 4 eggs
- ¼ cup parmesan cheese, grated

Directions:

1. Set to sauté on medium heat. Add walnuts and cook, stirring frequently, 3-5 minutes or until golden brown. Transfer to small bowl to cool.
2. Add oil and let it get hot. Once oil is hot, add onions and Brussel sprouts and cook 5 minutes, stirring occasionally.
3. Stir in mushrooms, salt, and pepper and cook 10-12 minutes until vegetables are tender. Add garlic and cook 1 minute more.
4. Pour in broth and cook until liquid has evaporated, about 3 minutes.
5. Make 4 "well" in vegetable mixture and crack an egg in each. Add tender-crisp lid and set to air fryer function on 350°F. Bake 8-10 minutes, or until whites are cooked through.
6. Chop the walnut and sprinkle over top with parmesan cheese and serve.

Nutrition Info:

- Calories 261,Total Fat 18g,Total Carbs 14g,Protein 13g,Sodium 399mg.

Deviled Eggs

Servings: 6
Cooking Time: 20 Min

Ingredients:

- 10 large eggs
- ¼ cup cream cheese /32.5ml
- ¼ cup mayonnaise /62.5ml
- 1 cup water /250ml
- ¼ tsp chili powder /1.25g
- salt and ground black pepper to taste

Directions:

1. Add water to the Foodi's pot. Insert the eggs into the steamer basket; place into the pot. Seal the pressure lid, choose Pressure, set to High, and set the timer to 5 minutes. Press Start.When ready, release the pressure quickly.
2. Drop eggs into an ice bath to cool for 5 minutes. Press Start. Peel eggs and halve them.
3. Transfer yolks to a bowl and use a fork to mash; stir in cream cheese, and mayonnaise. Add pepper and salt for seasoning. Ladle yolk mixture into egg white halves.

Almond Quinoa Porridge

Servings: 6
Cooking Time: 1 Minute
Ingredients:

- 1¼ cups water
- 1 cup almond milk
- 1½ cups uncooked quinoa, rinsed
- 1 tablespoon choc zero maple syrup
- 1 cinnamon stick
- Pinch of salt

Directions:

1. In the Ninja Foodi's insert, add all ingredients and stir to combine well.
2. Close the Ninja Foodi's lid with the pressure lid and place the pressure valve in the "Seal" position.
3. Select "Pressure" mode and set it to "High" for 1 minute.
4. Press the "Start/Stop" button to initiate cooking.
5. Now turn the pressure valve to "Vent" and do a "Quick" release.
6. Open the Ninja Foodi's lid, and with a fork, fluff the quinoa.
7. Serve warm.

Nutrition Info:

- Calories: 186; Fat: 2.6 g; Carbohydrates: 4.8 g; Protein: 6 g

Spinach And Gruyère Cheese Quiche

Servings:6
Cooking Time: 20 Minutes
Ingredients:

- 8 eggs
- ½ cup milk
- 1 teaspoon sea salt
- 1 teaspoon freshly ground black pepper
- 1 cup shredded Gruyère cheese
- 1 tablespoon extra-virgin olive oil
- 1 yellow onion, chopped
- 2 garlic cloves, minced
- 2 cups fresh spinach
- 1 refrigerated piecrust, at room temperature

Directions:

1. Select SEAR/SAUTÉ and set to HI. Select START/STOP to begin. Allow the pot to preheat for 5 minutes.
2. In a large mixing bowl, whisk together the eggs, milk, salt, and pepper. Stir in the Gruyère cheese.
3. Put the oil, onion, and garlic in the preheated pot and stir occasionally for 5 minutes. Add the spinach and cook sauté another 5 minutes.
4. Pour the egg mixture over the vegetables and gently stir for 1 minute (this will allow the egg mixture to temper well and ensure that it cooks evenly under the crust).
5. Lay the piecrust evenly on top of the filling mixture, folding over the edges if necessary. Make a small cut in the center of the piecrust so that steam can escape during baking.
6. Close the crisping lid. Select BROIL and set the time to 10 minutes. Select START/STOP to begin. Check the crust after 5 minutes to check for desired crispness.
7. When cooking is complete, remove the pot and place it on a heat-resistant surface. Let the quiche rest for 5 to 10 minutes before serving.

Nutrition Info:

- Calories: 303,Total Fat: 21g,Sodium: 584mg,Carbohydrates: 16g,Protein: 14g.

Banana Coconut Loaf

Servings: 8
Cooking Time: 35 Minutes
Ingredients:

- Nonstick cooking spray
- 1 ¼ cup whole wheat flour
- ½ cup coconut flakes, unsweetened
- 2 tsp baking powder
- ½ tsp baking soda
- ½ tsp salt
- 1 cup banana, mashed
- ¼ cup coconut oil, melted
- 2 tbsp. honey

Directions:

1. Select the bake function on heat cooker to 350°F. Spray an 8-inch loaf pan with cooking spray.
2. In a large bowl, combine flour, coconut, baking powder, baking soda, and salt.
3. In a separate bowl, combine banana, oil, and honey. Add to dry ingredients and mix well. Spread batter in prepared pan.
4. Secure the tender-crisp lid and bake 30-35 minutes or until loaf passes the toothpick test.
5. Remove pan from the cooker and let cool 10 minutes. Invert loaf to a wire rack and cool completely before slicing.

Nutrition Info:

- Calories 201,Total Fat 11g,Total Carbs 26g,Protein 3g,Sodium 349mg.

Baked Eggs & Kale

Servings: 4
Cooking Time: 25 Minutes
Ingredients:

- 1 tbsp. olive oil
- 6 cups kale, remove stems & chop
- 2 cloves garlic, diced fine
- ¼ cup ricotta cheese, fat free
- ¼ cup feta, fat free, crumbled
- 4 eggs
- 1/3 cup grape tomatoes, halved

- ¼ tsp pepper
- ½ tsp salt

Directions:

1. Add oil to the cooking pot and select sauté on medium heat.
2. Add the kale and garlic and cook until kale is wilted, about 2-3 minutes.
3. In a small bowl, combine ricotta and feta cheeses.
4. Make 4 small indents in the kale mixture and crack an egg into each one.
5. Drop the cheese mixture by tablespoons around the eggs.
6. Top with tomatoes, pepper, and salt. Secure the tender-crisp lid, set to air fryer function at 350°F and bake 20-25 minutes or until egg whites are cooked through. Serve immediately.

Nutrition Info:

- Calories 154,Total Fat 12g,Total Carbs 7g,Protein 7g,Sodium 410mg.

Mediterranean Quiche

Servings: 6
Cooking Time: 45 Minutes

Ingredients:

- Nonstick cooking spray
- 2 cups potatoes, grated
- ¾ cup feta cheese, fat free, crumbled
- 1 tbsp. olive oil
- 1 cup grape tomatoes, halved
- 3 cups baby spinach
- 2 eggs
- 2 egg whites
- ¼ cup skim milk
- ½ tsp salt
- ¼ tsp pepper

Directions:

1. Select bake function and heat to 375°F. Spray an 8-inch round pan with cooking spray.
2. Press the potatoes on the bottom and up sides of the prepared pan. Place in the cooker. Secure the tender-crisp lid and bake 10 minutes.
3. Remove pan from the cooker and sprinkle half the feta cheese over the bottom of the crust.
4. Set cooker to sauté function on medium heat. Add the oil and heat until hot.
5. Add the tomatoes and spinach and cook until spinach has wilted, about 2-3 minutes. Place over the feta cheese.
6. In a medium bowl, whisk together eggs, milk, salt, and pepper. Pour over spinach mixture and top with remaining feta cheese.
7. Place the pan back in the cooking pot and secure the tender-crisp lid. Set temperature to 375°F and bake 30 minutes or until eggs are completely set and starting to brown. Let cool 10 minutes before serving.

Nutrition Info:

- Calories 145,Total Fat 8g,Total Carbs 12g,Protein 7g,Sodium 346mg.

Sweet Bread Pudding

Servings: 3
Cooking Time: 45 Min

Ingredients:

- 8 slices of bread
- 2 eggs
- ¼ cup sugar /32.5g
- ¼ cup honey /62.5ml
- 1 cup milk /250ml
- ½ cup buttermilk /125ml
- 4 tbsp raisins /60g
- 2 tbsp chopped hazelnuts /30g
- 2 tbsp butter, softened /30g
- ½ tsp vanilla extract /2.5ml
- Cinnamon for garnish

Directions:

1. Beat the eggs along with the buttermilk, honey, milk, vanilla, sugar, and butter. Stir in raisins and hazelnuts. Cut the bread into cubes and place it in a bowl.
2. Pour the milk mixture over the bread. Let soak for about 10 minutes. Close the crisping lid and cook the bread pudding for 25 minutes on Roast mode. Leave the dessert to cool for 5 minutes, then invert onto a plate and sprinkle with cinnamon to serve.

Omelets In The Jar

Servings: 5
Cooking Time: 8 Minutes

Ingredients:

- 10 eggs
- 1/3 cup heavy cream
- 2/3 cup of shredded cheese
- 1 green pepper, chopped
- 1 ham steak, chopped
- 1/2 lb. bacon, cooked and chopped
- 5 mason jars or other jars
- 1 cup of water

Directions:

1. Grease the mason jars with canola spray.
2. Whisk 2 eggs with 1 tbsp cream in a bowl then pour it into a jar.
3. Add 1 tbsp of ham, green peppers, and cheese to the same jar.
4. Repeat the same steps to fill remaining jars.
5. Pour 1 cup water in the Ninja Food pot and place trivet over it.
6. Set all the mason jars over the trivet.
7. Secure the Ninja Foodi lid and turn its pressure handle to 'Closed' position.

8. Select Pressure mode for 8 minutes at 350 °F.
9. Once done, release the steam naturally then remove the lid.
10. Drizzle bacon and cheese over each jar.
11. Serve fresh.

Nutrition Info:

- Calories 111; Total Fat 8.3 g; Total Carbs 1.9 g; Protein 7.4 g

Pumpkin Steel Cut Oatmeal

Servings: 4
Cooking Time: 25 Min

Ingredients:

- ½ cup pumpkin seeds, toasted /65g
- 1 cup pumpkin puree /250ml
- 2 cups steel cut oats /260g
- 3 cups water /750ml
- 1 tbsp butter /15g
- 3 tbsp maple syrup /45ml
- ¼ tsp cinnamon /1.25g
- ½ tsp salt /2.5g

Directions:

1. Melt butter on Sear/Sauté. Add in cinnamon, oats, salt, pumpkin puree and water. Seal the pressure lid, choose Pressure, set to High, and set the timer to 10 minutes; press Start. When cooking is complete, do a quick release.
2. Open the lid and stir in maple syrup and top with toasted pumpkin seeds to serve.

Ham, Egg, And Cheese Breakfast Pockets

Servings:4
Cooking Time: 29 Minutes

Ingredients:

- 5 large eggs, divided
- 1 tablespoon extra-virgin olive oil
- Sea salt
- Freshly ground black pepper
- 1 tube refrigerated crescent rolls
- 4 ounces thinly sliced ham
- 1 cup shredded Cheddar cheese
- Cooking spray

Directions:

1. Select SEAR/SAUTÉ and set to MD:HI. Select START/STOP and let preheat for 5 minutes.
2. Lightly whisk 4 eggs in a medium bowl.
3. Once unit has preheated, add the oil and beaten eggs. Season with salt and pepper. Whisk the eggs until they just begin to set, cooking until soft and translucent, 3 to 5 minutes. Remove the eggs from the pot and set aside.
4. In a small bowl, whisk the remaining egg.
5. Remove the crescent rolls from the tube and divide them into 4 rectangles. Gently roll out each rectangle until it is 6-by-4 inches. Top one half of each rectangle with ham, cheese, and scrambled eggs, leaving about a ½-inch border.
6. Brush the edges of the filled dough with water. Fold over the rectangle and press firmly to seal. Brush the top of each pocket with the egg.
7. Place Cook & Crisp Basket in pot. Coat 2 pastries well on both sides with cooking spray and arrange them in the basket in a single layer. Close crisping lid.
8. Select AIR CRISP, set temperature to 375°F, and set time to 12 minutes. Select START/STOP to begin.
9. After 6 minutes, open lid, remove basket, and use silicone-tipped tongs to flip the breakfast pockets. Lower basket back into pot and close lid to continue cooking, until golden brown.
10. When cooking is complete, check for your desired crispiness. Place the pockets on a wire rack to cool. Repeat steps 7, 8, and 9 with the remaining 2 pastries.

Nutrition Info:

- Calories: 501,Total Fat: 34g,Sodium: 1131mg,Carbohydrates: 24g,Protein: 24g.

Cinnamon Sugar Donuts

Servings:4
Cooking Time: 10 Minutes

Ingredients:

- ⅔ cup all-purpose flour, plus additional for dusting
- 3 tablespoons granulated sugar, divided
- ½ teaspoon baking powder
- ¼ teaspoon, plus ½ tablespoon cinnamon
- ¼ teaspoon sea salt
- 2 tablespoons cold unsalted butter, cut into small pieces
- ¼ cup plus 1½ tablespoons whole milk
- Cooking spray

Directions:

1. In a medium bowl, mix together the flour, 1 tablespoon of sugar, baking powder, ¼ teaspoon of cinnamon, and salt.
2. Use a pastry cutter or two forks to cut in the butter, breaking it up into little pieces until the mixture resembles coarse cornmeal. Add the milk and continue to mix together until the dough forms a ball.
3. Place the dough on a lightly floured work surface and knead it until a smooth ball forms, about 30 seconds. Divide the dough into 8 equal pieces and roll each piece into a ball.
4. Place the Cook & Crisp Basket in the pot. Close crisping lid. Select AIR CRISP, set temperature to 350°F, and set time to 3 minutes. Press START/STOP to begin.
5. Once preheated, coat the basket with cooking spray. Place the dough balls in the basket, leaving room between each. Spray them with cooking spray. Close crisping lid.
6. Select AIR CRISP, set temperature to 350°F, and set time to 10 minutes. Press START/STOP to begin.
7. In a medium bowl, combine the remaining 2 tablespoons of sugar and ½ tablespoon of cinnamon.

8. When cooking is complete, open lid. Place the dough balls in the bowl with the cinnamon sugar and toss to coat. Serve immediately.

Nutrition Info:

- Calories: 192,Total Fat: 7g,Sodium: 126mg,Carbohydrates: 31g,Protein: 3g.

Baked Eggs In Spinach

Servings: 4

Cooking Time: 20 Minutes

Ingredients:

- 2 tsp olive oil
- 2 cloves garlic, diced fine
- 4 cups baby spinach
- ½ cup parmesan cheese, reduced fat
- 4 eggs
- 1 tomato, diced fine

Directions:

1. Select sauté function on medium heat. Add oil to the pot and heat.
2. Add the spinach and garlic and cook, stirring, about 2 minutes, or until spinach has wilted. Drain off excess liquid.
3. Stir in parmesan cheese. Make 4 small indents in the spinach. Crack an egg into each indent.
4. Set to air fryer function at 350°F. Secure the tender-crisp lid and bake 15-20 minutes or until egg whites are cooked and yolks are still slightly runny.
5. Let cool 5 minutes, serve topped with tomatoes.

Nutrition Info:

- Calories 139,Total Fat 10g,Total Carbs 3g,Protein 12g,Sodium 280mg.

Ham & Hash Brown Casserole

Servings: 12

Cooking Time: 7 Hours

Ingredients:

- Nonstick cooking spray
- 30 oz. hash browns, shredded & frozen
- 1 lb. ham, diced
- 1 onion, diced
- 1 red bell pepper, diced
- 1 orange bell pepper, diced
- 1 ½ cups cheddar cheese, grated
- 12 eggs
- 1 cup milk
- 4 oz. green chilies, diced
- 1 tbsp. Dijon mustard
- ½ tsp garlic powder
- ½ tsp pepper
- ¼ tsp salt

Directions:

1. Spray the cooking pot with cooking spray.
2. Layer half the hash browns, ham, onions, peppers, and cheese in the pot. Repeat layers.
3. In a large bowl, whisk together the eggs, milk, green chilies, and seasonings until combined. Pour over ingredients in the cooking pot.
4. Secure the lid and set to slow cooker function on low heat. Set the timer for 7 hours. Casserole is done when the eggs are set.

Nutrition Info:

- Calories 348,Total Fat 18g,Total Carbs 22g,Protein 23g,Sodium 893mg.

Broccoli, Ham, And Cheddar Frittata

Servings:6

Cooking Time: 40 Minutes

Ingredients:

- 1 head broccoli, cut into 1-inch florets
- 1 tablespoon canola oil
- Kosher salt
- Freshly ground black pepper
- 12 large eggs
- ¼ cup whole milk
- 1½ cups shredded white Cheddar cheese, divided
- 3 tablespoons unsalted butter
- ½ medium white onion, diced
- 1 cup diced ham

Directions:

1. Place Cook & Crisp Basket in the pot. Close crisping lid. Select AIR CRISP, setting temperature to 390°F, and set time to 5 minutes. Select START/STOP to begin preheating.
2. In a large bowl, toss the broccoli with the oil and season with salt and pepper.
3. Once unit is preheated, open lid and add the broccoli to basket. Close crisping lid.
4. Select AIR CRISP, set temperature to 390°F, and set time to 15 minutes. Select START/STOP to begin.
5. In a separate large bowl, whisk together the eggs, milk, and 1 cup of cheese.
6. After 7 minutes, open lid. Remove basket and shake the broccoli. Return basket to pot and close lid to continue cooking.
7. After 8 minutes, check the broccoli for desired doneness. When cooking is complete, remove broccoli and basket from pot.
8. Select SEAR/SAUTÉ and set to HI. Select START/STOP to begin.
9. After 5 minutes, add the butter. Melt for 1 minute, then add the onion and cook for 3 minutes, stirring occasionally.
10. Add the ham and broccoli and cook, stirring occasionally, for 2 minutes.
11. Add the egg mixture, season with salt and pepper, and stir. Close crisping lid.

12. Select BAKE/ROAST, set temperature to 400°F, and set time to 15 minutes. Select STOP/START to begin.
13. After 5 minutes, open lid and sprinkle the remaining ½ cup of cheese on top. Close lid to continue cooking.
14. When cooking is complete, remove pot from unit and let the frittata sit for 5 to 10 minutes before serving.

Nutrition Info:

- Calories: 404,Total Fat: 30g,Sodium: 671mg,Carbohydrates: 10g,Protein: 27g.

Ham Breakfast Casserole

Servings: 4
Cooking Time: 10 Minutes

Ingredients:

- 4 whole eggs
- 1 tablespoons milk
- 1 cup ham, cooked and chopped
- ½ cup cheddar cheese, shredded
- ¼ teaspoon salt
- ¼ teaspoon black pepper

Directions:

1. Take a baking pan small enough to fit into your Ninja Foodi bowl, and grease it well with butter.
2. Take a medium bowl and whisk in eggs, milk, salt, pepper and add ham, cheese, and stir.
3. Pour mixture into baking pan and lower the pan into your Ninja Foodi.
4. Set your Ninja Foodi Air Crisp mode and Air Crisp for 325 °F for 7 minutes.
5. Remove pan from eggs and enjoy.

Nutrition Info:

- Calories: 169; Fat: 13g; Carbohydrates: 1g; Protein: 12g

Spinach Turkey Cups

Servings: 4
Cooking Time: 23 Minutes

Ingredients:

- 1 tablespoon unsalted butter
- 1-pound fresh baby spinach
- 4 eggs
- 7 ounces cooked turkey, chopped
- 4 teaspoons unsweetened almond milk
- Black pepper and salt, as required

Directions:

1. Select the "Sauté/Sear" setting of Ninja Foodi and place the butter into the pot.
2. Press the "Start/Stop" button to initiate cooking and heat for about 2-3 minutes.
3. Add the spinach and cook for about 3 minutes or until just wilted.
4. Press the "Start/Stop" button to pause cooking and drain the liquid completely.
5. Transfer the spinach into a suitable and set aside to cool slightly.
6. Set the "Air Crisp Basket" in the Ninja Foodi's insert.
7. Close the Ninja Foodi's lid with a crisping lid and select "Air Crisp."
8. Set its cooking temperature to 355 °F for 5 minutes.
9. Press the "Start/Stop" button to initiate preheating.
10. Divide the spinach into 4 greased ramekins, followed by the turkey.
11. Crack 1 egg into each ramekin and drizzle with almond milk.
12. Sprinkle with black pepper and salt.
13. After preheating, Open the Ninja Foodi's lid.
14. Place the ramekins into the "Air Crisp Basket."
15. Close the Ninja Foodi's lid with a crisping lid and select "Air Crisp."
16. Set its cooking temperature to 355 °F for 20 minutes.
17. Press the "Start/Stop" button to initiate cooking.
18. Open the Ninja Foodi's lid and serve hot.

Nutrition Info:

- Calories: 200; Fat: 10.2g; Carbohydrates: 4.5g; Protein: 23.4g

Apple Pie Oatmeal

Servings: 8
Cooking Time: 8 Hours

Ingredients:

- 2 cups steel cut oats
- 7 cups water
- 2 apples peel, core & chop
- ¾ tsp vanilla
- ½ tsp cinnamon
- ¼ tsp ginger
- ¼ tsp nutmeg

Directions:

1. Add all the ingredients to the cooking pot and stir to combine.
2. Add the lid and set to slow cooking on low heat. Cook 6-8 hours, stirring occasionally.
3. When oatmeal is done, stir well before serving.

Nutrition Info:

- Calories 172,Total Fat 3g,Total Carbs 31g,Protein 7g,Sodium 1mg.

Cinnamon Apple Bread

Servings: 10
Cooking Time: 55 Minutes
Ingredients:

- Butter flavored cooking spray
- ½ cup coconut flour
- 1 ½ cup almond flour, sifted
- ¾ cup Stevia
- 1 tsp baking soda
- 2 tbsp. cinnamon
- 5 eggs
- 1 cup applesauce, unsweetened

Directions:

1. Set to bake function on 350°F. Lightly spray a loaf pan with cooking spray.
2. In a large bowl, combine both flours, Stevia, cinnamon, and baking soda.
3. In a medium bowl, whisk the eggs and applesauce together. Add to dry ingredients and stir to combine.
4. Pour into prepared pan and place in the cooker. Add the tender-crisp lid and bake 45-55 minutes, or until bread passes the toothpick test.
5. Let cool 15 minutes, then invert onto serving plate and slice.

Nutrition Info:

- Calories 189,Total Fat 10g,Total Carbs 30g,Protein 7g,Sodium 162mg.

Very Berry Puffs

Servings: 3
Cooking Time: 20 Min
Ingredients:

- 3 pastry dough sheets
- 2 cups cream cheese /260g
- 1 tbsp honey /15ml
- 2 tbsp mashed raspberries /30g
- 2 tbsp mashed strawberries /30g
- ¼ tsp vanilla extract /1.25ml

Directions:

1. Divide the cream cheese between the dough sheets and spread it evenly. In a small bowl, combine the berries, honey, and vanilla. Divide the mixture between the pastry sheets. Pinch the ends of the sheets, to form puff.
2. You can seal them by brushing some water onto the edges, or even better, use egg wash. Lay the puffs into a lined baking dish.
3. Place the dish into the Ninja Foodi, close the crisping lid and cook for 15 minutes on Air Crisp mode at 370 °F or 188°C. Once the timer beeps, check the puffs to ensure they're puffed and golden. Serve warm.

Spanish Potato And Chorizo Frittata

Servings:4
Cooking Time: 20 Minutes
Ingredients:

- 4 eggs
- 1 cup milk
- Sea salt
- Freshly ground black pepper
- 1 potato, diced
- ½ cup frozen corn
- 1 chorizo sausage, diced
- 8 ounces feta cheese, crumbled
- 1 cup water

Directions:

1. In a medium bowl, whisk together the eggs and milk. Season with salt and pepper.
2. Place the potato, corn, and chorizo in the Multi-Purpose Pan or an 8-inch baking pan. Pour the egg mixture and feta cheese over top. Cover the pan with aluminum foil and place on the Reversible Rack. Make sure it's in the lower position.
3. Pour the water into the pot. Assemble pressure lid, making sure the pressure release valve is in the SEAL position.
4. Select PRESSURE and set to HI. Set time to 20 minutes. Select START/STOP to begin.
5. When pressure cooking is complete, quick release the pressure by moving the pressure release valve to the VENT position. Carefully remove lid when unit has finished releasing pressure.
6. Remove the pan from pot and place it on a cooling rack for 5 minutes, then serve.

Nutrition Info:

- Calories: 361,Total Fat: 24g,Sodium: 972mg,Carbohydrates: 17g,Protein: 21g.

Spinach Casserole

Servings: 4
Cooking Time: 5 Minutes
Ingredients:

- 4 whole eggs
- 1 tablespoons milk
- 1 tomato, diced
- ½ cup spinach
- ¼ teaspoon salt
- ¼ teaspoon black pepper

Directions:

1. Take a baking pan small enough to fit Ninja Foodi and grease it with butter.
2. Take a medium bowl and whisk in eggs, milk, salt, pepper, add veggies to the bowl and stir.
3. Pour egg mixture into the baking pan and lower the pan into the Ninja Foodi .
4. Close Air Crisping lid and Air Crisp for 325 degrees for 7 minutes.
5. Remove the pan from eggs, and enjoy hot.

Nutrition Info:

- Calories: 78; Fat: 5g; Carbohydrates: 1 g; Protein: 7 g

Zucchini Pancakes

Servings: 6

Cooking Time: 10 Minutes

Ingredients:

- 1 cup almond milk, unsweetened
- 1 egg
- 2 tbsp. honey
- 1 tbsp. coconut oil, melted
- 1 tsp vanilla
- ½ cup zucchini, grated
- 1 ½ cup oat flour
- 2 tsp cinnamon
- 1 tsp baking powder
- ¼ tsp salt
- Nonstick cooking spray

Directions:

1. In a large bowl, combine milk, egg, honey, oil, vanilla, and zucchini.
2. In a separate bowl, stir together remaining ingredients. Add to zucchini mixture and mix just until combined.
3. Spray the cooking pot with cooking spray. Set to sauté on medium heat.
4. Pour batter, ¼ cup at a time, into cooking pot. Cook 3-4 minutes or until bubble form in the middle. Flip and cook another 2-3 minutes. Repeat with remaining batter. Serve immediately with your favorite toppings.

Nutrition Info:

- Calories 188,Total Fat 7g,Total Carbs 27g,Protein 6g,Sodium 132mg.

Waffle Bread Pudding With Maple-jam Glaze

Servings:6

Cooking Time: 25 Minutes

Ingredients:

- 2 whole eggs
- 4 egg yolks
- 1 cup heavy (whipping) cream
- ½ teaspoon ground cinnamon
- ¼ cup granulated sugar
- 1 teaspoon vanilla extract
- 20 waffles, cut in sixths
- 1 cup water
- ⅓ cup desired jam
- raspberry)
- ⅓ cup maple syrup

Directions:

1. In a large mixing bowl, combine the eggs, egg yolks, cream, cinnamon, sugar, and vanilla. Whisk well to combine. Add the waffle pieces and toss very well to incorporate. The waffles should be completely soaked through with cream sauce, with some extra residual cream sauce at the bottom of the bowl.
2. Place the waffle mixture in the Ninja Multi-Purpose Pan or 8-inch round baking dish. Press down gently to ensure ingredients are well packed into the pan. Cover the pan tightly with plastic wrap.
3. Add the water to the pot. Place the pan on the Reversible Rack and place rack in pot. Assemble pressure lid, making sure the pressure release valve is in the SEAL position.
4. Select PRESSURE and set to HI. Set time to 15 minutes. Select START/STOP to begin.
5. Place the jam and maple syrup in a small bowl and mix well to combine.
6. When pressure cooking is complete, quick release the pressure by moving the pressure release valve to the VENT position. Carefully remove lid when unit has finished releasing pressure.
7. Remove rack from pot, then remove the plastic wrap from the pan. Pour the jam and syrup mixture over top of waffles. Place rack and pan back in pot. Close crisping lid.
8. Select BROIL and set time to 10 minutes. Select START/STOP to begin.
9. When cooking is complete, open lid and remove rack from pot. Serve the bread pudding warm.

Nutrition Info:

- Calories: 640,Total Fat: 30g,Sodium: 765mg,Carbohydrates: 82g,Protein: 12g.

Bacon And Sausage Cheesecake

Servings: 6

Cooking Time: 25 Min

Ingredients:

- 8 eggs, cracked into a bowl
- 8 oz. breakfast sau sage; chopped /240g
- 4 slices bread, cut into ½ -inch cubes
- 1 large green bell pepper; chopped
- 1 large red bell pepper; chopped
- 1 cup chopped green onion /130g
- ½ cup milk /125ml
- 2 cups water /500ml
- 1 cup grated Cheddar cheese /130g
- 3 bacon slices; chopped
- 1 tsp red chili flakes /5g
- Salt and black pepper to taste

Directions:

1. Add the eggs, sausage chorizo, bacon slices, green and red bell peppers, green onion, chili flakes, cheddar cheese, salt, pepper, and milk to a bowl and use a whisk to beat them together.
2. Grease a bundt pan with cooking spray and pour the egg mixture into it. After, drop the bread slices in the egg

mixture all around while using a spoon to push them into the mixture.

3. Open the Ninja Foodi, pour in water, and fit the rack at the center of the pot. Place bundt pan on the rack and seal the pressure lid. Select Pressure mode on High pressure for 6 minutes, and press Start/Stop.

4. Once the timer goes off, press Start/Stop, do a quick pressure release. Run a knife around the egg in the bundt pan, close the crisping lid and cook for another 4 minutes on Bake/Roast on 380 °F or 194°C.

5. When ready, place a serving plate on the bundt pan, and then, turn the egg bundt over. Use a knife to cut the egg into slices. Serve with a sauce of your choice.

Deviled Eggs

Servings: 4
Cooking Time: 10 Minutes

Ingredients:

- 8 large eggs
- 1 cup of water
- Guacamole
- Sliced Radishes
- Mayonnaise
- Furikake

Directions:

1. Add water to the inner insert of your Ninja Foodi.
2. Place the steamer rack inside the pot and set the eggs on top of the rack.
3. Lock pressure lid and cook on "HIGH" pressure for 6 minutes.
4. Release Pressure naturally over 10 minutes and transfer the eggs to a suitable full of icy water.
5. Peel after 5 minutes.
6. Cut in half and decorate with guacamole, sliced radish, mayo and enjoy.

Nutrition Info:

- Calories: 70; Fat: 6g; Carbohydrates: 1g; Protein: 3g

Beef, Pork & Lamb

Pork Asado

Servings: 6
Cooking Time: 1 Hour

Ingredients:

- 1 ½ lbs. pork picnic or shoulder, cut in 2-inch cubes
- ¼ cup soy sauce
- ½ cup lemon juice
- 1 ½ cups water
- ¼ cup olive oil
- 1 onion, peeled & sliced into ¼-inch thick rings
- 2 potatoes, peeled & sliced in ½-inch thick strips
- Salt and pepper to taste

Directions:

1. Add the pork, soy sauce, lemon juice, and water to the cooking pot. Set to sauté on med-high heat and bring to a boil.
2. Add lid and set to pressure cook on high. Set timer for 10 minutes. When timer goes off, use quick release to remove the pressure. Transfer pork and cooking liquid to a bowl.
3. Add the oil to the cooking pot and set to sauté on med-high. Add onions and cook about 1 minute. Use a slotted spoon to transfer them to a bowl.
4. Add potatoes to the pot and cook until tender and lightly browned. Transfer to bowl with onions.
5. Return just the pork to the pot and cook until browned. Drain off fat. Add the reserved cooking liquid and bring to a boil. Season with salt and pepper. Cook about 5 minutes until liquid is reduced.
6. Place pork on a serving platter and place potatoes and onions around it. Pour the sauce over all and serve.

Nutrition Info:

- Calories 327,Total Fat 13g,Total Carbs 25g,Protein 27g,Sodium 882mg.

Ground Beef Stuffed Empanadas

Servings: 2
Cooking Time: 60 Min

Ingredients:

- ¼ pound ground beef /112.5g
- 2 small tomatoes; chopped
- 8 square gyoza wrappers
- 1 egg, beaten
- 1 garlic clove; minced
- ½ white onion; chopped
- 6 green olives, pitted and chopped
- 1 tbsp olive oil /15ml
- ¼ tsp cumin powder /1.25g
- ¼ tsp paprika /1.25g
- ⅛ tsp cinnamon powder /0.625g

Directions:

1. Choose Sear/Sauté on the pot and set to Medium High. Choose Start/Stop to preheat the pot. Put the oil, garlic, onion, and beef in the preheated pot and cook for 5 minutes, stirring occasionally, until the fragrant and the beef is no longer pink.
2. Stir in the olives, cumin, paprika, and cinnamon and cook for an additional 3 minutes. Add the tomatoes and cook for 1 more minute.
3. Spoon the beef mixture into a plate and allow cooling for a few minutes.
4. Meanwhile, put the Crisping Basket in the pot. Close the crisping lid; choose Air Crisp, set the temperature to 400°F or 205°C, and the time to 5 minutes. Press Start.
5. Lay the gyoza wrappers on a flat surface. Place 1 to 2 tbsps of the beef mixture in the middle of each wrapper. Brush the edges of the wrapper with egg and fold in half to form a triangle. Pinch the edges together to seal.
6. Place 4 empanadas in a single layer in the preheated Basket. Close the crisping lid. Choose Air Crisp, set the temperature to 400°F or 205°C, and set the time to 7 minutes. Choose Start/Stop to begin frying.
7. Once the timer is done, remove the empanadas from the basket and transfer to a plate. Repeat with the remaining empanadas.

Beef Bourguignon

Servings: 6
Cooking Time: 9 Hours
Ingredients:
- 5 slices bacon, chopped fine
- 3 lbs. beef chuck, cut in 1-inch cubes
- 1 cup red cooking wine
- 2 cups beef broth, low sodium
- ½ cup tomato sauce
- ¼ cup soy sauce
- ¼ cup flour
- 3 cloves garlic, chopped fine
- 2 tbsp. thyme, chopped fine
- 5 carrots, sliced
- 1 lb. baby potatoes
- 8 oz. mushrooms, sliced
- 2 tbsp. fresh parsley, chopped

Directions:
1. Add the bacon to the cooking pot and set to sauté on med high. Cook until crisp. Transfer to a bowl.
2. Season the beef with salt and pepper. Add to the pot and brown on all sides. Add to the bacon.
3. Add the wine to the pot and stir to scrape up the brown bits from the bottom of the pot. Simmer 2-3 minutes to reduce.
4. Stir in broth, tomato sauce, and soy sauce. Slowly whisk in flour.
5. Add the beef and bacon back to the pot along with remaining ingredients, except parsley, and stir to mix. Add the lid and set to slow cook on low. Cook 8-10 hours or until beef is tender. Stir and serve garnished with parsley.

Nutrition Info:
- Calories 649,Total Fat 28g,Total Carbs 28g,Protein 69g,Sodium 1344mg.

Chunky Pork Meatloaf With Mashed Potatoes

Servings: 4
Cooking Time: 55 Min
Ingredients:
- 2 pounds potatoes; cut into large chunks /900g
- 12 ounces pork meatloaf /360g
- 2 garlic cloves; minced
- 2 large eggs
- 12 individual saltine crackers, crushed
- 1¾ cups full cream milk; divided /438ml
- 1 cup chopped white onion /130g
- ½ cup heavy cream /125ml
- ¼ cup barbecue sauce /62.5ml
- 1 tbsp olive oil /15ml
- 3 tbsp chopped fresh cilantro /45g
- 3 tbsp unsalted butter /45g
- ¼ tsp dried rosemary /1.25g
- 1 tsp yellow mustard /5g
- 1 tsp Worcestershire sauce /5ml
- 2 tsp salt /10g
- ½ tsp black pepper /2.5g

Directions:
1. Select Sear/Sauté and adjust to Medium. Press Start to preheat the pot for 5 minutes. Heat the olive oil until shimmering and sauté the onion and garlic in the oil. Cook for about 2 minutes until the onion softens. Transfer the onion and garlic to a plate and set aside.
2. In a bowl, crumble the meatloaf mix into small pieces. Sprinkle with 1 tsp of salt, the pepper, cilantro, and thyme. Add the sautéed onion and garlic. Sprinkle the crushed saltine crackers over the meat and seasonings.
3. In a small bowl, beat ¼ cup of milk, the eggs, mustard, and Worcestershire sauce. Pour the mixture on the layered cracker crumbs and gently mix the ingredients in the bowl with your hands. Shape the meat mixture into an 8-inch round.
4. Cover the reversible rack with aluminum foil and carefully lift the meatloaf into the rack. Pour the remaining 1½ cups of milk and the heavy cream into the inner pot. Add the potatoes, butter, and remaining salt. Place the rack with meatloaf over the potatoes in the upper position in the pot.
5. Seal the pressure lid, choose Pressure; adjust the pressure to High and the cook time to 25 minutes; press Start. After cooking, perform a quick pressure release, and carefully open the pressure lid. Brush the meatloaf with the barbecue sauce.

6. Close the crisping lid; choose Broil and adjust the cook time to 7 minutes. Press Start to begin grilling. When the top has browned, remove the rack, and transfer the meatloaf to a serving platter. Mash the potatoes in the pot. Slice the meatloaf and serve with the mashed potatoes.

Korean Pork Chops

Servings: 4
Cooking Time: 10 Minutes
Ingredients:

- ½ cup soy sauce, low sodium
- 4 tbsp. honey
- 12 cloves garlic, chopped
- 4 tsp ginger
- 2 tsp sesame oil
- 2 tbsp. sweet chili sauce
- 4 top loin pork chops
- 2 tsp olive oil

Directions:

1. In a medium bowl, whisk together soy sauce, honey, garlic, ginger, sesame oil, and chili sauce until smooth. Reserve ½ the marinade for later.
2. Add the pork chops to the bowl and turn to coat. Let sit 10 minutes.
3. Add the olive oil to the cooking pot and set to sauté on med-high heat.
4. Add the pork chops and cook 5 minutes until browned. Turn the chops over and add the reserved marinade to the pot. Cook another 5 minutes or until chops are cooked through. Let rest 3 minutes before serving.

Nutrition Info:

- Calories 364,Total Fat 8g,Total Carbs 24g,Protein 46g,Sodium 2218mg.

Pot Roast With Broccoli

Servings: 4
Cooking Time: 35 Min
Ingredients:

- 2 lb. beef chuck roast /900g
- 1 packet onion soup mix
- 2 red bell peppers, seeded and quartered
- 1 yellow onion, quartered
- 1 cup chopped broccoli /130g
- 1 cup beef broth /250ml
- 3 tbsp olive oil; divided into 2 /45ml
- Salt to taste

Directions:

1. Season the chuck roast with salt and set aside. Select Sear/Sauté mode on the Foodi cooker. Add the olive oil, and once heated, add the chuck roast. Sear for 5 minutes on each side. Then, pour in the beef broth.
2. In a zipper bag, add broccoli, onions, peppers, the remaining olive oil, and onion soup. Close the bag and shake the mixture to coat the vegetables well. Use tongs to remove the vegetables into the pot and stir with a spoon.
3. Close the lid, secure the pressure valve, and select Pressure mode on High pressure for 18 minutes. Press Start/Stop.
4. Once the timer has stopped, do a quick pressure release, and open the pressure lid. Make cuts on the meat inside the pot and close the crisping lid.
5. Cook on Air Crisp mode for about 10 minutes, at 380 °F or 194°C, until nice and crispy. Plate and serve with the vegetables and a drizzle of the sauce in the pot.

Thai Roasted Beef

Servings: 2
Cooking Time: 4 Hours 20 Min
Ingredients:

- 1 lb. ground beef /450g
- Thumb-sized piece of ginger; chopped
- 3 chilies, deseeded and chopped
- 4 garlic cloves; chopped
- Juice of 1 lime
- 2 tbsp oil /30ml
- 2 tbsp fish sauce/30ml
- 2 tbsp soy sauce /30ml
- 2 tbsp mirin /30ml
- 2 tbsp coriander; chopped /30g
- 2 tbsp basil; chopped /30g
- ½ tsp salt /2.5g
- ½ tsp pepper /2.5g
- 1 tsp brown sugar

Directions:

1. Place all ingredients, except beef, salt, and pepper, in a blender; pulse until smooth. Season the beef with salt and pepper. Place the meat and Thai mixture in a zipper bag. Shake well to combine and let marinate in the fridge for about 4 hours.
2. Place the beef in the Foodi basket and cook for about 12 minutes, or a little more for well done, on Air Crisp mode at 350 °F or 177°C. Let sit for 5 minutes before serving.

Pork And Ricotta Meatballs With Cheesy Grits

Servings:8
Cooking Time: 26 Minutes
Ingredients:

- 2 pounds ground pork
- 1 cup whole milk ricotta cheese
- 2 eggs
- 1 cup panko bread crumbs
- 4 garlic cloves, minced
- ¼ cup parsley, minced, plus more for garnishing
- 1½ cups grated Parmesan cheese, divided

- 2 tablespoons kosher salt, divided
- 1 teaspoon freshly ground black pepper
- 2 tablespoons canola oil
- 4 cups whole milk
- 1 cup coarse ground grits

Directions:

1. In a large bowl, combine the pork, ricotta, eggs, bread crumbs, garlic, parsley, ½ cup of Parmesan, 1 tablespoon of salt, and pepper. Use your hands or a sturdy spatula to mix well.
2. Use a 3-ounce ice cream scoop to portion the mixture into individual meatballs. Use your hands to gently form them into balls.
3. Select SEAR/SAUTÉ and set to HI. Select START/STOP to begin. Let preheat for 5 minutes.
4. Add the oil. Add half the meatballs and sear for 6 minutes, flipping them after 3 minutes. Remove from the pot and repeat with the remaining meatballs. Remove the second batch of meatballs from the pot.
5. Add the milk, grits, and remaining 1 tablespoon of salt and stir. Gently place meatballs back in the pot. They will sink slightly when placed in the milk. Assemble pressure lid, making sure pressure release valve is in the SEAL position.
6. Select PRESSURE and set to HI. Set time to 6 minutes. Select START/STOP to begin.
7. When pressure cooking is complete, quick release the pressure by moving the pressure release valve to the VENT position. Carefully remove lid when unit has finished releasing pressure.
8. Sprinkle the remaining 1 cup of Parmesan cheese over the top of the grits and meatballs. Close crisping lid.
9. Select BROIL and set time to 8 minutes. Select START/STOP to begin.
10. When cooking is complete, serve immediately.

Nutrition Info:

- Calories: 544,Total Fat: 32g,Sodium: 763mg,Carbohydrates: 28g,Protein: 37g.

Southern-style Lettuce Wraps

Servings:6

Cooking Time: 30 Minutes

Ingredients:

- 3 pounds boneless pork shoulder, cut into 1- to 2-inch cubes
- 2 cups light beer
- 1 cup brown sugar
- 1 teaspoon chipotle chiles in adobo sauce
- 1 cup barbecue sauce
- 1 head iceberg lettuce, quartered and leaves separated
- 1 cup roasted peanuts, chopped or ground
- Cilantro leaves

Directions:

1. Place the pork, beer, brown sugar, chipotle, and barbecue sauce in the pot. Assemble pressure lid, making sure the pressure release valve is in the SEAL position.
2. Select PRESSURE and set to HI. Set the timer to 30 minutes. Select START/STOP to begin.
3. When pressure cooking is complete, quick release the pressure by turning the pressure release valve to the VENT position. Carefully remove lid when unit has finished releasing pressure.
4. Using a silicone-tipped utensil, shred the pork in the pot. Stir to mix the meat in with the sauce.
5. Place a small amount of pork in a piece of lettuce. Top with peanuts and cilantro to serve.

Nutrition Info:

- Calories: 811,Total Fat: 58g,Sodium: 627mg,Carbohydrates: 22g,Protein: 45g.

Creole Dirty Rice

Servings: 6

Cooking Time: 15 Minutes

Ingredients:

- 1 tbsp. olive oil
- 1 lb. lean ground beef
- 1 stalk celery, sliced
- ½ green bell pepper, chopped
- 2 tbsp. garlic, chopped fine
- 1 onion, chopped
- 4 tbsp. fresh parsley, chopped
- 2 tbsp. creole seasoning
- 5 cups brown rice, cooked

Directions:

1. Add the oil to the cooking pot and set to sauté on med-high heat.
2. Add the beef, celery, bell pepper, garlic, and onion and cook, breaking up beef with a spatula, until meat is no longer pink and vegetables are tender, about 6-8 minutes.
3. Add the parsley and Creole seasoning and mix well.
4. Add the rice and cook, stirring occasionally, about 5 minutes or until heated through. Serve.

Nutrition Info:

- Calories 386,Total Fat 15g,Total Carbs 43g,Protein 19g,Sodium 57mg.

Fresh Kielbasa And Braised Sweet And Sour Cabbage

Servings:6

Cooking Time: 1 Hour

Ingredients:

- 1½ pounds fresh kielbasa sausage links
- ½ stick (¼ cup) unsalted butter
- ½ medium onion, thinly sliced
- 2 garlic cloves, minced
- 1 large head red cabbage, cut into ¼-inch slices
- ¼ cup granulated sugar
- ⅓ cup apple cider vinegar
- ½ cup water
- 2 teaspoons caraway seeds
- Kosher salt
- Freshly ground black pepper

Directions:

1. Insert Cook & Crisp Basket into pot and close crisping lid. Select AIR CRISP, set temperature to 390°F, and set time to 15 minutes. Select START/STOP to begin. Let preheat for 5 minutes.
2. Add the sausage to the basket. Close lid and cook for 10 minutes.
3. When cooking is complete, open lid and remove basket and sausage. Set aside.
4. Select SEAR/SAUTÉ and set to HI. Select START/STOP to begin.
5. Add the butter and let it heat for 5 minutes. Add the onion and garlic and cook for 3 minutes.
6. Add the cabbage, sugar, vinegar, water, and caraway seeds, and season with salt and pepper. Assemble pressure lid, making sure the pressure release valve is in the SEAL position.
7. Select PRESSURE and set to HI. Set time to 10 minutes. Select START/STOP to begin.
8. When pressure cooking is complete, quick release the pressure by moving the pressure release valve to the VENT position.
9. Select SEAR/SAUTÉ and set to HI. Set time to 10 minutes. Select START/STOP to begin.
10. After 5 minutes, open lid and add the sausage to the top of cabbage. Close lid and continue cooking.
11. When cooking is complete, open lid and serve.

Nutrition Info:

- Calories: 351,Total Fat: 19g,Sodium: 588mg,Carbohydrates: 24g,Protein: 23g.

Pork Chops With Squash Purée And Mushroom Gravy

Servings: 4

Cooking Time: 45 Min

Ingredients:

- 4 pork chops
- 1 pound butternut squash; cubed /450g
- 2 sprigs rosemary, leaves removed and chopped
- 2 sprigs thyme, leaves removed and chopped
- 4 cloves garlic; minced
- 1 cup mushrooms; chopped /130g
- 1 cup chicken broth /250ml
- 1 tbsp olive oil /15ml
- 2 tbsp olive oil /30ml
- 1 tbsp soy sauce /15ml
- 1 tsp cornstarch 5g

Directions:

1. Set on Sear/Sauté, set to Medium High, and choose Start/Stop to preheat the pot and heat rosemary, thyme and 1 tbsp or 15ml of olive oil. Add the pork chops and sear for 1 minute for each side until lightly browned.
2. Sauté garlic and mushrooms in the pressure cooker for 5-6 minutes until mushrooms are tender. Add soy sauce and chicken broth. Transfer pork chops to a wire trivet and place it into the pressure cooker. Over the chops, place a cake pan. Add butternut squash in the pot and drizzle with 1 tbsp olive oil.
3. Seal the pressure lid, choose Pressure, set to High, and set the timer to 10 minutes. Press Start. When ready, release the pressure quickly. Remove the pan and trivet from the pot. Stir cornstarch into the mushroom mixture for 2 to 3 minutes until the sauce thickens.
4. Transfer the mushroom sauce to an immersion blender and blend until you attain the desired consistency. Scoop sauce into a cup with a pour spout. Smash the squash into a purée. Set pork chops on a plate and ladle squash puree next to them. Top the pork chops with gravy.

Corned Cabbage Beef

Servings: 4

Cooking Time: 100 Minutes

Ingredients:

- 1 corned beef brisket
- 4 cups of water
- 1 small onion, peeled and quartered
- 3 garlic cloves, smashed and peeled
- 2 bay leaves
- 3 whole black peppercorns
- 1/2 teaspoon allspice berries
- 1 teaspoon dried thyme
- 5 medium carrots
- 1 cabbage, cut into wedges

Directions:

1. Stir in corned beef, onion, garlic cloves, water, allspice, peppercorn, thymes to the Ninja Foodi.
2. Lock up the lid and cook for about 90 minutes at "HIGH" pressure.
3. Allow the pressure to release naturally once done.

4. Open up and transfer the meat to your serving plate.
5. Cover it with tin foil and allow it to cool for 15 minutes.
6. Stir in carrots and cabbage to the lid and let them cook for 10 minutes at "HIGH" pressure.
7. Once done, do a quick release. Take out the prepped veggies and serve with your corned beef.

Nutrition Info:

- Calories: 297; Fats: 17g; Carbohydrates:1g; Protein: 14g

Roasted Pork With Apple Gravy

Servings: 6

Cooking Time: 3 Hours 30 Minutes

Ingredients:

- 1 tbsp. fennel seeds, toasted
- 2 tsp peppercorns
- 2 tbsp. fresh thyme, chopped
- 2 tbsp. fresh rosemary, chopped
- 4 cloves garlic, chopped
- 2 tsp salt
- 4 tbsp. olive oil, divided
- 4-5 lbs. pork shoulder, boneless & fat trimmed
- 4 Fuji apples, peeled, cored & cut in wedges
- 1 onion, cut in 12 wedges
- ½ cup dry white wine
- ½ cup water
- ½ tsp Dijon mustard

Directions:

1. Place fennel seeds, peppercorns, thyme, rosemary, garlic, and 2 teaspoons salt into a spice or coffee grinder and grind to a paste.
2. Transfer to a small bowl and stir in 2 tablespoons olive oil. Rub mixture evenly over the pork. Wrap with plastic wrap and refrigerate overnight.
3. Place the apples and onions in the cooking pot and drizzle with remaining oil, toss to coat. Place the pork on top of the apples and onions.
4. Add the tender-crisp lid and set to roast on 450°F. Cook 30 minutes.
5. Remove the lid and add the wine. Cover roast with foil. Add the tender-crisp lid and reduce heat to 325°F. Cook 2 ½ - 3 hours or until pork falls apart when stuck with a fork.
6. Transfer pork to a serving plate and tent with foil to keep warm.
7. Transfer apples and onions to a blender. Add ½ cup water and the mustard and pulse to puree. Mixture should be the consistency of gravy, if not add more water.
8. Slice the pork and serve topped with gravy.

Nutrition Info:

- Calories 111,Total Fat 3g,Total Carbs 4g,Protein 15g,Sodium 229mg.

Layered Taco Casserole

Servings: 8

Cooking Time: 35 Minutes

Ingredients:

- 2 lbs. lean ground beef
- 1 tsp garlic, chopped fine
- 2 tbsp. chili powder
- 1 tsp onion powder
- ½ cup salsa
- ¼ cup water
- 16 oz. re-fried beans, low fat
- ½ cup sour cream, low fat
- 1 cup cheddar cheese, low fat, grated
- ¼ cup green onion, chopped

Directions:

1. Add the beef to the cooking pot and set to sauté on med-high heat. Cook, breaking up with spatula, until no longer pink. Stir in garlic, chili powder, and onion powder and cook 1 minute more.
2. Stir in salsa and water and cook, stirring occasionally, until liquid has reduced.
3. Spread beans on top of the meat. Top with sour cream then sprinkle the cheese evenly over the top.
4. Add the tender-crisp lid and set to bake on 350°F. Bake 25-30 minutes or until hot and bubbly.
5. Let cool slightly then serve garnished with green onions.

Nutrition Info:

- Calories 360,Total Fat 22g,Total Carbs 11g,Protein 28g,Sodium 513mg.

Tender Beef & Onion Rings

Servings: 6

Cooking Time: 25 Minutes

Ingredients:

- 2 lb. chuck roast, cubed
- ¼ cup soy sauce, low sodium
- 1 tbsp. lemon juice
- ½ tsp pepper
- 1 cup water
- 3 tbsp. olive oil
- 3 cloves garlic, chopped fine
- 1 onion, sliced & separated in rings

Directions:

1. In a large bowl, combine beef, soy sauce, lemon juice, and pepper, mix well. Cover and let sit 1 hour.
2. Add the beef mixture to the cooking pot. Stir in water. Add the lid and set to pressure cook on high. Set timer for 20 minutes. When the timer goes off, use natural release to remove the pressure.
3. Use a slotted spoon to transfer beef to a bowl.
4. Set cooker to sauté on medium heat. Cook until sauce reduces and thickens, about 3-4 minutes.
5. Stir in oil and garlic. Add the beef back to the pot and cook until sauce turns a light brown, about 4-5 minutes. Add

the onion rings and cook 2 minutes, or until onions are almost soft. Serve.

Nutrition Info:

- Calories 529,Total Fat 29g,Total Carbs 4g,Protein 62g,Sodium 1059mg.

Italian Beef Steak

Servings: 8

Cooking Time: 4 Hours

Ingredients:

- Nonstick cooking spray
- 2 lbs. round steak, cut in 1-inch pieces
- ½ tsp salt
- ¼ tsp pepper
- 1 onion, sliced thin
- 1 tsp oregano
- 1 tsp basil
- 1 tsp rosemary
- ½ tsp thyme
- 4 cloves garlic, chopped fine
- ½ cup balsamic vinegar
- 28 oz. tomatoes, diced & undrained

Directions:

1. Spray the cooking pot with cooking spray.
2. Season the beef with salt and pepper and add it to the cooking pot.
3. Top the beef with onion and herbs to cover it evenly. Sprinkle the garlic overall then add the vinegar and tomatoes, do not stir.
4. Add the lid and set to slow cook on high. Cook 4 hours or until beef is tender. Stir to mix and serve over pasta or rice.

Nutrition Info:

- Calories 200,Total Fat 9g,Total Carbs 9g,Protein 26g,Sodium 218mg.

Barbecue Pork Ribs

Servings: 2

Cooking Time: 4 H 35 Min

Ingredients:

- 1 lb. pork ribs /450g
- 3 garlic cloves; chopped
- 1 tbsp honey, plus more for brushing /15ml
- 4 tbsp barbecue sauce /60ml
- 1 tsp black pepper /5g
- 1 tsp sesame oil /5ml
- ½ tsp five spice powder /2.5g
- 1 tsp salt /5g
- 1 tsp soy sauce /5ml

Directions:

1. Chop the ribs into smaller pieces and place in a large bowl. In a separate bowl, whisk together all of the other ingredients. Add to the bowl with the pork, and mix until the pork is thoroughly coated. Cover the bowl, place it in the fridge, and let it marinade for about 4 hours.
2. Place the ribs in the basket of the Foodi. Close the crisping lid and cook for 15 minutes on Air Crisp mode at 350 °F or 177°C. After, brush the ribs with some honey and cook for 15 more minutes.

One Pot Ham & Rice

Servings: 4

Cooking Time: 10 Minutes

Ingredients:

- 2 tbsp. water
- ¼ cup celery, chopped
- ¼ cup onion, chopped
- ¼ cup green bell pepper, chopped
- ¼ cup fresh parsley, chopped
- ½ tsp garlic powder
- ¼ tsp pepper
- Nonstick cooking spray
- 5 slices lean deli ham, chopped
- 2 cups brown rice, cooked
- 2 eggs, beaten
- 1 green onion, sliced

Directions:

1. Add water to the cooking pot and set to sauté on medium heat.
2. Add the celery, onion, peppers, parsley, garlic powder, and pepper and cook until water evaporates and vegetables are tender, about 4-5 minutes.
3. Spray the vegetables and pot with cooking spray. Add ham and cook 1-2 minutes until heated through.
4. Stir in rice and mix well. Pour in eggs and cook until they are completely set, stirring occasionally.
5. Sprinkle with green onions and serve immediately.

Nutrition Info:

- Calories 184,Total Fat 4g,Total Carbs 25g,Protein 11g,Sodium 413mg.

Bunless Burgers

Servings:4

Cooking Time: 10 Minutes

Ingredients:

- ¼ teaspoon onion powder
- ¼ teaspoon garlic powder
- ¼ teaspoon Italian seasoning
- Dash Himalayan pink salt
- 1 pound ground beef

Directions:

1. Place the Cook & Crisp Basket into the cooking pot. Select AIR CRISP, set the temperature to 375°F, and set the time to 5 minutes to preheat. Select START/STOP to begin.
2. In a small bowl, stir together the onion powder, garlic powder, Italian seasoning, and salt.

3. Divide the ground beef into 4 equal portions and shape each into a patty. Season both side of the patties with the seasoning mix and place them on a sheet of parchment paper.
4. Once the unit is preheated, add the burgers to the basket, working in batches as needed. Close the crisping lid.
5. Select AIR CRISP, set the temperature to 375°F, and set the time to 8 to 10 minutes. Select START/STOP to begin. Cook the burgers until cooking is complete; no need to flip the burgers!

Nutrition Info:

- Calories: 172,Total Fat: 8g,Sodium: 82mg,Carbohydrates: 0g,Protein: 23g.

Beef Pho With Swiss Chard

Servings: 6
Cooking Time: 1 Hr 10 Min

Ingredients:

- 2 pounds Beef Neck Bones /900g
- 10 ounces sirloin steak /300g
- 8 ounces rice noodles /240g
- 1 yellow onion, quartered
- A handful of fresh cilantro; chopped
- 2 scallions; chopped
- 2 jalapeño peppers; sliced
- ¼ cup minced fresh ginger /32.5g
- 9 cups water /2250ml
- 2 cups Swiss chard; chopped /260g
- 2 tsp coriander seeds /10g
- 2 tsp ground cinnamon /10g
- 2 tsp ground cloves /10g
- 2 tbsp coconut oil /30ml
- 3 tbsp sugar /45g
- 2 tbsp fish sauce /30ml
- 2 ½ tsp kosher salt /12.5g
- Freshly ground black pepper to taste

Directions:

1. Melt the oil on Sear/Sauté. Add ginger and onions and cook for 4 minutes until the onions are softened. Stir in cloves, cinnamon and coriander seeds and cook for 1 minute until soft. Add in water, salt, beef meat and bones.
2. Seal the pressure lid, choose Pressure, set to High, and set the timer to 30 minutes. Press Start. Release pressure naturally for 10 minutes.
3. Transfer the meat to a large bowl; cover with it enough water and soak for 10 minutes. Drain the water and slice the beef. In hot water, soak rice noodles for 8 minutes until softened and pliable; drain and rinse with cold water. Drain liquid from cooker into a separate pot through a fine-mesh strainer; get rid of any solids.
4. Add fish sauce and sugar to the broth; transfer into the Foodi and simmer on Sear/Sauté. Place the noodles in four separate soup bowls. Top with steak slices, scallions, swiss chard; sliced jalapeño pepper, cilantro, red onion, and pepper. Spoon the broth over each bowl to serve.

Adobo Steak

Servings: 4
Cooking Time: 25 Minutes

Ingredients:

- 2 cups of water
- 8 steaks, cubed, 28 ounces pack
- Pepper to taste
- 1 and 3/4 teaspoons adobo seasoning
- 1 can 8 ounces tomato sauce
- 1/3 cup green pitted olives
- 2 tablespoons brine
- 1 small red pepper
- 1/2 a medium onion, sliced

Directions:

1. Chop peppers, onions into ¼ inch strips.
2. Prepare beef by seasoning with adobo and pepper.
3. Add into Ninja Foodi.
4. Stir in remaining ingredients and Lock lid, cook on “HIGH” pressure for 25 minutes.
5. Release pressure naturally.
6. Serve and enjoy.

Nutrition Info:

- Calories: 154; Fat: 5g; Carbohydrates: 3g; Protein: 23g

Beef Stir Fry

Servings: 4
Cooking Time: 11 Minutes

Ingredients:

- 1 lb. beef sirloin, sliced into strips
- 1 tablespoon vegetable oil
- 1-1/2 lb. broccoli florets
- 1 red bell pepper, sliced into strips
- 1 yellow pepper, sliced into strips
- 1 green bell pepper, sliced into strips
- 1/2 cup onion, sliced into strips
- Marinade:
- 1/4 cup of hoisin sauce
- 1 teaspoon sesame oil
- 2 teaspoons garlic, minced
- 1 teaspoon of ground ginger
- 1 tablespoon soy sauce
- 1/4 cup of water

Directions:

1. Put all the marinade ingredients in a suitable. Divide it in half.
2. Soak the beef in the marinade for 20 minutes. Toss the vegetables in the other half.
3. Place the vegetables in the Ninja Foodi basket. Seal the crisping lid.
4. Select air crisp. Cook at 200 °F for 5 minutes.

5. Remove the vegetables and set them aside. Put the meat on the basket.
6. Seal and cook at 360 °For 6 minutes.

Nutrition Info:

- Calories: 390; Fat: 13g; Carbohydrate: 28.9g; Protein: 41.3g

Pulled Pork Tacos

Servings: 5
Cooking Time: 1 Hr 25 Min

Ingredients:

- 2 pounds pork shoulder, trimmed; cut into chunks /900g
- 3 cups shredded cabbage /390g
- 5 taco tortillas
- 1 cup beer /250ml
- 1 cup vegetable broth /250ml
- 1/4 cup plus 2 tbsp lemon juice /92.5ml
- 1/4 cup mayonnaise /62.5ml
- 3 tbsp sugar /45g
- 2 tbsp honey /30ml
- 3 tsp taco seasoning /15g
- 1 tsp ground black pepper /5g
- 2 tsp mustard /10g

Directions:

1. In a bowl, combine sugar, taco seasoning, and black pepper; rub the mixture onto pork pieces to coat well. Allow to settling for 30 minutes. Into the Foodi, add 1/4 cup or 62.5ml lemon juice, broth, pork and beer.
2. Seal the pressure lid, choose Pressure, set to High, and set the timer to 50 minutes. Press Start. Meanwhile in a large bowl, mix mayonnaise, mustard, 2 tbsp lemon juice, cabbage and honey until well coated.
3. Release pressure naturally for 15 minutes before doing a quick release. Transfer the pork to a cutting board and Allow cooling before using two forks to shred. Skim and get rid of fat from liquid in the pressure cooker. Return pork to the pot and mix with the liquid. Top the pork with slaw on taco tortillas before serving.

Pork Sandwiches With Slaw

Servings: 8
Cooking Time: 20 Min

Ingredients:

- 2 lb. chuck roast /900g
- 1 white onion; sliced
- 2 cups beef broth /500ml
- ¼ cup sugar /32.5g
- 1 tsp Spanish paprika /5g
- 1 tsp garlic powder /5g
- 2 tbsp apple cider vinegar /30ml
- Salt to taste
- Assembling:
- 4 Buns, halved
- 1 cup red cabbage, shredded /130g
- 1 cup white cabbage, shredded /130g
- 1 cup white Cheddar cheese, grated /130g
- 4 tbsp mayonnaise /60ml

Directions:

1. Place the pork roast on a clean flat surface and sprinkle with paprika, garlic powder, sugar, and salt. Use your hands to rub the seasoning on the meat.
2. Open the Foodi, add beef broth, onions, pork, and apple cider vinegar. Close the lid, secure the pressure valve, and select Pressure mode on High pressure for 12 minutes. Press Start/Stop.
3. Once the timer has ended, do a quick pressure release. Remove the roast to a cutting board, and use two forks to shred them. Return to the pot, close the crisping lid, and cook for 3 minutes on Air Crisp at 300 °F or 149°C.
4. In the buns, spread the mayo, add the shredded pork, some cooked onions from the pot, and shredded red and white cabbage. Top with the cheese.

Peanut Sauce Beef Satay

Servings: 4
Cooking Time: 60 Min

Ingredients:

- 1 pound flank steak /450g
- 1 tbsp coconut aminos /15g
- 1 tbsp lime juice /15ml
- 1 tbsp coconut oil /15ml
- 1½ tsp red curry paste /7.5ml
- ½ tsp salt /2.5g
- For the Cucumber Relish
- 1 serrano chile; cut into thin rounds
- ½ cucumber
- ½ cup rice vinegar /125ml
- ¼ cup water /62.5ml
- 2 tbsp sugar /30g
- 1 tsp salt /5g
- For the Sauce
- 1 cup coconut milk /250ml
- ½ cup peanut butter /65g
- ⅓ cup water /88ml
- 1 tbsp lime juice /15ml
- 1 tbsp onion; minced /15g
- 1 tbsp coconut oil /15ml
- 1 tsp garlic; minced /5g
- 2 tsp red curry paste /10g
- 1 tsp brown sugar /5g

Directions:

1. Season both sides of the steak with salt. Put in a resealable plastic bag, set aside, and make the marinade. In a small bowl, whisk the lime juice, curry paste, coconut aminos, and coconut oil. Pour the marinade over the steak,

seal the bag, and massage the bag to coat the meat. Set aside for 20 minutes. While the steak marinates; cut the cucumber into ¼-inch slices, then into quarters.
2. In a bowl, whisk the vinegar, water, sugar, and salt until the sugar and salt dissolve. Add the cucumber pieces. Refrigerate until needed.
3. To make the sauce, on the Foodi, choose Sear/Sauté and adjust to Medium-High. Press Start to preheat the pot for 5 minutes. Then, heat the coconut oil until shimmering and sauté the onion and garlic in the pot. Cook for 1 to 2 minutes or until fragrant. Stir in the coconut milk, curry paste, and brown sugar.
4. Seal the pressure lid, choose Pressure; adjust the pressure to High and the cook time to 0 minutes. Press Start. After cooking, perform a quick pressure release, and carefully open the lid. Pour in the water and mix.
5. Remove the meat from the marinade, holding the meat above the bag for a while to drain the excess marinade, put on the reversible rack, and put the rack with the steak in the upper position of the pot above the sauce.
6. Close the crisping lid; choose Broil, adjust the cook time to 14 minutes, and press Start to begin cooking. After about 7 minutes, open the lid and turn the steak. Close the lid and begin broiling.
7. Transfer the steak to a cutting board and allow resting for a few minutes. While the steak cools, mix the peanut butter and lime juice into the sauce. Taste and adjust the seasoning. Cut the steak into thin slices and serve with the peanut sauce and cucumber relish.

Corned Beef

Servings: 4
Cooking Time: 60 Minutes
Ingredients:

- 4 pounds beef brisket
- 2 garlic cloves, peeled and minced
- 2 yellow onions, peeled and sliced
- 11 ounces celery, sliced
- 1 tablespoon dried dill
- 3 bay leaves
- 4 cinnamon sticks, cut into halves
- Black pepper and salt to taste
- 17 ounces of water

Directions:

1. Take a suitable and stir in beef, add water and cover, let it soak for 2-3 hours.
2. Drain and transfer to the Ninja Foodi.
3. Stir in celery, onions, garlic, bay leaves, dill, cinnamon, dill, salt, pepper and the rest of the water to the Ninja Foodi.
4. Stir and combine it well.
5. Lock and secure the Ninja Foodi's lid, then cook on "HIGH" pressure for 50 minutes.
6. Release pressure naturally over 10 minutes.
7. Transfer meat to cutting board and slice, divide amongst plates and pour the cooking liquid alongside veggies over the servings.
8. Enjoy.

Nutrition Info:

- Calories: 289; Fat: 21g; Carbohydrates: 14g; Protein: 9g

Lamb Tagine

Servings:8
Cooking Time: 55 Minutes
Ingredients:

- 1 cup couscous
- 2 cups water
- 3 tablespoons extra-virgin olive oil, divided
- 2 yellow onions, diced
- 3 garlic cloves, minced
- 2 pounds lamb stew meat, cut into 1- to 2-inch cubes
- 1 cup dried apricots, sliced
- 2 cups chicken stock
- 2 tablespoons ras el hanout seasoning
- 1 can chickpeas, drained
- Kosher salt
- Freshly ground black pepper
- 1 cup toasted almonds, for garnish

Directions:

1. Place the couscous in the pot and pour in the water. Assemble pressure lid, making sure the pressure release valve is in the SEAL position.
2. Select PRESSURE and set to HI. Set time to 5 minutes. Select START/STOP to begin.
3. When pressure cooking is complete, quick release the pressure by turning the pressure release valve to the VENT position. Carefully remove lid when unit has finished releasing pressure.
4. Stir 1 tablespoon of oil into the couscous, then transfer the couscous to a bowl.
5. Select SEAR/SAUTÉ and set to MD:HI. Select START/STOP to begin. Let preheat for 3 minutes
6. Add the remaining 2 tablespoons of oil, onion, garlic, and lamb. Sauté for 7 to 10 minutes, stirring frequently.
7. Add the apricots, chicken stock, and ras el hanout. Stir to combine. Assemble pressure lid, making sure the pressure release valve is in the SEAL position.
8. Select PRESSURE and set to HI. Set time to 30 minutes. Select START/STOP to begin.
9. When pressure cooking is complete, quick release the pressure by turning the pressure release valve to the VENT position. Carefully remove lid when unit has finished releasing pressure.
10. Stir in the chickpeas.
11. Select SEAR/SAUTÉ and set to MD:LO. Select START/STOP to begin. Let the mixture simmer for 10 minutes. Season with salt and pepper.

12. When cooking is complete, ladle the tagine over the couscous. Garnish with the toasted almonds.

Nutrition Info:

- Calories: 596,Total Fat: 21g,Sodium: 354mg,Carbohydrates: 65g,Protein: 39g.

Crusted Pork Chops

Servings: 6

Cooking Time: 12 Minutes

Ingredients:

- Cooking spray
- 6 pork chops
- Black pepper and salt to taste
- 1/2 cup bread crumbs
- 2 tablespoons Parmesan cheese, grated
- 1/4 cup cornflakes, crushed
- 1-1/4 teaspoon sweet paprika
- 1/2 teaspoon onion powder
- 1/2 teaspoon garlic powder
- 1/4 teaspoon chilli powder
- 1 egg, beaten

Directions:

1. Season the pork chops liberally with black pepper and salt.
2. In a suitable, mix the rest of the ingredients except the egg.
3. Beat the egg in a suitable. Dip the pork chops in the egg.
4. Coat the pork with the breading. Place the pork on the Ninja Foodi basket.
5. Set it to air crisp and close the crisping lid.
6. Cook at 400 °F for about 12 minutes, flipping halfway through.

Nutrition Info:

- Calories: 310; Fat: 21.3g; Carbohydrate: 8.2g; rotein: 20.3g

Pork Italiana

Servings: 8

Cooking Time:x

Ingredients:

- 2 tbsp. olive oil, divided
- 1 ½ lb. pork loin, cut in 3/4-inch cubes
- 1 green bell pepper, chopped
- 2 onions, chopped
- 2 cloves garlic, chopped fine
- 1 ½ tsp salt
- 1 bay leaf
- 8 oz. tomatoes, undrained
- ¼ tsp pepper
- 2 cups brown rice
- 4 cups water
- 2 chicken bouillon cube
- ½ cup sherry
- 1/8 tsp saffron
- ½ tsp water
- 1 cup green peas
- 4 oz. pimentos, drained
- 12 green olives

Directions:

1. Add 1 tablespoon oil to the cooking pot and set to sauté on med-high heat.
2. Add the pork and cook until browned on all sides, stirring occasionally. Transfer to a bowl.
3. Add remaining oil, bell pepper, onion, and garlic. Cook until pepper is tender, about 5 minutes.
4. Return pork to the pot and stir in salt, bay leaf, tomatoes, and pepper, mix well.
5. Add rice, water, bouillon, and sherry. Place the saffron in a small bowl and add ½ teaspoon water, stir until saffron dissolves. Stir into pork mixture.
6. Bring pork mixture to a boil. Reduce heat to low, cover, and simmer 15-20 minutes until pork is tender and rice is cooked.
7. Serve garnished with peas, olives, and pimientos.

Nutrition Info:

- Calories 369,Total Fat 9g,Total Carbs 45g,Protein 25g,Sodium 741mg.

Asian-style Meatballs

Servings:8

Cooking Time: 20 Minutes

Ingredients:

- 1 pound frozen beef meatballs
- 1¼ cups garlic-hoisin sauce
- ¼ cup soy sauce
- ½ cup rice vinegar
- 2 tablespoons brown sugar
- ½ tablespoon sriracha
- 2 tablespoons freshly squeezed lime juice
- 2 tablespoons cornstarch
- 2 tablespoons water
- 1 head butter lettuce

Directions:

1. Place the meatballs, hoisin sauce, soy sauce, rice vinegar, brown sugar, sriracha, and lime juice in the pot and stir. Assemble pressure lid, making sure the pressure release valve is in the SEAL position.
2. Select PRESSURE and set to HI. Set the time to 20 minutes. Select START/STOP to begin.
3. When pressure cooking is complete, quick release the pressure by turning the pressure release valve to the VENT position. Carefully remove the lid when the unit has finished releasing pressure.
4. Transfer the meatballs to a serving bowl.
5. In a small bowl, mix together the cornstarch and water until smooth. Pour this mixture into the pot, whisking it into

the sauce. Once sauce has thickened, pour it over the meatballs.

6. Serve the meatballs in lettuce cups with the toppings of your choice, such as sesame seeds, sliced scallions, chopped peanuts, and julienned cucumber.

Nutrition Info:

- Calories: 337,Total Fat: 18g,Sodium: 2070mg,Carbohydrates: 41g,Protein: 9g.

Barbecue Juicy Pork Chops

Servings: 4
Cooking Time: 100 Min

Ingredients:

- 4 bone-in pork chops
- 1½ cups chicken broth /375ml
- 1 tbsp freshly ground black pepper /15g
- 1 tbsp olive oil /15ml
- 4 tbsp barbecue sauce /60ml
- 3 tbsp brown sugar /45g
- 1 tbsp salt /15g
- 1½ tbsp smoked paprika /22.5g
- 2 tsp garlic powder /10g

Directions:

1. Choose Sear/Sauté and set to High. Choose Start/Stop to preheat the pot. In a small bowl, mix the brown sugar, salt, paprika, garlic powder, and black pepper. Season both sides of the pork with the rub. Heat the oil in the preheated pot and sear the pork chops, one at a time, on both sides, about 5 minutes per chop. Set aside.
2. Pour the chicken broth into the pot and with a wooden spoon, scrape the bottom of the pot of any browned bits. Place the Crisping Basket in the upper position of the pot. Put the pork chops in the basket and brush with 2 tbsps of barbecue sauce.
3. Seal the pressure lid, choose Pressure and set to High. Set the time to 5 minutes, then Choose Start/Stop to begin cooking. When the timer is done, perform a natural pressure release for 10 minutes, then a quick pressure release, and carefully open the lid.
4. Apply the remaining barbecue sauce on both sides of the pork and close the crisping lid. Choose Broil and set the time to 3 minutes. Press Start/Stop to begin. When ready, check for your desired crispiness and remove the pork from the basket.

Spicy Thai Basil Beef

Servings:8
Cooking Time: 20 Minutes

Ingredients:

- 2 pounds ground beef
- 2 tablespoons sriracha
- 4 tablespoons fish sauce
- 3 tablespoons soy sauce
- Zest of 2 limes
- Juice of 2 limes
- 3 tablespoons brown sugar
- 2 shallots, diced
- 2 tablespoons minced garlic
- 1 red bell pepper, diced
- 1 bunch Thai basil leaves
- 6 scallions, sliced

Directions:

1. Select SEAR/SAUTÉ and set temperature to HI. Select START/STOP to begin. Let preheat for 5 minutes.
2. Add the ground beef. Cook, stirring occasionally, until the beef is fully cooked, 3 to 5 minutes.
3. In a small bowl, whisk together the sriracha, fish sauce, soy sauce, lime zest and juice, and brown sugar.
4. Once the beef is cooked, add the shallot and garlic and cook until soft, about 2 minutes.
5. Add sauce mixture and stir. Let boil until reduced slightly, about 5 minutes.
6. Add the bell pepper and basil. Cook just until the basil wilts, about 1 minute.
7. When cooking is complete, garnish with the scallions and serve over rice, if desired.

Nutrition Info:

- Calories: 269,Total Fat: 17g,Sodium: 1137mg,Carbohydrates: 6g,Protein: 22g.

Beef Tips & Mushrooms

Servings: 8
Cooking Time: 5 Hours

Ingredients:

- 2 tbsp. olive oil
- 3 lbs. beef stew meat
- Salt & pepper, to taste
- 3 cups beef broth, low sodium
- 1 pkg. dry onion soup mix
- 1 tbsp. Worcestershire sauce
- 1 onion chopped
- 2 cups mushrooms, sliced
- 3 cloves garlic, chopped fine
- ¼ cup water
- 3 tbsp. cornstarch

Directions:

1. Add the oil to the cooking pot and set to sauté on med-high heat.
2. Season the beef with salt and pepper. Add to the pot, in batches, and cook until browned on all sides. Transfer to a bowl until all the beef has been seared.
3. Return all the beef to the pot and add broth, soup mix, onions, mushrooms, and garlic, stir to combine.
4. Add the lid and set to slow cook on low. Cook 5-6 hours until beef is tender.
5. 30 minutes before the beef tips are done, whisk together the water and cornstarch until smooth and stir into the beef

mixture. Stir well before serving over noodles, mashed potatoes or mashed cauliflower to keep it low carb.

Nutrition Info:

- Calories 285,Total Fat 11g,Total Carbs 9g,Protein 40g,Sodium 1178mg.

Beef Brisket & Carrots

Servings: 10
Cooking Time: 8 Hours 15 Minutes

Ingredients:

- 4 -5 lb. beef brisket,
- 1 ½ tsp salt
- 3 onions, sliced
- 6 cloves garlic, chopped fine
- 1 sprig thyme
- 1 sprig rosemary
- 4 bay leaves
- 2 cups beef broth, low sodium
- 3 carrots, peeled & sliced ½-inch thick
- 1 tbsp. mustard

Directions:

1. Use a sharp knife and score the fat side of the brisket in parallel lines, being careful to only slice through the fat, not the meat. Repeat to create a cross-hatch pattern. Sprinkle with salt and let sit 30 minutes.
2. Set the cooker to sear on med-high and lay brisket, fat side down, in the pot. Cook 5-8 minutes to render the fat. Turn the brisket over and brown the other side. Transfer to a plate.
3. Add the onions and season with salt. Cook, stirring frequently, until onions are browned, about 5-8 minutes. Add the garlic and cook 1 minute more.
4. Stir in remaining ingredients. Add the brisket back to the pot, pushing it down to cover as much as possible by the broth.
5. Add the lid and set to slow cook on low. Cook 8-9 hours or until brisket is tender. Transfer brisket to cutting board and tent with foil. Let rest 10-15 minutes. Slice across the grain to serve with carrots, onions and some of the cooking liquid.

Nutrition Info:

- Calories 143,Total Fat 10g,Total Carbs 2g,Protein 10g,Sodium 833mg.

Skinny Cheesesteaks

Servings: 4
Cooking Time: 10 Minutes

Ingredients:

- ½ tbsp. olive oil
- 1 lb. lean sirloin steak, sliced in very thin strips
- ½ tsp salt
- ¼ tsp pepper
- 2 tsp oregano
- 1 onion, sliced in strips
- 1 green bell pepper, sliced in strips
- 1 red bell pepper, sliced in strips
- 8 large lettuce leaves
- ½ cup provolone cheese, low fat, grated
- 2 tbsp. cilantro, chopped

Directions:

1. Add the oil to the cooking pot and set to sauté on med-high heat.
2. Season the steak with salt and pepper and add to the pot along with the oregano, onion, and bell peppers. Cook, stirring frequently, 5-10 minutes until beef is cooked and vegetables are tender.
3. Place 2 lettuce leaves on each serving plate. Spoon beef mixture onto lettuce and tops with cheese and cilantro. Serve.

Nutrition Info:

- Calories 319,Total Fat 19g,Total Carbs 7g,Protein 29g,Sodium 444mg.

Baked Rigatoni With Beef Tomato Sauce

Servings: 4
Cooking Time: 75 Min

Ingredients:

- 2 pounds ground beef /900g
- 2 cans tomato sauce /720ml
- 16-ounce dry rigatoni /480g
- 1 cup cottage cheese /130g
- 1 cup shredded mozzarella cheese /130g
- ½ cup chopped fresh parsley /65g
- 1 cup water /250ml
- 1 cup dry red wine /250ml
- 1 tbsp butter /15g
- ½ tsp garlic powder /2.5g
- ½ tsp salt /2.5g

Directions:

1. Choose Sear/Sauté and set to High. Choose Start/Stop to preheat the pot. Melt the butter, add the beef and cook for 5 minutes, or until browned and cooked well. Stir in the tomato sauce, water, wine, and rigatoni; season with the garlic powder and salt.
2. Put the pressure lid together and lock in the Seal position. Choose Pressure, set to Low, and set the time to 2 minutes. Choose Start/Stop to begin cooking.
3. When the timer is done, perform a natural pressure release for 10 minutes, then a quick pressure release and carefully open the lid. Stir in the cottage cheese and evenly sprinkle the top of the pasta with the mozzarella cheese. Close the crisping lid.
4. Choose Broil, and set the time to 3 minutes. Choose Start/Stop to begin. Cook for 3 minutes, or until the cheese has melted, slightly browned, and bubbly. Garnish with the parsley and serve immediately.

Crispy Roast Pork

Servings: 4
Cooking Time: 50 Min
Ingredients:

- 4 pork tenderloins
- ¾ tsp garlic powder /3.75g
- 1 tsp five spice seasoning /5g
- ½ tsp white pepper /2.5g
- 1 tsp salt /5g
- Cooking spray

Directions:

1. Place the pork, white pepper, garlic powder, five seasoning, and salt into a bowl and toss to coat. Leave to marinate at room temperature for 30 minutes.
2. Place the pork into the Foodi basket, greased with cooking spray, close the crisping lid and cook for 20 minutes at 360 °F or 183°C. After 10 minutes, turn the tenderloins. Serve hot.

Lone Star Chili

Servings: 8
Cooking Time: 8 Hours
Ingredients:

- 2 tbsp. flour
- 2 lbs. lean beef chuck, cubed
- 1 tbsp. olive oil
- 1 onion, chopped fine
- 2 jalapeño peppers, chopped
- 4 cloves garlic, chopped fine
- 1 tbsp. cumin
- 4 oz. green chilies, drained & chopped
- 3 tbsp. Ancho chili powder
- 1 tsp crushed red pepper flakes
- 1 tsp oregano
- 3 cups beef broth, fat-free & low-sodium
- 28 oz. tomatoes, diced, undrained
- ¼ cup Greek yogurt, fat free
- 3 tbsp. green onions, chopped

Directions:

1. Place the flour in a large Ziploc bag. Add the beef and toss to coat.
2. Add the oil to the cooking pot and set to sauté on med-high.
3. Add the beef and cook, stirring occasionally, until browned on all sides. Add the onions and jalapenos and cook until soft. Stir in the garlic and cook 1 minute more.
4. Stir in remaining ingredients, except yogurt and green onions, mix well. Add the lid and set to slow cook on low. Cook 7-8 hours until chili is thick and beef is tender.
5. Ladle into bowls and top with a dollop of yogurt and green onions. Serve.

Nutrition Info:

- Calories 267,Total Fat 9g,Total Carbs 8g,Protein 36g,Sodium 317mg.

Chipotle Beef Brisket

Servings: 4
Cooking Time: 1 Hr 10 Min
Ingredients:

- 2 pounds, beef brisket /900g
- 1 cup beef broth/250ml
- ¼ cup red wine /62.5ml
- 2 tbsp olive oil /30ml
- 1 tbsp Worcestershire sauce /15ml
- ½ tsp ground cumin /2.5g
- ½ tsp garlic powder /2.5g
- 1 tsp chipotle powder /5g
- ¼ tsp cayenne pepper/1.25g
- 2 tsp smoked paprika /10g
- ½ tsp dried oregano /2.5g
- ½ tsp salt /2.5g
- ½ tsp ground black pepper /2.5g
- A handful of parsley; chopped

Directions:

1. In a bowl, combine oregano, cumin, cayenne pepper, garlic powder, salt, paprika, pepper, Worcestershire sauce and chipotle powder; rub the seasoning mixture on the beef to coat. Warm olive oil on Sear/Sauté. Add in beef and cook for 3 to 4 minutes each side until browned completely. Pour in beef broth and red wine.
2. Seal the pressure lid, choose Pressure, set to High, and set the timer to 50 minutes. Press Start. Release the pressure naturally, for about 10 minutes.
3. Place the beef on a cutting board and Allow cooling for 10 minutes before slicing. Arrange the beef slices on a serving platter, pour the cooking sauce over and scatter with parsley to serve.

Cuban Marinated Pork

Servings: 8
Cooking Time: 10 Hours
Ingredients:

- 4 lb. pork shoulder, bone in
- 1½ tsp salt
- 1 tsp pepper
- ½ cup fresh lime juice
- ¾ cup fresh orange juice
- Zest of 1 orange
- Zest of 1 lime
- ½ cup olive oil
- 8 cloves garlic, chopped fine
- 2 tsp oregano
- 2 tsp cumin
- ¼ cup cilantro, chopped

Directions:

1. Use a sharp knife to score the pork.
2. Add remaining ingredients to the cooking pot and stir to mix. Top with pork.
3. Add the lid and set to slow cook on low. Cook 8-10 hours or until meat is almost tender.
4. Line a baking sheet with foil and place the pork on it. Drain cooking liquid into a large bowl.
5. Add the pork back to the pot and add the tender-crisp lid. Set to roast on 400°F. Cook pork 15-20 minutes until browned.
6. Transfer pork to a cutting board and let rest 10 minutes. Slice and serve topped with some of the reserved cooking liquid.

Nutrition Info:

- Calories 452,Total Fat 24g,Total Carbs 6g,Protein 50g,Sodium 575mg.

Barbeque Sticky Baby Back Ribs With

Servings: 6
Cooking Time: 40 Min

Ingredients:

- 1 reversible rack baby back ribs; cut into bones
- 1/3 cup ketchup /88ml
- 1 cup barbecue sauce /250ml
- ½ cup apple cider /125ml
- 1 tbsp mustard powder /15g
- 1 tbsp smoked paprika /15g
- 2 tbsp olive oil /30ml
- 1 tbsp dried oregano/15g
- ½ tsp ground black pepper /2.5g
- ½ tsp salt /2.5g

Directions:

1. In a bowl, thoroughly combine salt, mustard powder, smoked paprika, oregano, and black pepper. Rub the mixture over the ribs. Warm oil on Sear/Sauté.
2. Add in the ribs and sear for 1 to 2 minutes for each side until browned. Pour apple cider and barbecue sauce into the pot. Turn the ribs to coat.
3. Seal the pressure lid, choose Pressure, set to High, and set the timer to 30 minutes. Press Start. When ready, release the pressure quickly.
4. Place the Cook & Crisp Basket in the pot. Close the crisping lid, choose Air Crisp, set the temperature to 390°F or 199°C, and the time to 5 minutes.
5. Place the ribs with the sauce in the Cook & Crisp Basket. Close the Crisping Lid. Preheat the unit by selecting Air Crisp, setting the temperature to 390°F or 199°C, and setting the time to 7 minutes. Press Start. When ready, the ribs should be sticky with a brown dark color. Transfer the ribs to a serving plate. Baste with the sauce to serve.

Pork Pie

Servings:8
Cooking Time: 45 Minutes

Ingredients:

- 2 tablespoons extra-virgin olive oil
- 1 pound ground pork
- 1 yellow onion, diced
- 1 can black beans, drained
- 1 cup frozen corn kernels
- 1 can green chiles
- 2 tablespoons chili powder
- 1 box cornbread mix
- 1½ cups milk
- 1 cup shredded Cheddar cheese

Directions:

1. Select SEAR/SAUTÉ and set temperature to MED. Select START/STOP to begin. Let preheat for 3 minutes.
2. Add the olive oil, pork, and onion. Brown the pork, stirring frequently to break the meat into smaller pieces, until cooked through, about 5 minutes.
3. Add the beans, corn, chiles, and chili powder and stir. Simmer, stirring frequently, about 10 minutes.
4. In a medium bowl, combine the cornbread mix, milk, and cheese. Pour it over simmering mixture in an even layer. Close crisping lid.
5. Select BAKE/ROAST, set temperature to 360°F, and set time for 25 minutes. Select START/STOP to begin.
6. After 20 minutes, use wooden toothpick to check if cornbread is done. If the toothpick inserted into the cornbread does not come out clean, close lid and cook for the remaining 5 minutes.
7. When cooking is complete, open lid. Let cool for 10 minutes before slicing and serving.

Nutrition Info:

- Calories: 491,Total Fat: 24g,Sodium: 667mg,Carbohydrates: 47g,Protein: 24g.

Ham, Ricotta & Zucchini Fritters

Servings: 4
Cooking Time: 10 Minutes

Ingredients:

- 1 ½ tbsp. butter, unsalted
- 1/3 cup milk
- ½ cup ricotta cheese
- 2 eggs
- 1 ½ tsp baking powder
- ½ tsp salt
- ¼ tsp pepper
- 1 cup flour
- ¼ cup fresh basil, chopped
- 3 oz. ham, cut in strips
- ½ zucchini, cut into matchsticks

Directions:

1. Spray the fryer basket with cooking spray. Place in the cooking pot.
2. Place the butter in a large microwave safe bowl and microwave until melted.
3. Whisk milk and ricotta into melted butter until smooth. Whisk in eggs until combined.
4. Stir in baking powder, salt, and pepper until combined. Stir in flour, until combined.
5. Fold in basil, ham and zucchini until distributed evenly. Drop batter by ¼ cups into fryer basket, these will need to be cooked in batches.
6. Add the tender-crisp lid and set to air fry on 375°F. Cook fritters 4-5 minutes per side until golden brown and cooked through. Serve immediately.

Nutrition Info:

- Calories 180,Total Fat 10g,Total Carbs 15g,Protein 7g,Sodium 451mg.

Beef And Bacon Chili

Servings: 6

Cooking Time: 1 Hr

Ingredients:

- 2 pounds stewing beef, trimmed /900g
- 29 ounces canned whole tomatoes /870g
- 15 ounces canned kidney beans, drained and rinsed /450g
- 4 ounces smoked bacon; cut into strips /120g
- 1 chipotle in adobo sauce, finely chopped
- 1 onion; diced
- 2 bell peppers; diced
- 3 garlic cloves; minced
- 2 cups beef broth /500ml
- 1 tbsp ground cumin/15g
- 2 tsp olive oil; divided /10ml
- 1 tsp chili powder /5g
- ½ tsp cayenne pepper /2.5g
- 4 tsp salt; divided /20g
- 1 tsp freshly ground black pepper; divided /5g

Directions:

1. Set on Sear/Sauté, set to Medium High, and choose Start/Stop to preheat the pot and fry the bacon until crispy, about 5 minutes. Set aside.
2. Rub the beef with ½ tsp or 5g black pepper and 1 tsp or 5g salt. In the bacon fat, brown beef for 5-6 minutes; transfer to a plate.
3. Warm the oil. Add in garlic, peppers and onion and cook for 3 to 4 minutes until soft. Stir in cumin, cayenne pepper, the extra pepper and salt; chopped chipotle, and chili powder and cook for 30 seconds until soft.
4. Return beef and bacon to the pot with vegetables and spices; add in tomatoes and broth.
5. Seal the pressure lid, choose Pressure, set to High, and set the timer to 45 minutes. Press Start. When ready, release the pressure quickly. Stir in beans. Let simmer on Keep Warm for 10 minutes until flavors combine.

Basque Lamb Stew

Servings: 6

Cooking Time: 6 Hours

Ingredients:

- 3 ½ lbs. lamb shoulder, cut in 2-inch pieces
- 6 cloves garlic, chopped fine, divided
- 1 tbsp. fresh rosemary, chopped
- ½ cup dry white wine
- 2 tbsp. olive oil
- 1 onion, chopped
- ½ tsp salt
- 2 tsp sweet paprika
- 10 oz. roasted red bell peppers, cut in ½-inch strips
- 1 tomato, peeled, seeded, & chopped
- 2 tbsp. fresh parsley, chopped
- 1 bay leaf
- 1 cup dry red wine, full bodied
- 1 cup chicken broth, low sodium
- ½ tsp pepper

Directions:

1. Place the lamb in a large bowl and add half the garlic, the rosemary, wine. Cover and refrigerated 2-3 hours.
2. Add the oil to the cooking pot and set to sear.
3. Add the lamb, season with salt, and cook just until brown on the outside. Transfer to bowl.
4. Add the onion to the pot and cook, stirring to scrape up the brown bits on the bottom of the pot. Cook until onions are soft. Add the garlic and cook 1 minute more.
5. Return the lamb to the pot along with remaining ingredients, stir to mix well.
6. Add the lid and set to slow cook on high. Cook 4-6 hours until lamb is tender. Stir to mix, discard the bay leaf and serve.

Nutrition Info:

- Calories 108,Total Fat 5g,Total Carbs 2g,Protein 11g,Sodium 229mg.

Butter Pork Chops

Servings: 4
Cooking Time: 10 Minutes

Ingredients:

- 4 pork chops
- Black pepper and salt, to taste
- 2 tablespoons butter
- 2 teaspoons garlic, minced
- 1/2 cup herbed chicken stock
- 1/2 cup heavy whip cream
- 1/2 a lemon, juiced

Directions:

1. Season the four pork chops with black pepper and salt.
2. Select "Sauté" mode on Ninja Foodi and add oil to heat up.
3. Add pork chops and sauté both sides until the golden, total for 6 minutes.
4. Remove thighs to a platter and keep it on the side.
5. Add garlic and cook for 2 minutes.
6. Whisk in chicken stock, heavy cream, lemon juice and bring the sauce to simmer and reintroduce the pork chops.
7. Lock and secure the Ninja Foodi's lid and cook for 10 minutes on "HIGH" pressure.
8. Release pressure naturally over 10 minutes.
9. Serve warm and enjoy.

Nutrition Info:

- Calories: 294; Fat: 26g; Carbohydrates: 4g; Protein: 12g

Mexican Pork Stir Fry

Servings: 4
Cooking Time: 15 Minutes

Ingredients:

- 12 oz. pork tenderloin
- 4 slices hickory bacon, chopped
- 1 chipotle chili, chopped
- 1 tbsp. olive oil
- 1 tsp cumin
- 1 tsp oregano
- 2 cloves garlic, chopped
- 1 red bell pepper, cut in strips
- 1 onion, halved & sliced thin
- 3 cups lettuce, chopped

Directions:

1. Slice tenderloin in half lengthwise, and then cut crosswise thinly. Toss pork, bacon and chipotle pieces together in small bowl; set aside.
2. Add oil, cumin, oregano, and garlic to the cooking pot. Set to sauté on med-high heat.
3. Add bell pepper and onion and cook, stirring frequently, 3-4 minutes until tender-crisp. Transfer to a bowl.
4. Add pork mixture to the pot and cook, stirring frequently, 3-4 minutes until bacon is crisp and pork is no longer pink.
5. Return vegetables to the pot and cook until heated through. Serve over a bed of lettuce.

Nutrition Info:

- Calories 322,Total Fat 18g,Total Carbs 5g,Protein 34g,Sodium 192mg.

Jamaican Pork

Servings: 4
Cooking Time: 25 Minutes

Ingredients:

- 1 tbsp. butter
- 1 tsp curry powder
- 2 bananas, sliced ½-inch thick
- 1 lb. pork tenderloin, cubed
- ½ tsp salt
- ½ cup pineapple juice, unsweetened
- ¼ cup onion, chopped fine
- ¼ cup coconut flakes, unsweetened

Directions:

1. Add butter to the cooking pot and set to sauté on medium heat.
2. Once the butter has melted, stir in curry powder until foamy.
3. Add bananas and cook until golden brown, about 3-5 minutes. Transfer to a plate.
4. Add pork and cook until golden brown, about 6-8 minutes. Season with salt.
5. Stir in pineapple juice and onion. Cover, reduce heat, and simmer 10 minutes until pork is tender.
6. Stir in coconut and bananas and toss gently to combine. Serve over cooked rice.

Nutrition Info:

- Calories 247,Total Fat 7g,Total Carbs 21g,Protein 25g,Sodium 100mg.

Pot Roast With Biscuits

Servings: 6

Cooking Time: 75 Min

Ingredients:

- 1 chuck roast /1350g
- 1 pound small butternut squash; diced /450g
- 1 small red onion, peeled and quartered
- 2 carrots, peeled and cut into 1-inch pieces
- 6 refrigerated biscuits
- 1 bay leaf
- ⅔ cup dry red wine /176ml
- ⅔ cup beef broth /176ml
- ¾ cup frozen pearl onions /98g
- 2 tbsp olive oil /30ml
- 1½ tsp salt /7.5g
- 1 tsp dried oregano leaves /5g
- ¼ tsp black pepper /1.25g

Directions:

1. On the Foodi, choose Sear/Sauté and adjust to Medium-High. Press Start to preheat the pot. Heat the olive oil until shimmering. Season the beef on both sides with salt and add to the pot. Cook, undisturbed, for 3 minutes or until deeply browned. Flip the roast over and brown the other side for 3 minutes. Transfer the beef to a wire rack.
2. Pour the oil out of the pot and add the wine to the pot. Stir with a wooden spoon, scraping the bottom of the pot to let off any browned bits. Bring to a boil and cook for 1 to 2 minutes or until the wine has reduced by half.
3. Mix in the beef broth, oregano, bay leaf, black pepper, and red onion. Stir to combine and add the beef with its juices. Seal the pressure lid and choose Pressure; adjust the pressure to High and the cook time to 35 minutes. Press Start to begin cooking.
4. After cooking, perform a quick pressure release. Carefully open the pressure lid.
5. Add the butternut squash, carrots, and pearl onions to the pot. Lock the pressure lid into place, set to Seal position and Choose Pressure; adjust the pressure to High and the cook time to 2 minutes. Press Start to cook the vegetables.
6. After cooking, perform a quick pressure release, and open the lid. Transfer the beef to a cutting board and cover with aluminum foil.
7. Put the reversible rack in the upper position of the pot and cover with a circular piece of aluminum foil. Put the biscuits on the rack and put the rack in the pot.
8. Close the crisping lid and Choose Bake/Roast; adjust the temperature to 300°F and the cook time to 15 minutes. Press Start. After 8 minutes, open the lid and carefully flip the biscuits over. After baking, remove the rack and biscuits. Allow the biscuits to cool for a few minutes before serving.
9. While the biscuits cook, remove the foil from the beef and cut it against the grain into slices. Remove and discard the bay leaf and transfer the beef to a serving platter. Spoon the vegetables and the sauce over the beef. Serve with the biscuits.

Poultry

Korean Barbecued Satay

Servings: 4
Cooking Time: 4h 15 Min

Ingredients:

- 1 lb. boneless; skinless chicken tenders /450g
- ½ cup pineapple juice /125ml
- ½ cup soy sauce /125ml
- ⅓ cup sesame oil /84ml
- 4 scallions; chopped
- 1 pinch black pepper
- 4 cloves garlic; chopped
- 2 tsp sesame seeds, toasted /10g
- 1 tsp fresh ginger, grated /5g

Directions:

1. Skew each tender and trim any excess fat. Mix the other ingredients in one large bowl. Add the skewered chicken and place in the fridge for 4 to 24 hours.
2. Preheat the Foodi to 370 For 188°C. Using a paper towel, pat the chicken dry. Fry for 10 minutes on Air Crisp mode.

Chicken Thighs With Cabbage

Servings: 4
Cooking Time: 35 Min

Ingredients:

- 1 pound green cabbage, shredded /450g
- 4 slices pancetta; diced
- 4 chicken thighs, boneless skinless
- 1 cup chicken broth /250ml
- 1 tbsp Dijon mustard/15g
- 1 tbsp lard /15g
- Fresh parsley; chopped
- salt and ground black pepper to taste

Directions:

1. Warm lard on Sear/Sauté. Fry pancetta for 5 minutes until crisp. Set aside. Season chicken with pepper and salt. Sear in Foodi for 2 minutes each side until browned. In a bowl, mix mustard and chicken broth.
2. In your Foodi, add pancetta and chicken broth mixture. Seal the pressure lid, choose Pressure, set to High, and set the timer to 6 minutes. Press Start. When ready, release the pressure quickly.
3. Open the lid, mix in green cabbage, seal again, and cook on High Pressure for 2 minutes. When ready, release the pressure quickly. Serve with sprinkled parsley.

Turkey Croquettes

Servings: 10
Cooking Time: 20 Minutes

Ingredients:

- Nonstick cooking spray
- 2 ½ cups turkey, cooked
- 1 stalk celery, chopped
- 2 green onions, chopped
- ½ cup cauliflower, cooked
- ½ cup broccoli, cooked
- 1 cup stuffing, cooked
- 1 cup cracker crumbs
- 1 egg, lightly beaten
- 1/8 tsp salt
- 1/8 tsp pepper
- 1 cup French fried onions, crushed

Directions:

1. Spray the fryer basket with cooking spray.
2. Add the turkey, celery, onion, cauliflower, and broccoli to a food processor and pulse until finely chopped. Transfer to a large bowl.
3. Stir in stuffing and 1 cup of the cracker crumbs until combined.
4. Add the egg, salt and pepper and stir to combine. Form into 10 patties.
5. Place the crushed fried onions in a shallow dish. Coat patties on both sides in the onions and place in the basket. Lightly spray the tops with cooking spray.
6. Add the tender-crisp lid and set to air fry on 375°F. Cook 5-7 minutes until golden brown. Flip over and spray with cooking spray again, cook another 5-7 minutes. Serve immediately.

Nutrition Info:

- Calories 133,Total Fat 4g,Total Carbs 16g,Protein 9g,Sodium 449mg.

Healthy Chicken Stew

Servings: 4
Cooking Time: 4 Hours

Ingredients:

- 1 large potato, peeled & chopped
- 2 carrots, peeled & sliced
- ½ tsp salt
- ¼ tsp pepper
- 2 cloves garlic, chopped fine
- 3 cups chicken broth, low sodium
- 2 bay leaves
- 2 chicken breasts, boneless, skinless & cut in pieces
- ½ tsp thyme
- ¼ tsp basil
- 1 tsp paprika
- 2 tbsp. cornstarch
- ½ cup water

- 1 cup green peas

Directions:

1. Add the potatoes, carrots, salt, pepper, garlic, broth, bay leaves, chicken, thyme, basil, and paprika to the cooking pot, stir to mix.
2. Add the lid and set to slow cook on high. Cook 4 hours or until vegetables and chicken are tender.
3. In a small bowl, whisk together cornstarch and water until smooth. Stir into the cooking pot along with the peas.
4. Recover and cook another 15 minutes. Stir well before serving.

Nutrition Info:

- Calories 187,Total Fat 2g,Total Carbs 25g,Protein 17g,Sodium 1038mg.

Spicy Onion Crusted Chicken Tenders

Servings: 6

Cooking Time: 10 Minutes

Ingredients:

- Nonstick cooking spray
- ½ cup hot pepper sauce
- 2 cups French-fried onions, crushed
- 1 ½ lbs. chicken tenders

Directions:

1. Spray fryer basket with cooking spray.
2. Pour the hot sauce in a shallow dish.
3. In a separate shallow dish, place the crushed onions.
4. Dip each piece of chicken in the hot sauce then coat with onions. Place in a single layer in the fryer basket, these will need to be cooked in batches.
5. Add the tender-crisp lid and to air fry on 400°F. Cook chicken 10 minutes, until golden brown and cooked through, turning over halfway through cooking tine. Serve immediately.

Nutrition Info:

- Calories 154,Total Fat 3g,Total Carbs 6g,Protein 24g,Sodium 541mg.

Buffalo Chicken And Navy Bean Chili

Servings: 6

Cooking Time: 45 Min

Ingredients:

- 1 ½ pounds chicken sausage; sliced /675g
- 1 can diced tomatoes with green chilies /420g
- 2 cans navy beans, drained and rinsed /420g
- 1 can crushed tomatoes /840g
- ¾ cup Buffalo wing sauce /188ml
- 1 shallot; diced
- ½ cup fennel; chopped /65g
- ¼ cup minced garlic /32.5g
- 1 tbsp olive oil /15ml
- 1 tbsp smoked paprika /15ml
- 2 tsp chili powder /10g
- 2 tsp ground cumin /10g
- ½ tsp salt /2.5g
- ½ tsp ground white pepper /2.5g

Directions:

1. Warm oil on Sear/Sauté. Add the sausages and brown for 5 minutes, turning frequently. Set aside on a plate.
2. In the same fat, sauté onion, roasted red peppers, fennel, and garlic for 4 minutes until soft; season with paprika, cumin, pepper, salt, and chili powder.
3. Stir in crushed tomatoes; diced tomatoes with green chilies, buffalo sauce, and navy beans. Return the sausages to the pot.
4. Seal the pressure lid, choose Pressure, set to High, and set the timer to 30 minutes. Press Start. When ready, do a quick pressure release. Spoon chili into bowls and serve warm.

Crunchy Chicken & Almond Casserole

Servings: 6

Cooking Time: 30 Minutes

Ingredients:

- Nonstick cooking spray
- 3 cups chicken breast, cooked & chopped
- ¾ cup mozzarella cheese, grated
- 10 ¾ oz. condensed cream of chicken soup, low fat
- ¼ cup skim milk
- 1 cup red bell pepper, chopped
- ¼ cup celery, chopped
- ¼ cup green onions, sliced
- ¼ tsp pepper
- ¼ cup cornflakes, crushed
- ¼ cup almonds, sliced

Directions:

1. Spray the cooking pot with cooking spray.
2. In a large bowl, combine chicken, cheese, soup, milk, bell pepper, celery, green onions, and pepper. Pour into the pot.
3. In a small bowl, combine cornflakes and almonds, sprinkle over the top of the chicken mixture.
4. Add the tender-crisp lid and set to bake on 400°F. Bake 30 minutes until casserole is hot and bubbly. Turn off the heat and let sit 10 minutes before serving.

Nutrition Info:

- Calories 266,Total Fat 13g,Total Carbs 7g,Protein 28g,Sodium 526mg.

Chicken With Rice And Peas

Servings: 4
Cooking Time: 30 Min
Ingredients:

- 4 boneless; skinless chicken breasts; sliced
- 1 onion; chopped
- 1 celery stalk; diced
- 1 garlic clove; minced
- 2 cups chicken broth; divided /500ml
- 1 cup long grain rice /130g
- 1 cup frozen green peas /130g
- 1 tbsp oil olive /15ml
- 1 tbsp tomato puree /15ml
- ½ tsp paprika /2.5g
- ¼ tsp dried oregano/1.25g
- ¼ tsp dried thyme /1.25g
- ⅛ tsp cayenne pepper /0.625g
- ⅛ tsp ground white pepper /0.625g
- Salt to taste

Directions:

1. Season chicken with garlic powder, oregano, white pepper, thyme, paprika, cayenne pepper, and salt. Warm the oil on Sear/Sauté. Add in onion and cook for 4 minutes until fragrant. Mix in tomato puree to coat.
2. Add ¼ cup or 65ml chicken stock into the Foodi to deglaze the pan, scrape the pan's bottom to get rid of browned bits of food. Mix in celery, rice, and the seasoned chicken. Add in the remaining broth to the chicken mixture.
3. Seal the pressure lid, choose Pressure, set to High, and set the timer to 8 minutes. Press Start. Once ready, do a quick release. Mix in green peas, cover with the lid and let sit for 5 minutes. Serve warm.

Chicken Fajitas With Avocado

Servings: 4
Cooking Time: 30 Min
Ingredients:

- 4 chicken breasts, boneless and skinless
- 1 can diced tomatoes /720g
- 3 bell peppers, julienned
- 1 shallot; chopped
- 4 garlic cloves; minced
- 4 flour tortillas
- 1 avocado; sliced
- 1 taco seasoning
- 2 tbsp cilantro; chopped /30g
- 1 tbsp olive oil /15ml
- Juice of 1 lemon
- salt and pepper to taste

Directions:

1. In a bowl, mix taco seasoning and chicken until evenly coated. Warm oil on Sear/Sauté. Sear chicken for 2 minutes per side until browned. To the chicken, add tomatoes, shallot, lemon juice, garlic, and bell peppers; season with pepper and salt.
2. Seal the pressure lid, choose Pressure, set to High, and set the timer to 4 minutes. Press Start. When ready, release the pressure quickly.
3. Move the bell peppers and chicken to tortillas. Add avocado slices and serve.

Chicken Breasts

Servings: 4
Cooking Time: 15 Min
Ingredients:

- 4 boneless; skinless chicken breasts
- 1/4 cup dry white wine /62.5ml
- 1 cup water /250ml
- ½ tsp marjoram /2.5g
- ½ tsp sage /2.5g
- ½ tsp rosemary /2.5g
- ½ tsp mint /2.5g
- ½ tsp salt /2.5g

Directions:

1. Sprinkle salt over the chicken and set in the pot of the Foodi. Mix in mint, rosemary, marjoram, and sage. Pour wine and water around the chicken.
2. Seal the pressure lid, choose Pressure, set to High, and set the timer to 6 minutes. Press Start. Release the pressure naturally for 10 minutes.

Basil Cheddar Stuffed Chicken

Servings: 4
Cooking Time: 25 Min
Ingredients:

- 2 large chicken breasts, skinless
- 4 cherry tomatoes, halved
- 4 slices cheddar cheese
- A handful of fresh basil leaves
- 2 tbsp olive oil /30ml
- Salt and pepper to taste

Directions:

1. With a sharp knife; cut a slit into the side of each chicken breast. Put 2 slices of cheese, 3-4 basil leaves, and 4 cherry tomato halves into each slit. Use toothpicks to keep the chicken breasts closed.
2. Season the meat with salt and pepper, and brush with some olive oil. Grease the Foodi basket with the remaining olive oil and place the chicken breasts in the basket; close the crisping lid and cook for 12 minutes at 370 °F or 188°C.
3. After 6 minutes, turn the breasts over. Once ready, leave to sit the chicken breasts, then slice each one in half and serve with salad.

Salsa Chicken With Feta

Servings: 6
Cooking Time: 30 Min
Ingredients:

- 2 pounds boneless skinless chicken drumsticks /900g
- 1 cup feta cheese, crumbled /130g
- 1 ½ cups hot tomato salsa /375ml
- 1 onion; chopped
- ¼ tsp salt /1.25g

Directions:

1. Sprinkle salt over the chicken; set in the inner steel pot of Foodi. Stir in salsa to coat the chicken. Seal the pressure lid, choose Pressure, set to High, and set the timer to 15 minutes. Press Start. When ready, do a quick pressure release.
2. Press Sear/Sauté and cook for 5 to 10 minutes as you stir until excess liquid has evaporated. Top with feta cheese and serve.

Thyme Turkey Nuggets

Servings: 2
Cooking Time: 20 Min
Ingredients:

- 8 oz. turkey breast, boneless and skinless /240g
- 1 cup breadcrumbs /130g
- 1 egg, beaten
- 1 tbsp dried thyme /15g
- ½ tsp dried parsley /2.5g
- Salt and pepper, to taste

Directions:

1. Mince the turkey in a food processor. Transfer to a bowl. Stir in the thyme and parsley, and season with salt and pepper.
2. Take a nugget-sized piece of the turkey mixture and shape it into a ball, or another form. Dip it in the breadcrumbs, then egg, then in the breadcrumbs again. Place the nuggets onto a prepared baking dish. Close the crisping lid and cook for 10 minutes on Air Crisp mode at 350 °F or 177°C

Honey Garlic Chicken

Servings: 4
Cooking Time: 30 Min
Ingredients:

- 4 boneless; skinless chicken breast; cut into chunks
- 4 garlic cloves, smashed
- 1 onion; diced
- ½ cup honey /125ml
- 1 tbsp cornstarch /15g
- 1 tbsp water /15ml
- 2 tbsp lime juice /30ml
- 3 tbsp soy sauce /45ml
- 2 tsp sesame oil /10ml
- 1 tsp rice vinegar /5ml
- Salt and black pepper to taste

Directions:

1. Mix garlic, onion and chicken in your Foodi. In a bowl, combine honey, sesame oil, lime juice, soy sauce, and rice vinegar; pour over the chicken mixture.
2. Seal the pressure lid, choose Pressure, set to High, and set the timer to 15 minutes. Press Start. When ready, release the pressure quickly.
3. Mix water and cornstarch until well dissolved; stir into the sauce. Press Sear/Sauté. Simmer the sauce and cook for 2 to 3 minutes as you stir until thickened.

Chicken Wings With Lemon

Servings: 4
Cooking Time: 40 Min
Ingredients:

- 8 chicken wings
- ½ cup chicken broth /125ml
- 2 lemons, juiced
- ½ dried oregano
- 2 tbsp olive oil /30ml
- ½ tsp cayenne pepper /2.5g
- ½ tsp chili powder /2.5g
- ½ tsp garlic powder /2.5g
- ½ tsp onion powder /2.5g
- Sea salt and ground black pepper to taste

Directions:

1. Coat the chicken wings with olive oil; season with chili powder, onion powder, salt, oregano, garlic powder, cayenne, and pepper.
2. In the steel pot of the Foodi, add your wings and chicken broth. Seal the pressure lid, choose Pressure, set to High, and set the timer to 4 minutes. Press Start. When ready, do a quick pressure release. Preheat an oven to high.
3. Onto a greased baking sheet, place the wings in a single layer and drizzle over the lemon juice. Bake for 5 minutes until skin is crispy.

Chicken Burrito Bowl

Servings:4
Cooking Time: 10 Minutes
Ingredients:

- 1 pound boneless, skinless chicken breasts, cut into 1-inch chunks
- 1 tablespoon chili powder
- 1½ teaspoons cumin
- 1 teaspoon sea salt
- 1 teaspoon freshly ground black pepper
- ½ teaspoon paprika
- ¼ teaspoon garlic powder
- ¼ teaspoon onion powder
- ¼ teaspoon cayenne pepper

- ¼ teaspoon dried oregano
- 1 cup chicken stock
- ¼ cup water
- 1¼ cups of your favorite salsa
- 1 can corn kernels, drained
- 1 can black beans, rinsed and drained
- 1 cup rice
- ¾ cup shredded Cheddar cheese

Directions:

1. Add the chicken, chili powder, cumin, salt, black pepper, paprika, garlic powder, onion powder, cayenne pepper, oregano, chicken stock, water, salsa, corn, and beans and stir well.
2. Add the rice to the top of the ingredients in the pot. Assemble pressure lid, making sure the pressure release valve is in the SEAL position.
3. Select PRESSURE and set to HI. Set time to 10 minutes. Select START/STOP to begin.
4. When pressure cooking is complete, quick release the pressure by moving the pressure release valve to the VENT position. Carefully remove lid when the unit has finished releasing pressure.
5. Add the cheese and stir. Serve immediately.

Nutrition Info:

- Calories: 570,Total Fat: 11g,Sodium: 1344mg,Carbohydrates: 77g,Protein: 45g.

Sweet Garlicky Chicken Wings

Servings: 4

Cooking Time: 20 Min

Ingredients:

- 16 chicken wings
- 4 garlic cloves; minced
- ¾ cup potato starch /98g
- ¼ cup butter /32.5g
- ¼ cup honey /62.5ml
- ½ tsp salt /2.5g

Directions:

1. Rinse and pat dry the wings, and place them in a bowl. Add the starch to the bowl, and mix to coat the chicken.
2. Place the chicken in a baking dish that has been previously coated lightly with cooking oil. Close the crisping lid and cook for 5 minutes on Air Crisp mode at 370 °F or 188°C.
3. Meanwhile, whisk the rest of the ingredients together in a bowl. Pour the sauce over the wings and cook for another 10 minutes.

Chicken Chickpea Chili

Servings: 4

Cooking Time: 25 Min

Ingredients:

- 1 pound boneless; skinless chicken breast; cubed /450g
- 2 cans chickpeas, drained and rinsed /435g
- 1 jalapeño pepper; diced
- 1 lime; cut into six wedges
- 3 large serrano peppers; diced
- 1 onion; diced
- ½ cup chopped fresh cilantro /65g
- ½ cup shredded Monterey Jack cheese /65g
- 2 ½ cups water; divided /675ml
- 1 tbsp olive oil /15ml
- 2 tbsp chili powder /30g
- 1 tsp ground cumin /5g
- 1 tsp minced fresh garlic /5g
- 1 tsp salt /5g

Directions:

1. Warm oil on Sear/Sauté. Add in onion, serrano peppers, and jalapeno pepper and cook for 5 minutes until tender; add salt, cumin and garlic for seasoning.
2. Stir chicken with vegetable mixture; cook for 3 to 6 minutes until no longer pink; add 2 cups or 500ml water and chickpeas.
3. Seal the pressure lid, choose Pressure, set to High, and set the timer to 5 minutes. Press Start. Release pressure naturally for 5 minutes. Press Start. Stir chili powder with remaining ½ cup or 125ml water; mix in chili.
4. Press Sear/Sauté. Boil the chili as you stir and cook until slightly thickened. Divide chili into plates; garnish with cheese and cilantro. Over the chili, squeeze a lime wedge.

Creamy Chicken Carbonara

Servings:4

Cooking Time: 15 Minutes

Ingredients:

- 4 strips bacon, chopped
- 1 medium onion, diced
- 1½ pounds chicken breast, cut into ¾ inch-cubes
- 6 garlic cloves, minced
- 2 cups chicken stock
- 8 ounces dry spaghetti, with noodles broken in half
- 2 cups freshly grated Parmesan cheese, plus more for serving
- 2 eggs
- Sea salt
- Freshly ground black pepper

Directions:

1. Select SEAR/SAUTÉ and set to HI. Select START/STOP to begin. Let preheat for 5 minutes.
2. Add the bacon and cook, stirring frequently, for about 6 minutes, or until crispy. Using a slotted spoon, transfer the bacon to a paper towel-lined plate to drain. Leave any bacon fat in the pot.
3. Add the onion, chicken, and garlic and sauté for 2 minutes, until the onions start to become translucent and the garlic is fragrant.

4. Add the chicken stock and spaghetti noodles. Assemble pressure lid, making sure the pressure release valve is in the SEAL position.
5. Select PRESSURE and set to HI. Set time to 6 minutes. Select START/STOP to begin.
6. When pressure cooking is complete, allow pressure to naturally release for 5 minutes. After 5 minutes, quick release remaining pressure by moving the pressure release valve to the VENT position. Carefully remove lid when unit has finished releasing pressure.
7. Add the cheese and stir to fully combine. Close the crisping lid, leaving the unit off, to keep the heat inside and allow the cheese to melt.
8. Whisk the eggs until full beaten.
9. Open lid, select SEAR/SAUTÉ, and set to LO. Select START/STOP to begin. Add the eggs and stir gently to incorporate, taking care to ensure the eggs are not scrambling while you work toward your desired sauce consistency. If your pot gets too warm, turn unit off.
10. Add the bacon back to the pot and season with salt and pepper. Stir to combine. Serve, adding more cheese as desired.

Nutrition Info:

- Calories: 732,Total Fat: 28g,Sodium: 1518mg,Carbohydrates: 47g,Protein: 70g.

Sesame Chicken Wings

Servings: 4
Cooking Time: 65 Min

Ingredients:

- 24 chicken wings
- 2 garlic cloves; minced
- 2 tbsp honey /30ml
- 1 tbsp toasted sesame seeds /15g
- 2 tbsp sesame oil /30ml
- 2 tbsp hot garlic sauce /30ml

Directions:

1. Pour 1 cup of water into the Foodi's inner pot and place the reversible rack in the lower position of the pot. Place the chicken wings on the rack.
2. Seal the pressure lid, choose Pressure; adjust the pressure to High and the cook time to 10 minutes. Press Start to begin cooking the chicken.
3. While the wings cook, prepare the glaze. In a large bowl, whisk the sesame oil, hot garlic sauce, honey, and garlic.
4. After cooking, perform a quick pressure release, and carefully open the lid. Remove the rack from the pot and empty the water in the pot. Return the pot to the base.
5. Close the crisping lid and Choose Air Crisp; adjust the temperature to 375°F or 191°C and the time to 3 minutes to preheat the inner pot. Press Start.
6. Toss the wings in the sauce to properly coat. Put the wings in the Crisping Basket, leaving any excess sauce in the bowl.
7. Place the basket in the Foodi and close the crisping lid. Choose Air Crisp and adjust the cook time to 15 minutes. Press Start to commence crisping.
8. After 8 minutes, open the lid and use tongs to turn the wings. Close the lid to resume browning until the wings are crisp and the glaze set. Before serving, drizzle with any remaining sauce and sprinkle with the sesame seeds.

Sesame Crusted Chicken

Servings: 6
Cooking Time: 10 Minutes

Ingredients:

- Nonstick cooking spray
- 1 egg
- 2 tbsp. water
- ½ cup Italian-seasoned bread crumbs
- 2 tbsp. sesame seeds
- 1 tsp thyme
- 1 tsp garlic powder
- ¼ tsp salt
- ¼ tsp pepper
- 4 chicken breasts, boneless & skinless

Directions:

1. Spray the fryer basket with cooking spray and place it in the cooking pot.
2. In a shallow dish, whisk egg and water until combined.
3. In another shallow dish, combine remaining ingredients, mix well.
4. Place chicken between 2 sheets of plastic wrap and pound out to ¼-inch thick.
5. Dip chicken first in the egg then coat with bread crumb mixture. Place in the fryer basket.
6. Add the tender-crisp lid and set to air fry on 375°F. Cook chicken 10 minutes, turning over halfway through cooking time, or until chicken is no longer pink. Serve.

Nutrition Info:

- Calories 155,Total Fat 5g,Total Carbs 7g,Protein 20g,Sodium 210mg.

Stacked Chicken Enchiladas With Roasted Veggies

Servings: 8
Cooking Time: 1 Hour 15 Minutes

Ingredients:

- Nonstick cooking spray
- 1 zucchini, cut in 1-inch pieces
- 1 yellow squash, cut in 1-inch pieces
- 1 eggplant, cut in 1-inch pieces
- 1 onion, cut in 1-inch pieces
- 1 tbsp. olive oil
- 1 tsp salt
- 2 cups chicken, cooked & chopped
- 20 oz. red enchilada sauce

- ½ tsp chili powder
- 1 jalapeno, seeded & chopped
- 10 small corn tortillas
- 10 oz. Monterey Jack cheese, grated

Directions:

1. Spray the fryer basket with cooking spray.
2. Place the vegetables in a large bowl and drizzle oil over them. Sprinkle with salt and toss to coat.
3. Place the vegetables in the fryer basket and add the tender-crisp lid. Set to bake on 475°F. Bake 45 minutes or until vegetables are light brown, mixing them up as they cook a few times.
4. In a medium bowl, mix the chicken with 2-3 tablespoons enchilada sauce.
5. Place the roasted vegetables back in the large bowl and add the jalapeno and pimentos, mix well.
6. Spray the cooking pot with cooking spray. Pour just enough enchilada sauce to cover the bottom of the cooking pot.
7. Lay 3 tortillas, overlapping them, in the pot and top with a thin layer of sauce. Add 1/3 of the cheese, ½ the vegetable mixture and half the chicken. Repeat this layer again. Top with remaining tortillas and pour remaining sauce over the top then sprinkle on remaining cheese.
8. Add the tender-crisp lid and set to bake on 350°F. Bake 30 minutes until sauce is hot and bubbling and cheese has started to brown. Serve.

Nutrition Info:

- Calories 107,Total Fat 5g,Total Carbs 8g,Protein 8g,Sodium 373mg.

Paprika Chicken

Servings: 4

Cooking Time: 5 Minutes

Ingredients:

- 4 chicken breasts, skin on
- Black pepper and salt, to taste
- 1 tablespoon olive oil
- ½ cup sweet onion, chopped
- ½ cup heavy whip cream
- 2 teaspoons smoked paprika
- ½ cup sour cream
- 2 tablespoons fresh parsley, chopped

Directions:

1. Season the four chicken breasts with black pepper and salt.
2. Select "Sauté" mode on your Ninja Foodi and add oil; let the oil heat up.
3. Add chicken and sear both sides until properly browned, should take about 15 minutes.
4. Remove chicken and transfer them to a plate.
5. Take a suitable skillet and place it over medium heat; stir in onion.
6. Sauté for 4 minutes until tender.
7. Stir in cream, paprika and bring the liquid to a simmer.
8. Return chicken to the skillet and alongside any juices.
9. Transfer the whole mixture to your Ninja Foodi and lock lid, cook on "HIGH" pressure for 5 minutes.
10. Release pressure naturally over 10 minutes.
11. Stir in sour cream, serve and enjoy.

Nutrition Info:

- Calories: 389; Fat: 30g; Carbohydrates: 4g; Protein: 25g

Spicy Southern Chicken

Servings: 4

Cooking Time: 20 Minutes

Ingredients:

- Nonstick cooking spray
- 1 tsp onion powder
- 1 tsp garlic powder
- 1 tsp oregano
- 1 tsp pepper
- 1 tsp thyme
- ½ tsp cayenne pepper
- 2 tsp paprika
- 1 tsp salt
- 2 lbs. chicken breasts, boneless & skinless

Directions:

1. Spray the cooking pot with cooking spray.
2. In a medium bowl, combine the spices and seasonings until well mixed.
3. Coat all sides of the chicken with the spice mixture. Place in the pot.
4. Add the tender-crisp lid and set to roast on 425°F. Cook 20 minutes or until chicken is cooked through. Let rest 5 minutes before serving.

Nutrition Info:

- Calories 257,Total Fat 6g,Total Carbs 2g,Protein 47g,Sodium 501mg.

Turkey & Squash Casserole

Servings: 8

Cooking Time: 55 Minutes

Ingredients:

- 2 tsp olive oil
- 1 onion, chopped
- 1 lb. zucchini, sliced ¼-inch thick
- 1 lb. yellow squash, sliced ¼-inch thick
- 14 ½ oz. tomatoes, diced
- ¼ cup fresh basil, chopped
- 1 tsp garlic powder
- 10 ¾ oz. cream of chicken soup, low sodium
- 1 cup sour cream, fat free
- 1 cup sharp cheddar cheese, reduced fat, grated
- 4 cups turkey, cooked & chopped
- ½ tsp black pepper
- 2 tbsp. whole wheat bread crumbs

Directions:

1. Add the oil to the cooking pot and set to sauté on med-high heat.
2. Add the onion, zucchini, and yellow squash and cook until soft, about 10 minutes.
3. Transfer to a large bowl and stir in tomatoes, basil, and garlic powder.
4. In a medium bowl, combine soup, sour cream, cheese, turkey, and pepper, mix well.
5. Spread half the vegetable mixture on the bottom of the pot. Top with half the chicken mixture. Repeat. Sprinkle the bread crumbs over the top.
6. Add the tender-crisp lid and set to bake on 350°F. Bake 45 minutes or until hot and bubbly. Serve.

Nutrition Info:

- Calories 219,Total Fat 5g,Total Carbs 18g,Protein 25g,Sodium 469mg.

Indian Butter Chicken

Servings: 8

Cooking Time: 15 Minutes

Ingredients:

- 2 14 oz. cans tomatoes, diced & undrained
- 2 jalapeño peppers, seeded & chopped
- 2 tbsp. fresh ginger, peeled & chopped
- 1 tbsp. paprika
- 2 tsp cumin
- 2 tsp garam masala
- 2 tsp salt
- ½ cup butter, unsalted
- 10 chicken thighs, boneless & skinless
- 2 tbsp. cornstarch
- 2 tbsp. water
- ¾ cup heavy cream
- ¾ cup plain Greek yogurt
- ¼ cup cilantro, chopped & packed

Directions:

1. Add the tomatoes, jalapenos, ginger, paprika, cumin, garam masala, and salt to a food processor or blender, pulse until pureed.
2. Add the butter to the cooking pot and set to sauté on medium heat.
3. Once butter has melted, add chicken, a few at a time, and cook until nicely browned on all sides. Transfer chicken to a cutting board.
4. Add tomato mixture and cook, stirring up all the brown bits on the bottom of the pot. Turn off the heat.
5. Slice the chicken into bite-size pieces and return to the pot with the cooking juices, stir to mix.
6. Add the lid and set to pressure cook on high. Set the timer for 5 minutes. Once the timer goes off use quick release to remove the pressure.
7. In a small bowl, whisk together cornstarch and water until smooth. Add to the cooking pot and set to sauté on med-high heat. Bring to a boil and cook until sauce has thickened, about 1-2 minutes.
8. Turn off the heat and stir in sour cream, yogurt, and cilantro. Serve.

Nutrition Info:

- Calories 376,Total Fat 26g,Total Carbs 8g,Protein 27g,Sodium 1296mg.

Smoked Turkey & Collard Greens

Servings: 6

Cooking Time: 35 Minutes

Ingredients:

- 1 smoked turkey leg, cooked
- 1 cup onion, chopped
- 3 cloves garlic, chopped fine
- 1 ½ cups chicken broth, low sodium
- 1 lb. fresh collard greens
- ¼ tsp red pepper flakes
- 1 tbsp. apple cider vinegar

Directions:

1. Add the turkey leg, onion, garlic, red pepper flakes, and broth to the cooking pot, stir to mix.
2. Add the collard greens to the pot and mix.
3. Add the lid and set to pressure cook on high. Set timer for 35 minutes. Once the timer goes off, use the quick release to remove the pressure.
4. Transfer turkey leg to a cutting board and use a fork to shred the meat. Return the meat to the pot. Stir in the vinegar and serve immediately.

Nutrition Info:

- Calories 145,Total Fat 6g,Total Carbs 11g,Protein 16g,Sodium 786mg.

Bacon Lime Chicken

Servings: 4

Cooking Time: 30 Minutes

Ingredients:

- 8 chicken thighs, boneless & skinless
- 1 tsp salt
- 2 tsp honey
- 1 tsp granulated garlic
- 1 tsp granulated onion
- ½ tsp pepper
- 2 tsp lime juice
- ¼ tsp cayenne pepper
- 8 slices bacon

Directions:

1. Place the chicken and seasonings in a large bowl. Use your hands to mix and rub the seasonings into the meat until chicken is evenly coated.

2. Roll the chicken along the long side and wrap each with a slice of bacon.
3. Place chicken in the fryer basket, with bacon ends on the bottom. Add the tender-crisp lid and set to air fry on 400°F. Cook chicken 25-30 minutes, turning over halfway through cooking time. Serve hot.

Nutrition Info:

- Calories 371,Total Fat 23g,Total Carbs 6g,Protein 32g,Sodium 878mg.

Barbeque Chicken Drumettes

Servings: 4
Cooking Time: 30 Min

Ingredients:

- 2 lb. chicken drumettes, bone in and skin in /900g
- 1 stick butter; sliced in 5 pieces
- ½ cup chicken broth /125ml
- BBQ sauce to taste
- ½ tbsp cumin powder /7.5g
- ½ tsp onion powder /2.5g
- ¼ tsp Cayenne powder/1.25g
- ½ tsp dry mustard /2.5g
- ½ tsp sweet paprika /2.5g
- Salt and pepper, to taste
- Cooking spray

Directions:

1. Pour the chicken broth into the inner pot of Foodi P and insert the reversible rack. In a zipper bag, pour in dry mustard, cumin powder, onion powder, cayenne powder, salt, and pepper.
2. Add the chicken, close the bag and shake to coat the chicken well with the spices. You can toss the chicken in the spices in batches too.
3. Then, remove the chicken from the bag and place on the rack. Spread the butter slices on the drumsticks. Close the lid, secure the pressure valve, and select Pressure mode on High pressure for 10 minutes. Press Start/Stop.
4. Once the timer has ended, do a quick pressure release, and open the lid. Remove the chicken onto a clean flat surface like a cutting board and brush them with the barbecue sauce using the brush. Return to the rack and close the crisping lid. Cook for 10 minutes at 400 °F or 205°C on Air Crisp mode.

Chicken Cassoulet With Frijoles

Servings: 4
Cooking Time: 60 Min

Ingredients:

- 4 small chicken thighs, bone-in skin-on
- 2 pancetta slices; cut into thirds
- 1 medium carrot; diced
- ½ small onion; diced
- Olive oil, as needed
- ½ cup dry red wine /125ml
- 1 cup Pinto Beans Frijoles; soaked /130g
- 3 cups chicken stock /750ml
- 1 cup panko breadcrumbs /130g
- 1½ tsp salt /7.5g
- ¼ tsp black pepper /1.25g

Directions:

1. Season the chicken on both sides with salt and black pepper and set aside on a wire rack. On your Foodi, choose Sear/Sauté and adjust to Medium. Press Start to preheat the inner pot.
2. Add the pancetta slices in a single layer and cook for 3 to 4 minutes or until browned on one side. Turn and brown the other side. Remove the pancetta to a paper towel-lined plate.
3. Put the chicken thighs in the pot, and fry for about 6-7 minutes or until is golden brown on both sides. Use tongs to pick the chicken into a plate.
4. Carefully pour out all the fat in the pot leaving about 1 tbsp to coat the bottom of the pot. Reserve the remaining fat in a small bowl.
5. Sauté the carrots and onion in the pot for 3 minutes with frequent stirring, until the onion begins to brown. Stir in the wine while scraping off the brown bits at the bottom. Allow boiling until the wine reduces by one-third and stir in the beans and chicken stock.
6. Seal the pressure lid, choose pressure; adjust the pressure to High and the cook time to 25 minutes. Press Start to commence cooking.
7. When done cooking, perform a quick pressure release and carefully open the lid. Return the chicken to the pot and cook for 10 minutes.
8. Combine the breadcrumbs with the reserved fat until evenly mixed. When done cooking, perform a natural pressure release for 5 minutes, then a quick pressure release to let out any remaining steam, and carefully open the lid.
9. Crumble the pancetta over the cassoulet. Spoon the breadcrumbs mixture on top of the beans while avoiding the chicken as much as possible.
10. Close the crisping lid; choose Broil, adjust the cook time to 7 minutes, and press Start/Stop. When the cassoulet is ready, allow resting for a few minutes before serving.

Ginger Orange Chicken Tenders

Servings: 4

Cooking Time: 25 Minutes

Ingredients:

- Nonstick cooking spray
- 1 ½ lbs. chicken tenders
- 1 cup orange juice
- 2 tsp tamari, low sodium
- ½ tsp ginger
- 11 oz. mandarin oranges, drained

Directions:

1. Spray the fryer basket with cooking spray.
2. Place chicken in a single layer in the basket, these may need to be cooked in batches.
3. Add the tender-crisp lid and set to air fry on 350°F. Cook 10 minutes, turning over halfway through cooking time.
4. Add all the tenders to the cooking pot.
5. In a small bowl, whisk together orange juice, soy sauce, and ginger. Pour over chicken and stir to coat all the pieces.
6. Set to sauté on medium heat. Cover and cook chicken, stirring occasionally, about 10 minutes.
7. Add the orange slices and cook another 5 minutes. Serve.

Nutrition Info:

- Calories 259,Total Fat 5g,Total Carbs 17g,Protein 36g,Sodium 210mg.

Buttermilk Fried Chicken

Servings:4

Cooking Time: 30 Minutes

Ingredients:

- 1½ pounds boneless, skinless chicken breasts
- 1 to 2 cups buttermilk
- 2 large eggs
- ¾ cup all-purpose flour
- ¾ cup potato starch
- ½ teaspoon granulated garlic, divided
- 1 teaspoon salt, divided
- 2 teaspoons freshly ground black pepper, divided
- 1 cup bread crumbs
- ½ cup panko bread crumbs
- Olive oil or cooking spray

Directions:

1. In a large bowl, combine the chicken breasts and buttermilk, turning the chicken to coat. Cover the bowl with plastic wrap and refrigerate the chicken to soak at least 4 hours or overnight.
2. In a medium shallow bowl, whisk the eggs. In a second shallow bowl, stir together the flour, potato starch, ¼ teaspoon of granulated garlic, ½ teaspoon of salt, and 1 teaspoon of pepper. In a third shallow bowl, stir together the bread crumbs, panko, remaining ¼ teaspoon of granulated garlic, remaining ½ teaspoon of salt, and remaining 1 teaspoon of pepper.
3. Working one piece at a time, remove the chicken from the buttermilk, letting the excess drip into the bowl. Dredge the chicken in the flour mixture, coating well on both sides. Then dip the chicken in the eggs, coating both sides. Finally, dip the chicken in the bread crumb mixture, coating both sides and pressing the crumbs onto the chicken. Spritz both sides of the coated chicken pieces with olive oil.
4. Place the Cook & Crisp Basket into the unit.
5. Select AIR CRISP, set the temperature to 400°F, and set the time to 30 minutes. Select START/STOP to begin and allow to preheat for 5 minutes.
6. Spritz both sides of the coated chicken pieces with olive oil. Working in batches as needed, place the chicken breasts in the Cook & Crisp Basket, ensuring the chicken pieces do not touch each other.
7. After 12 minutes, turn the chicken with a spatula so you don't tear the breading. Close the crisping lid and continue to cook, checking the chicken for an internal temperature of 165°F.
8. When cooking is complete, transfer the chicken to a wire rack to cool.

Nutrition Info:

- Calories: 574,Total Fat: 7g,Sodium: 995mg,Carbohydrates: 67g,Protein: 51g.

Butter Chicken

Servings: 6

Cooking Time: 30 Min

Ingredients:

- 2 pounds boneless; skinless chicken legs /900g
- 3 Roma tomatoes, pureed in a blender
- 1 can coconut milk, refrigerated overnight /435ml
- 1 large onion; minced
- ½ cup chopped fresh cilantro; divided /65g
- 2 tbsp Indian curry paste /30ml
- 2 tbsp dried fenugreek /30g
- 1 tbsp Kashmiri red chili powder /15g
- 2 tbsp butter /30g
- 1 tbsp grated fresh ginger /15g
- 1 tbsp minced fresh garlic /15g
- 1 tsp salt /5g
- 2 tsp sugar /10g
- ½ tsp ground turmeric /2.5g
- 1 tsp garam masala /5g
- Salt to taste

Directions:

1. Set your Foodi to Sear/Sauté, set to Medium High, and choose Start/Stop to preheat the pot and melt butter. Add in 1 tsp salt and onion. Cook for 2 to 3 minutes until fragrant. Stir in ginger, turmeric, garlic, and red chili powder to coat; cook for 2 more minutes.

2. Place water and coconut cream into separate bowls. Stir the water from the coconut milk can, pureed tomatoes, and chicken with the onion mixture. Seal the pressure lid, choose Pressure, set to High, and set the timer to 8 minutes. Press Start. When ready, release the pressure quickly.
3. Stir sugar, coconut cream, fenugreek, curry paste, half the cilantro, and garam masala through the chicken mixture; apply salt for seasoning. Simmer the mixture and cook for 10 minutes until the sauce thickens, on Sear/Sauté. Garnish with the rest of the cilantro before serving.

Turkey Breakfast Sausage

Servings: 8
Cooking Time: 10 Minutes
Ingredients:

- Nonstick cooking spray
- 1 lb. ground turkey
- ½ tsp sage
- ½ tsp marjoram
- ¾ tsp thyme
- ¼ tsp cayenne pepper
- ¼ tsp allspice
- ¼ tsp black pepper
- ¾ tsp salt
- 1 clove garlic, chopped fine
- ¼ cup maple syrup

Directions:
1. Spray the fryer basket with cooking spray and place in the cooking pot.
2. In a large bowl, mix all ingredients until combined. Form into 8 patties.
3. Place the sausage patties in the fryer basket in a single layer. Add the tender-crisp lid and set to air fry on 375°F. Cook about 10 minutes until browned on the outside and cooked through, turning over halfway through cooking time. Serve.

Nutrition Info:

- Calories 126,Total Fat 7g,Total Carbs 7g,Protein 11g,Sodium 252mg.

Cheesy Chipotle Chicken

Servings: 6
Cooking Time: 35 Minutes
Ingredients:

- 15 oz. fire roasted tomatoes
- ¼ cup red onion, chopped
- 1 clove garlic
- ½ cup cilantro, chopped, packed
- 2 chipotle chili peppers in adobo sauce
- 1 tsp adobo sauce
- 1 tsp fresh lime juice
- 1 tsp salt
- 1 ½ lbs. chicken, cut in 3-inch pieces
- 1 cup Monterey Jack cheese, grated

Directions:
1. Add the tomatoes, onion, garlic, cilantro, chipotle peppers, lime juice, and salt to a food processor or blender. Pulse until vegetables are chopped but not until the salsa is smooth.
2. Place the chicken in the cooking pot. Pour the salsa over the tops. Turn the chicken to coat with salsa on all sides.
3. Add the tender-crisp lid and set to bake on 350°F. Bake 25 minutes. Remove the lid and sprinkle the cheese over the top.
4. Recover and bake another 10 minutes or until chicken is cooked through and cheese is melted and starting to brown. Serve.

Nutrition Info:

- Calories 92,Total Fat 4g,Total Carbs 2g,Protein 12g,Sodium 342mg.

Creamy Turkey And Mushroom Ragu

Servings:4
Cooking Time: 40 Minutes
Ingredients:

- 2 tablespoons unsalted butter
- 1 pound ground turkey
- 8 ounces cremini mushrooms, sliced
- 1 can condensed cream of celery soup
- 4 cups chicken stock
- 1 package egg noodles
- 16 ounces frozen peas
- 1 cup sour cream
- ¾ cup grated Parmesan cheese
- Kosher salt
- Freshly ground black pepper

Directions:
1. Select SEAR/SAUTÉ and set to MED. Press START/STOP to begin. Let preheat for 3 minutes.
2. Add the butter, ground turkey, and mushrooms. Using a silicone-tipped utensil, break up the turkey as it browns, about 10 minutes.
3. Add the condensed soup and stock. Whisk well to combine. Bring to a simmer for 15 minutes.
4. Add the egg noodles and peas and stir well. Cook until the noodles are tender and cooked through, 8 to 10 minutes.
5. Select START/STOP to stop cooking. Stir in sour cream and Parmesan cheese until melted and incorporated. Season with salt and pepper. Serve immediately.

Nutrition Info:

- Calories: 854,Total Fat: 39g,Sodium: 1714mg,Carbohydrates: 79g,Protein: 48g.

Buttered Turkey

Servings: 6
Cooking Time: 25 Min

Ingredients:

- 6 turkey breasts, boneless and skinless
- 1 stick butter, melted
- 2 cups panko breadcrumbs /260g
- ½ tsp cayenne pepper /2.5g
- ½ tsp black pepper /2.5g
- 1 tsp salt /5g

Directions:

1. In a bowl, combine the panko breadcrumbs, half of the black pepper, the cayenne pepper, and half of the salt.
2. In another bowl, combine the melted butter with salt and pepper. Brush the butter mixture over the turkey breast.
3. Coat the turkey with the panko mixture. Arrange on a lined Foodi basket. Close the crisping lid and cook for 15 minutes at 390 °F or 199°C on Air Crisp mode, flipping the meat after 8 minutes.

Herb Roasted Drumsticks

Servings: 3
Cooking Time: 40 Minutes

Ingredients:

- Nonstick cooking spray
- 1 tsp paprika
- ¼ tsp salt
- ½ tsp garlic powder
- ¼ tsp onion powder
- ¼ tsp dried thyme
- ¼ tsp pepper
- 6 chicken drumsticks, skin removed, rinsed & patted dry
- ½ tbsp. butter, melted

Directions:

1. Place the rack in the cooking pot and spray it with cooking spray.
2. In a small bowl, combine spices, mix well.
3. Place chicken on the rack and sprinkle evenly over chicken. Drizzle with melted butter.
4. Add the tender-crisp lid and set to roast on 375°F. Bake 35-40 minutes until juices run clear. Serve.

Nutrition Info:

- Calories 319,Total Fat 12g,Total Carbs 0g,Protein 50g,Sodium 505mg.

Apricot Bbq Duck Legs

Servings: 6
Cooking Time: 8 Hours

Ingredients:

- Nonstick cooking spray
- 2 cups spicy BBQ sauce
- 1 cup apricot preserves
- 1 tsp ginger
- 1 tbsp. garlic powder
- 2 tbsp. Worcestershire sauce
- 4 lbs. duck legs

Directions:

1. Spray the cooking pot with cooking spray.
2. In a medium bowl, whisk together BBQ sauce, preserves, ginger, garlic powder, and Worcestershire until combined. Reserve ½ cup of the sauce.
3. Add the duck to the cooking pot and pour the sauce over. Stir to coat the duck.
4. Add the lid and select slow cook on low. Cook 6-8 hours or until duck is tender.
5. Add the tender-crisp lid and set to broil. Cook another 2-3 minutes to caramelize the duck legs. Turn the legs over and repeat. Serve.

Nutrition Info:

- Calories 651,Total Fat 26g,Total Carbs 44g,Protein 61g,Sodium 1027mg.

Mini Turkey Loaves

Servings: 6
Cooking Time: 35 Minutes

Ingredients:

- 6 tbsp. barbecue sauce, divided
- 2 tbsp. water
- 2/3 cup oats
- 2 egg whites, lightly beaten
- 2 tsp chili powder
- 2 tsp Worcestershire sauce
- ½ tsp salt
- 1 lb. ground turkey
- 1 onion, chopped fine
- ½ green bell pepper, chopped fine

Directions:

1. Place the rack in the cooking pot and top with a sheet of foil.
2. In a large bowl, combine 3 tablespoons barbecue sauce and water, stir to mix well.
3. Stir in the oats, egg whites, chili powder, Worcestershire, and salt and mix well.
4. Add the turkey, onion, and bell pepper and mix to combine. Form into 6 small oval-shaped loaves and place on the foil.
5. Add the tender-crisp lid and set to bake on 375°F. Bake 30 minutes.
6. Open the lid and spread the remaining barbecue sauce over the tops of the meatloaves. Bake another 5 minutes. Serve.

Nutrition Info:

- Calories 250,Total Fat 11g,Total Carbs 21g,Protein 17g,Sodium 448mg.

Chicken Pasta With Pesto Sauce

Servings: 8
Cooking Time: 30 Min

Ingredients:

- 4 chicken breast, boneless, skinless; cubed
- 8 oz. macaroni pasta /240g
- 1 garlic clove; minced
- 1/4 cup Asiago cheese, grated /32.5g
- 2 cups fresh collard greens, trimmed /260g
- ¼ cup cream cheese, at room temperature /32.5g
- 1 cup cherry tomatoes, halved /130g
- ½ cup basil pesto sauce /125ml
- 3½ cups water /875ml
- 1 tbsp butter /15g
- 1 tbsp salt; divided/15g
- 1 tsp freshly ground black pepper to taste /5g
- Freshly chopped basil for garnish

Directions:

1. To the inner steel pot of the Foodi, add water, chicken, 2 tsp salt, butter, and macaroni, and stir well to mix and be submerged in water.
2. Seal the pressure lid, choose Pressure, set to High, and set the timer to 2 minutes. Press Start. When ready, release the pressure quickly. Press Start/Stop, open the lid, get rid of ¼ cup water from the pot.
3. Set on Sear/Sauté. Into the pot, mix in collard greens, pesto sauce, garlic, remaining 1 tsp o 5g salt, cream cheese, tomatoes, and black pepper. Cook, for 1 to 2 minutes as you stir, until sauce is creamy.
4. Place the pasta into serving plates; top with asiago cheese and basil before serving.

Chicken Stroganoff With Fetucini

Servings: 4
Cooking Time: 35 Min

Ingredients:

- 2 large boneless skinless chicken breasts
- 8 ounces fettucini /240g
- ½ cup sliced onion /65g
- ½ cup dry white wine /125ml
- 1 cup sautéed mushrooms /130g
- ¼ cup heavy cream /62.5ml
- 1 ½ cups water /375ml
- 2 cups chicken stock /500ml
- 2 tbsp butter /30g
- 1 tbsp flour /15g
- 2 tbsp chopped fresh dill to garnish /30g
- ½ tsp Worcestershire sauce /2.5ml
- 1½ tsp salt /7.5g

Directions:

1. Season the chicken on both sides with salt and set aside. Choose Sear/Sauté and adjust to Medium. Press Start to preheat the pot. Melt the butter and sauté the onion until brown, about 3 minutes.
2. Mix in the flour to make a roux, about 2 minutes and gradually pour in the dry white wine while stirring and scraping the bottom of the pot to release any browned bits. Allow the white wine to simmer and to reduce by two-thirds.
3. Pour in the water, chicken stock, 1 tbsp or 15g of salt, and fettucini. Mix and arrange the chicken on top of the fettucini.
4. Lock the pressure lid to Seal. Choose Pressure; adjust the pressure to High and the cook time to 5 minutes; press Start. When done pressure-cooking, perform a quick pressure release.
5. Transfer the chicken breasts to a cutting board to cool slightly, and then cut into bite-size chunks. Return the chicken to the pot and stir in the Worcestershire sauce and mushrooms. Add the heavy cream and cook until the mixture stops simmering. Ladle the stroganoff into bowls and garnish with dill.

Cordon Bleu Casserole

Servings: 4
Cooking Time: 30 Minutes

Ingredients:

- Nonstick cooking spray
- 2 cups chicken, cooked & shredded
- 4 oz. deli ham, low sodium, chopped
- 3 oz. cream cheese, low fat, soft
- 2 tbsp. butter, melted
- 1 tbsp. Dijon mustard
- ¼ cup skim milk
- 1 tbsp. white wine
- ¼ tsp pepper
- ½ cup Swiss cheese, grated
- 1 cup broccoli florets

Directions:

1. Spray cooking pot with cooking spray.
2. Lay the chicken on the bottom of the pot.
3. In a medium bowl, combine cream cheese, butter, mustard, milk, wine, and pepper, mix well.
4. Stir in ¼ cup Swiss cheese and broccoli. Spread over chicken. Sprinkle remaining cheese over top.
5. Add the tender-crisp lid and set to bake on 350°F. Bake 25-30 minutes until top is golden brown and casserole is heated through. Serve.

Nutrition Info:

- Calories 381,Total Fat 25g,Total Carbs 6g,Protein 33g,Sodium 568mg.

Greek Chicken With Potatoes

Servings: 4

Cooking Time: 40 Min

Ingredients:

- 4 potatoes, peeled and quartered
- 4 boneless skinless chicken drumsticks
- 2 lemons, zested and juiced
- 1 cucumber, thinly sliced
- 2 Serrano peppers, stemmed, cored, and chopped
- 1 cup packed watercress /130g
- ½ cup cherry tomatoes, quartered /65g
- ¼ cup Kalamata olives, pitted/32.5g
- ¼ cup hummus /32.5g
- ¼ cup feta cheese, crumbled /32.5g
- 4 cups water /1000ml
- 3 tbsp finely chopped parsley /45g
- 1 tbsp olive oil /15ml
- 2 tsp fresh oregano /10g
- ¼ tsp freshly ground black pepper /1.25g
- Lemon wedges; for serving
- Salt to taste

Directions:

1. In the cooker, add water and potatoes. Set trivet over them. In a baking bowl, mix lemon juice, olive oil, black pepper, oregano, zest, salt, and red pepper flakes. Add chicken drumsticks in the marinade and stir to coat.
2. Set the bowl with chicken on the trivet in the inner pot. Seal the lid, select Pressure and set the time to 15 minutes on High pressure. Press Start.
3. When ready, do a quick pressure release. Take out the bowl with chicken and the trivet from the pot. Drain potatoes and add parsley and salt.
4. Split the potatoes among four serving plates and top with watercress, cucumber slices, hummus, cherry tomatoes, chicken, olives, and feta cheese. Each bowl should be garnished with a lemon wedge.

Chicken And Broccoli

Servings: 4

Cooking Time: 20 Minutes

Ingredients:

- 3 pounds boneless chicken, cut into thin strips
- 1 tablespoon olive oil
- 1 yellow onion, peeled and chopped
- 1/2 cup beef stock
- 1-pound broccoli florets
- 2 teaspoons toasted sesame oil
- 2 tablespoons arrowroot
- For Marinade
- 1 cup coconut aminos
- 1 tablespoon sesame oil
- 2 tablespoons fish sauce
- 5 garlic cloves, peeled and minced
- 3 red peppers, dried and crushed
- 1/2 teaspoon Chinese five-spice powder
- Toasted sesame seeds, for serving

Directions:

1. Take a suitable and mix in coconut aminos, fish sauce, 1 tablespoon sesame oil, garlic, five-spice powder, crushed red pepper and stir.
2. Stir in chicken strips to the bowl and toss to coat.
3. Keep it on the side for 10 minutes.
4. Select "Sauté" mode on your Ninja Foodi and stir in oil, let it heat up, add onion and stir cook for 4 minutes.
5. Stir in chicken and marinade, stir cook for 2 minutes.
6. Add stock and stir.
7. Lock the pressure lid of Ninja Foodi and cook on "HIGH" pressure for 5 minutes.
8. Release pressure naturally over 10 minutes.
9. Mix arrowroot with 1/4 cup liquid from the pot and gently pour the mixture back to the pot and stir.
10. Place a steamer basket in the Ninja Foodi's pot and stir in broccoli to the steamer rack, Lock and secure the Ninja Foodi's lid.
11. Then cook on "HIGH" pressure mode for 3 minutes more, quick-release pressure.
12. Divide the dish between plates and serve with broccoli, toasted sesame seeds and enjoy.

Nutrition Info:

- Calories: 433; Fat: 27g; Carbohydrates: 8g; Protein: 20g

Chicken Coconut Curry

Servings: 6

Cooking Time: 20 Minutes

Ingredients:

- 2 tbsp. olive oil
- 1 sweet onion, chopped fine
- 1 lb. chicken breast, boneless, skinless & cut in 1-inch pieces
- 3 cloves garlic, chopped fine
- 1 tbsp. fresh ginger, chopped fine
- 2 tsp ground coriander
- 13 oz. coconut milk
- 1 ½ cups carrots, grated
- 2 tbsp. curry powder
- 1 tsp salt
- ½ tsp pepper
- 3 cups fresh spinach, packed
- 1 tbsp. lime juice
- ¼ cup cilantro, chopped fine

Directions:

1. Add the oil to the cooking pot and set to sauté on med-high heat.
2. Add the onion and cook about 5 minutes until it starts to soften.

3. Add the chicken and cook 5-6 minutes or until meat is no longer pink.
4. Add the garlic, ginger, and coriander and cook 1 minute, stirring frequently.
5. Stir in coconut milk, carrots, curry powder, salt, and pepper and mix well. Reduce heat to medium and simmer 5 minutes or until sauce has thickened.
6. Add the spinach and lime juice and stir to mix. Cook 2-3 minutes or until spinach has wilted. Serve immediately garnished with cilantro.

Nutrition Info:

- Calories 309,Total Fat 23g,Total Carbs 10g,Protein 20g,Sodium 464mg.

Lemon Chicken

Servings: 4
Cooking Time: 18 Minutes

Ingredients:

- 4 bone-in, skin-on chicken thighs
- Black pepper and salt to taste
- 2 tablespoons butter
- 2 teaspoons garlic, minced
- ½ cup herbed chicken stock
- ½ cup heavy whip cream
- ½ a lemon, juiced

Directions:

1. Season the four chicken thighs generously with black pepper and salt.
2. Set your Ninja Foodi to sauté mode and add oil, let it heat up.
3. Add thigh, Sauté on both sides for 6 minutes.
4. Remove thigh to a platter and keep it on the side.
5. Add garlic, cook for 2 minutes.
6. Whisk in chicken stock, heavy cream, lemon juice and gently stir.
7. Bring the mix to a simmer and reintroduce chicken.
8. Lock and secure the Ninja Foodi's lid and cook for 10 minutes on "HIGH" pressure.
9. Release pressure over 10 minutes.
10. Serve and enjoy.

Nutrition Info:

- Calories: 294; Fat: 26g; Carbohydrates: 4g; Protein: 12g

Garlic Chicken And Bacon Pasta

Servings:4
Cooking Time: 10 Minutes

Ingredients:

- 3 strips bacon, chopped
- ½ pound boneless, skinless chicken breast, cut into ½-pieces
- 1 teaspoon dried basil
- 1 teaspoon dried oregano
- ¼ teaspoon sea salt
- 1 tablespoon unsalted butter
- 3 garlic cloves, minced
- 1 cup chicken stock
- 1½ cups water
- 8 ounces dry penne pasta
- ½ cup half-and-half
- ½ cup grated Parmesan cheese, plus more for serving

Directions:

1. Select SEAR/SAUTÉ and set to HI. Select START/STOP to begin. Let preheat for 5 minutes.
2. Add the bacon and cook, stirring frequently, for about 5 minutes or until crispy. Using a slotted spoon, transfer the bacon to a paper towel-lined plate to drain.
3. Season the chicken with the basil, oregano, and salt, coating all the pieces.
4. Add the butter, chicken, and garlic and sauté for 2 minutes, until the chicken begins to brown and the garlic is fragrant.
5. Add the chicken stock, water, and penne pasta. Assemble pressure lid, making sure the pressure release valve is in the SEAL position.
6. Select PRESSURE and set to HI. Set time to 3 minutes. Select START/STOP to begin.
7. When pressure cooking is complete, allow pressure to naturally release for 2 minutes. After 2 minutes, quick release remaining pressure by moving the pressure release valve to the VENT position. Carefully remove lid when unit has finished releasing pressure.
8. Add the half-and-half, cheese, and bacon, and stir constantly to thicken the sauce and melt the cheese. Serve immediately, with additional Parmesan cheese to garnish.

Nutrition Info:

- Calories: 458,Total Fat: 18g,Sodium: 809mg,Carbohydrates: 45g,Protein: 30g.

Chicken & Black Bean Chowder

Servings: 6
Cooking Time: 6 Hours

Ingredients:

- 15 oz. black beans, rinsed & drained
- 3 chicken breasts, boneless & skinless
- 1 cup corn, frozen
- 16 oz. salsa
- 4 cups chicken broth, low sodium
- 4 oz. green chilies, diced
- ¼ cup cilantro, chopped
- 1 lime, cut in wedges

Directions:

1. Place all ingredients, except cilantro and limes, in the cooking pot, stir to mix well.
2. Add the lid and set to slow cook on low. Cook 5-6 hours until chicken is tender.
3. Transfer chicken to a cutting board and shred. Return to the pot and increase temperature to high. Cook 30 minutes.
4. Ladle into bowls and serve garnished with cilantro and a lime wedge.

Nutrition Info:

- Calories 350,Total Fat 8g,Total Carbs 29g,Protein 42g,Sodium 749mg.

Greek Chicken

Servings: 6
Cooking Time: 45 Min

Ingredients:

- 1 whole chicken; cut in pieces /1350g
- ½ cup olive oil /125ml
- 3 garlic cloves; minced
- Juice from 1 lemon
- ½ cup white wine /125ml
- 1 tbsp chopped fresh oregano /15g
- 1 tbsp fresh thyme /15g
- 1 tbsp fresh rosemary /15g
- Salt and black pepper, to taste

Directions:

1. In a large bowl, combine the garlic, rosemary, thyme, olive oil, lemon juice, oregano, salt, and pepper. Mix all ingredients very well and spread the mixture into the Foodi basket.
2. Stir in the chicken. Sprinkle with wine and cook for 45 minutes on Air Crisp mode at 380 °F or 194°C.

Fish & Seafood

Shrimp Fried Rice

Servings: 6
Cooking Time: 15 Minutes

Ingredients:

- 2 tbsp. sesame oil
- 2 tbsp. olive oil
- 1 lb. medium shrimp, peeled & deveined
- 1 cup frozen peas & carrots
- 1/2 cup corn
- 3 cloves garlic, chopped fine
- ½ tsp ginger
- 3 eggs, lightly beaten
- 4 cups brown rice, cooked
- 3 green onions, sliced
- 3 tbsp. tamari
- ½ tsp salt
- ½ tsp pepper

Directions:

1. Add the sesame and olive oils to the cooking pot and set to sauté on med-high heat.
2. Add the shrimp and cook 3 minutes, or until they turn pink, turning shrimp over halfway through. Use a slotted spoon to transfer shrimp to a plate.
3. Add the peas, carrots, and corn to the pot and cook 2 minutes until vegetables start to soften, stirring occasionally. Add the garlic and ginger and cook 1 minute more.
4. Push the vegetables to one side and add the eggs, cook to scramble, stirring frequently. Add the shrimp, rice, and onions and stir to mix all ingredients together.
5. Drizzle with tamari and season with salt and pepper, stir to combine. Cook 2 minutes or until everything is heated through. Serve immediately.

Nutrition Info:

- Calories 361,Total Fat 13g,Total Carbs 38g,Protein 24g,Sodium 1013mg.

Tuna Salad With Potatoes And Asparagus

Servings: 4
Cooking Time: 60 Minutes

Ingredients:

- 1½ pounds potatoes, quartered /675g
- 8 ounces asparagus, cut into three /240g
- 2 cans tuna, drained
- ½ cup pimento stuffed green olives /65g
- ½ cup coarsely chopped roasted red peppers /65g
- 1 cup water /250ml
- 2 tbsps chopped fresh parsley /30g
- 2 tbsps red wine vinegar; divided /30ml
- 3 tbsps olive oil /45ml
- ¼ tsp freshly ground black pepper /1.25g
- 1 tsp salt; divided, plus more as needed 5g

Directions:

1. Pour the water into the inner pot and set the reversible rack. Place the potatoes on the rack. Lock the pressure lid into place and set to Seal. Choose Pressure; adjust the pressure to High and the cook time to 4 minutes. Press Start/Stop.
2. After pressure cooking, perform a quick pressure release and carefully open the pressure lid. Take out the rack, empty the water in the pot, and return the pot to the base.
3. Arrange the potatoes and asparagus on the Crisping Basket. Drizzle the half of olive oil on them, and season with salt.
4. Place the basket in the pot. Close the crisping lid; choose Air Crisp, adjust the temperature to 375°F or 191°C, and the cook time to 12 minutes. Press Start.
5. After 8 minutes, open the lid, and check the veggies. The asparagus will have started browning and crisping. Gently toss with the potatoes and close the lid. Continue cooking for the remaining 4 minutes.
6. Take out the basket, pour the asparagus and potatoes into a salad bowl. Sprinkle with 1 tbsp of red wine vinegar and mix to coat.
7. In a bowl, pour the remaining oil, remaining vinegar, salt, and pepper. Whisk to combine.
8. To the potatoes and asparagus, add the roasted red peppers, olives, parsley, and tuna. Drizzle the dressing over the salad and mix to coat. Adjust the seasoning and serve immediately.

Tangy Catfish & Mushrooms

Servings: 4
Cooking Time: 10 Minutes

Ingredients:

- 2 tbsp. olive oil
- 4 catfish fillets
- 1/8 tsp salt
- ¼ tsp pepper
- 1 tbsp. fresh lemon juice
- ¼ lb. mushrooms, sliced
- 1 onion, chopped
- ¼ cup fresh parsley, chopped

Directions:

1. Add the oil to the cooking pot and set to sauté on medium heat.
2. Sprinkle the fish with salt and pepper and add to the pot. Drizzle lemon juice over the top.
3. Add the remaining ingredients and cook 3-4 minutes. Turn fish over and cook another 3-4 minutes or until it flakes with a fork and mushrooms are tender.
4. Transfer fish to serving plates and top with mushrooms. Serve immediately.

Nutrition Info:

- Calories 187,Total Fat 10g,Total Carbs 4g,Protein 20g,Sodium 131mg.

Italian Flounder

Servings: 4
Cooking Time: 70 Min

Ingredients:

- 4 flounder fillets
- 3 slices prosciutto; chopped
- 2 bags baby kale /180g
- ½ small red onion; chopped
- ½ cup whipping cream /125ml
- 1 cup panko breadcrumbs /130g
- 2 tbsps chopped fresh parsley /30g
- 3 tbsps unsalted butter, melted and divided /45g
- ¼ tsp fresh ground black pepper /1.25g
- ½ tsp salt; divided /2.5g

Directions:

1. On the Foodi, choose Sear/Sauté and adjust to Medium. Press Start to preheat the inner pot. Add the prosciutto and cook until crispy, about 6 minutes. Stir in the red onions and cook for about 2 minutes or until the onions start to soften. Sprinkle with half of the salt.
2. Fetch the kale into the pot and cook, stirring frequently until wilted and most of the liquid has evaporated, about 4-5 minutes. Mix in the whipping cream.
3. Lay the flounder fillets over the kale in a single layer. Brush 1 tbsp or 15ml of the melted butter over the fillets and sprinkle with the remaining salt and black pepper.
4. Close the crisping lid and choose Bake/Roast. Adjust the temperature to 300°F or 149°C and the cook time to 3 minutes. Press Start.
5. Combine the remaining butter, the parsley and breadcrumbs in a bowl.
6. When done cooking, open the crisping lid. Spoon the breadcrumbs mixture on the fillets.

7. Close the crisping lid and Choose Bake/Roast. Adjust the temperature to 400°F or 205°Cand the cook time to 6 minutes. Press Start.
8. After about 4 minutes, open the lid and check the fish. The breadcrumbs should be golden brown and crisp. If not, close the lid and continue to cook for an additional two minutes.

Salmon With Almonds, Cranberries, And Rice

Servings:4
Cooking Time: 10 Minutes
Ingredients:

- 1½ cups long-grain white rice, rinsed
- 1½ cups water
- ⅓ cup dry cranberries
- ⅓ cup slivered almonds
- Kosher salt
- 4 frozen salmon fillets
- ⅓ cup dry roasted sunflower seeds
- ¼ cup Dijon mustard
- ⅓ cup panko bread crumbs
- 1 tablespoon honey
- 1 tablespoon minced parsley

Directions:

1. Place the rice, water, cranberries, and almonds in the pot. Season with salt and stir. Place Reversible Rack in pot in the higher broil position. Place a circle of aluminum foil on top of the rack, then place the salmon fillets on the foil. Assemble pressure lid, making sure the pressure release valve is in the SEAL position.
2. Select PRESSURE and set to HI. Set time to 2 minutes. Select START/STOP to begin.
3. Add the sunflower seeds, mustard, bread crumbs, honey, and parsley to a small bowl and mix well.
4. When pressure cooking is complete, allow pressure to naturally release for 10 minutes. After 10 minutes, quick release remaining pressure by moving the pressure release valve to the VENT position. Carefully remove lid when unit has finished releasing pressure.
5. Using a spoon, spread a thick, even layer of the sunflower mixture across the top of each fillet. Close crisping lid.
6. Select BROIL and set time to 8 minutes. Select START/STOP to begin. When cooking is complete, open lid and remove the rack and salmon. Use a silicone-coated spatula to fluff the rice. Serve the salmon fillets over the rice.

Nutrition Info:

- Calories: 505,Total Fat: 10g,Sodium: 536mg,Carbohydrates: 75g,Protein: 28g.

Roasted Bbq Shrimp

Servings: 2
Cooking Time: 7 Minutes
Ingredients:

- 3 tablespoons chipotle in adobo sauce, minced
- 1/4 teaspoon salt
- 1/4 cup BBQ sauce
- 1/2 orange, juiced
- 1/2-pound large shrimps

Directions:

1. Toss shrimp with chipotles and rest of the ingredients in a suitable bowl.
2. Preheat Ninja Foodi by pressing the "Bake/Roast" mode and setting it to "400 °F" and timer to 7 minutes.
3. Let it preheat until you hear a beep.
4. Set shrimps over Grill Grate and lock lid, cook until the timer runs out.
5. Serve and enjoy.

Nutrition Info:

- Calories: 173; Fat: 2g; Carbohydrates: 21g; Protein: 17g

Steamed Sea Bass With Turnips

Servings: 4
Cooking Time: 15 Min
Ingredients:

- 4 sea bass fillets
- 4 sprigs thyme
- 1 lemon; sliced
- 2 turnips; sliced
- 1 white onion; sliced into thin rings
- 1½ cups water /375ml
- 2 tsp olive oil /30ml
- 2 pinches salt
- 1 pinch ground black pepper

Directions:

1. Add water to the Foodi. Set a reversible rack into the pot. Line a parchment paper to the bottom of steamer basket. Place lemon slices in a single layer on the reversible rack.
2. Arrange fillets on the top of the lemons, cover with onion and thyme sprigs and top with turnip slices.
3. Drizzle pepper, salt, and olive oil over the mixture. Put steamer basket onto the reversible rack. Seal lid and cook on Low for 8 minutes; press Start.
4. When ready, release pressure quickly. Serve over the delicate onion rings and thinly sliced turnips.

Baked Cod Casserole

Servings: 6
Cooking Time: 20 Minutes

Ingredients:

- Nonstick cooking spray
- 1 lb. mushrooms, chopped
- 1 onion, chopped
- ½ cup fresh parsley, chopped
- ½ tsp salt, divided
- ½ tsp pepper, divided
- 6 cod fillets
- ¾ cup dry white wine
- ¾ cup plain bread crumbs
- 2 tbsp. butter, melted
- 1 cup Swiss cheese, grated

Directions:

1. Spray the cooking pot with cooking spray.
2. In a medium bowl, combine mushrooms, onion, parsley, ¼ teaspoon salt, and ¼ teaspoon pepper and mix well. Spread evenly on the bottom of the cooking pot.
3. Place the fish on top of the mushroom mixture and pour the wine over them.
4. In a separate medium bowl, combine remaining ingredients and mix well. Sprinkle over the fish.
5. Add the tender-crisp lid and set to bake on 450°F. Bake 15-20 minutes or until golden brown and fish flakes easily with a fork. Serve immediately.

Nutrition Info:

- Calories 284,Total Fat 10g,Total Carbs 16g,Protein 27g,Sodium 693mg.

Caramelized Salmon

Servings: 4
Cooking Time: 10 Minutes

Ingredients:

- 1 tbsp. coconut oil, melted
- 1/3 cup Stevia brown sugar, packed
- 3 tbsp. fish sauce
- 1 ½ tbsp. soy sauce
- 1 tsp fresh ginger, peeled & grated
- 2 tsp lime zest, finely grated
- 1 tbsp. fresh lime juice
- ½ tsp pepper
- 4 salmon fillets
- 1 tbsp. green onions, sliced
- 1 tbsp. cilantro chopped

Directions:

1. Add the oil, brown sugar, fish sauce, soy sauce, ginger, zest, juice, and pepper to the cooking pot. Stir to mix.
2. Set to sauté on medium heat and bring mixture to a simmer, stirring frequently. Turn heat off.
3. Add the fish to the sauce making sure it is covered. Add the lid and set to pressure cooking on low. Set the timer for 1 minute.
4. When the timer goes off let the pressure release naturally for 5 minutes, the release it manually. Fish is done when it flakes with a fork.
5. Transfer fish to a serving dish with the caramelized side up.
6. Set cooker back to sauté on medium and cook sauce 3-4 minutes until it's thickened. Spoon over fish and garnish with chopped green onions and scallions. Serve.

Nutrition Info:

- Calories 316,Total Fat 18g,Total Carbs 5g,Protein 35g,Sodium 1514mg.

Kung Pao Shrimp

Servings: 4
Cooking Time: 15 Minutes

Ingredients:

- 1 tbsp. olive oil
- 1 red bell pepper, seeded & chopped
- 1 green bell pepper, seeded & chopped
- 3 cloves garlic, chopped fine
- 1 lb. large shrimp, peeled & deveined
- ¼ cup soy sauce
- 1 tsp sesame oil
- 1 tsp brown sugar
- 1 tsp Sriracha
- 1/8 tsp red pepper flakes
- 1 tsp cornstarch
- 1 tbsp. water
- ¼ cup peanuts
- ¼ cup green onions, sliced thin

Directions:

1. Add oil to the cooking pot and set to sauté on med-high heat.
2. Add the bell peppers and garlic and cook, 3-5 minutes, until pepper is almost tender.
3. Add the shrimp and cook until they turn pink, 2-3 minutes.
4. In a small bowl, whisk together soy sauce, sesame oil, brown sugar, Sriracha, and pepper flakes until combined.
5. In a separate small bowl, whisk together cornstarch and water until smooth. Whisk into sauce and pour over shrimp mixture. Add the peanuts.
6. Cook, stirring, until the sauce has thickened, about 2-3 minutes. Serve garnished with green onions.

Nutrition Info:

- Calories 212,Total Fat 11g,Total Carbs 10g,Protein 20g,Sodium 1729mg.

Tilapia With Spicy Pesto

Servings: 4
Cooking Time: 10 Minutes

Ingredients:

- Nonstick cooking spray
- 1 cup cilantro, packed
- 3 cloves garlic
- 2 tbsp. fresh lemon juice
- ¼ tsp salt
- 1/8 tsp red pepper
- 2 tbsp. olive oil
- 4 tilapia fillets

Directions:

1. Place the rack in the cooking pot. Spray a baking pan with cooking spray.
2. Place everything but the fish and oil in a food processor or blender and pulse until well chopped.
3. Slowly add the oil, with machine running, until combined.
4. Place the fish in the prepared pan and spread the pesto evenly over the top. Place on the rack.
5. Add the tender-crisp lid and set to bake on 400°F. Bake 10-12 minutes until fish flakes with a fork. Serve immediately.

Nutrition Info:

- Calories 174,Total Fat 9g,Total Carbs 1g,Protein 23g,Sodium 207mg.

Shrimp Egg Rolls

Servings: 10
Cooking Time: 10 Minutes

Ingredients:

- Nonstick cooking spray
- ¼ cup soy sauce, low sodium
- 2 tbsp. brown sugar
- 1 tsp ginger, grated
- 1 tsp garlic powder
- 5 cups coleslaw mix
- 2 green onions, sliced thin
- 3 tbsp. cilantro, chopped
- 1 cup small shrimp, chopped
- 10 egg roll wrappers

Directions:

1. Spray the fryer basket with cooking spray.
2. In a small bowl, whisk together, soy sauce, brown sugar, ginger, and garlic powder until combined.
3. In a large bowl, combine coleslaw, green onions, cilantro, and shrimp and mix well.
4. Pour the soy sauce over the coleslaw and toss well to coat. Let sit 15 minutes. After 15 minutes, place in a colander and squeeze to remove as much liquid as possible.
5. Place egg roll wrappers on a work surface. Spoon about 1/3 cup of shrimp mixture in the center of each wrapper. Fold opposite sides over filling, then one corner and roll up egg roll fashion. Place seam side down in fryer basket and spray lightly with cooking spray.
6. Add the tender-crisp lid and set to air fry on 425°F. Cook 8-10 minutes until golden brown and crisp, turning over halfway through cooking time.

Nutrition Info:

- Calories 138,Total Fat 1g,Total Carbs 24g,Protein 7g,Sodium 532mg.

Mussel Chowder With Oyster Crackers

Servings: 4
Cooking Time: 75 Min

Ingredients:

- 1 pound parsnips, peeled and cut into chunks /450g
- 3 cans chopped mussels, drained, liquid reserved /180g
- 1½ cups heavy cream /375ml
- 2 cups oyster crackers /260g
- ¼ cup white wine /62.5ml
- ¼ cup finely grated Pecorino Romano cheese/32.5g
- 1 cup clam juice /130g
- 2 thick pancetta slices, cut into thirds
- 1 bay leaf
- 2 celery stalks; chopped
- 1 medium onion; chopped
- 1 tbsp flour /15g
- 2 tbsps chopped fresh chervil/30g
- 2 tbsps melted ghee /30g
- ½ tsp garlic powder /2.5g
- 1 tsp salt; divided /5g
- 1 tsp dried rosemary /5g

Directions:

1. To preheat the Foodi, close the crisping lid and Choose Air Crisp; adjust the temperature to 375°F or 191°C and the time to 2 minutes; press Start. In a bowl, pour in the oyster crackers. Drizzle with the melted ghee, add the cheese, garlic powder, and ½ tsp or 2.5g of salt. Toss to coat the crackers. Transfer to the crisping basket.
2. Once the pot is ready, open the pressure lid and fix the basket in the pot. Close the lid and Choose Air Crisp; adjust the temperature to 375°F or 191°C and the cook time to 6 minutes; press Start.
3. After 3 minutes, carefully open the lid and mix the crackers with a spoon. Close the lid and resume cooking until crisp and lightly browned. Take out the basket and set aside to cool.
4. On the pot, choose Sear/Sauté and adjust to Medium. Press Start. Add the pancetta and cook for 5 minutes, turning once or twice, until crispy.
5. Remove the pancetta to a paper towel-lined plate to drain fat; set aside.

6. Sauté the celery and onion in the pancetta grease for 1 minute or until the vegetables start softening. Mix the flour into the vegetables to coat evenly and pour the wine over the veggies. Cook for about 1 minute or until reduced by about one-third.
7. Pour in the clam juice, the reserved mussel liquid, parsnips, remaining salt, rosemary, and bay leaf. Seal the pressure lid, choose Pressure; adjust the pressure to High and the cook time to 4 minutes. Press Start.
8. After cooking, perform a natural pressure release for 5 minutes. Stir in the mussels and heavy cream. Choose Sear/Sauté and adjust to Medium. Press Start to simmer to the chowder and heat the mussels. Carefully remove and discard the bay leaf after.
9. Spoon the soup into bowls and crumble the pancetta over the top. Garnish with the chervil and a handful of oyster crackers, serving the remaining crackers on the side.

Coconut Curried Mussels

Servings: 4
Cooking Time: 20 Minutes
Ingredients:
- 2 tbsp. water
- ½ cup onion, chopped fine
- ½ cup red bell pepper, seeded & chopped fine
- 3 cloves garlic, chopped fine
- ½ tsp pepper
- 2 tbsp. curry powder
- 1 cup coconut milk, unsweetened
- ½ cup vegetable broth
- 2 lbs. mussels, washed & cleaned
- ¼ cup cilantro, chopped

Directions:
1. Add the water, onion, bell pepper, and garlic to the cooking pot. Set to sauté on medium heat and cook, stirring occasionally until onions are soft, about 5-8 minutes, add more water if needed to prevent vegetables from sticking.
2. Stir in pepper, curry powder, coconut milk, and broth, stir well until smooth. Bring up to a simmer and add the mussels.
3. Add the lid and cook 5-6 minutes, or until all the mussels have opened. Discard any that do not open. Ladle into bowls and garnish with cilantro. Serve.

Nutrition Info:
- Calories 331,Total Fat 18g,Total Carbs 15g,Protein 29g,Sodium 664mg.

Lemon Cod Goujons And Rosemary Chips

Servings: 4
Cooking Time: 100 Min
Ingredients:
- 4 cod fillets, cut into strips
- 2 potatoes, cut into chips
- 4 lemon wedges to serve
- 2 eggs
- 1 cup arrowroot starch /130g
- 1 cup flour /130g
- 2 tbsps olive oil /30ml
- 3 tbsp fresh rosemary; chopped /45g
- 1 tbsp cumin powder /15g
- ½ tbsp cayenne powder /7.5g
- 1 tsp black pepper, plus more for seasoning /5g
- 1 tsp salt, plus more for seasoning /5g
- Zest and juice from 1 lemon
- Cooking spray

Directions:
1. Fix the Crisping Basket in the pot and close the crisping lid. Choose Air Crisp, set the temperature to 375°F or 191°C, and the time to 5 minutes. Choose Start/Stop to preheat the pot.
2. In a bowl, whisk the eggs, lemon zest, and lemon juice. In another bowl, combine the arrowroot starch, flour, cayenne powder, cumin, black pepper, and salt.
3. Coat each cod strip in the egg mixture, and then dredge in the flour mixture, coating well on all sides. Grease the preheated basket with cooking spray. Place the coated fish in the basket and oil with cooking spray.
4. Close the crisping lid. Choose Air Crisp, set the temperature to 375°F or 191°C, and the time to 15 minutes; press Start/Stop. Toss the potatoes with oil and season with salt and pepper.
5. After 15 minutes, check the fish making sure the pieces are as crispy as desired. Remove the fish from the basket.
6. Pour the potatoes in the basket. Close the crisping lid; choose Air Crisp, set the temperature to 400°F or 205°C, and the time to 24 minutes; press Start/Stop.
7. After 12 minutes, open the lid, remove the basket and shake the fries. Return the basket to the pot and close the lid to continue cooking until crispy.
8. When ready, sprinkle with fresh rosemary. Serve the fish with the potatoes and lemon wedges.

Pistachio Crusted Mahi Mahi

Servings: 6
Cooking Time: 20 Minutes
Ingredients:
- Nonstick cooking spray
- 6 fresh Mahi Mahi filets
- 2 tbsp. fresh lemon juice
- ½ tsp nutmeg
- ¼ tsp pepper
- ¼ tsp salt
- ½ cup pistachio nuts, chopped
- 2 tbsp. butter, melted

Directions:

1. Place the rack in the cooking pot. Lightly spray a small baking sheet with cooking spray.
2. Place the fish on the prepared pan. Season with lemon juice and spices. Top with pistachios and drizzle melted butter over the tops.
3. Place the pan on the rack and add the tender-crisp lid. Set to bake on 350°F. Cook fish 15-20 minutes or until it flakes easily with a fork. Serve immediately.

Nutrition Info:

- Calories 464,Total Fat 14g,Total Carbs 3g,Protein 77g,Sodium 405mg.

Shrimp Etouffee

Servings: 6
Cooking Time: 30 Minutes

Ingredients:

- ¼ cup olive oil
- ¼ cup flour
- 1 stalk celery, chopped
- 1 green bell pepper, chopped
- 2 jalapeno peppers, chopped
- ½ onion, chopped
- 4 cloves garlic, chopped
- 2 cups clam juice
- 1 tbsp. Cajun seasoning
- ½ tsp celery seed
- 1 tbsp. paprika
- 2 pounds shrimp, shell on, deveined
- 3 green onions, chopped
- Hot sauce to taste

Directions:

1. Add the oil to the cooking pot and set to sauté on medium heat. Whisk in the flour until smooth. Cook until a deep brown, whisking frequently, about 10 minutes.
2. Add celery, bell pepper, jalapeno, and onion and cook 4 minutes, stirring occasionally. Add the garlic and cook 2 minutes more.
3. Slowly stir in clam juice, a little at a time, until combined. The sauce should resemble syrup, add more juice if needed.
4. Add Cajun seasoning, celery seed, and paprika and mix well. Add the shrimp. Cover, reduce heat to low and cook 10 minutes.
5. Stir in green onions and hot sauce. Serve over rice.

Nutrition Info:

- Calories 83,Total Fat 3g,Total Carbs 6g,Protein 7g,Sodium 395mg.

Teriyaki Salmon

Servings: 4
Cooking Time: 15 Minutes

Ingredients:

- ½ cup brown sugar
- ½ cup soy sauce, low sodium
- ¼ cup cider vinegar
- 2 cloves garlic, chopped fine
- ¼ tsp pepper
- ½ tsp salt
- ½ tsp sesame oil
- 1 tbsp. water
- 1 tbsp. cornstarch
- 4 salmon filets
- 2 tbsp. green onions, sliced thin
- 2 tbsp. sesame seeds

Directions:

1. Set to sauté on medium heat. Add the brown sugar, soy sauce, vinegar, garlic, pepper, salt, and oil to the cooking pot. Stir until smooth.
2. In a small bowl, whisk together the water and cornstarch until smooth. Slowly whisk it into the sauce. Bring to a boil and cook 1-2 minutes until it starts to thicken. Reserve ¼ cup sauce.
3. Set cooker to bake on 400°F. Add the salmon to the pot and spoon sauce over the top. Add the tender-crisp lid and bake 15 minutes until salmon is firm to the touch but flakes easily.
4. Transfer salmon to serving plates and brush tops with reserved sauce. Garnish with green onion and sesame seeds and serve.

Nutrition Info:

- Calories 309,Total Fat 14g,Total Carbs 34g,Protein 38g,Sodium 2090mg.

Poached Flounder With Mango Salsa

Servings: 6
Cooking Time: 10 Minutes

Ingredients:

- 1 mango, peeled, pitted & chopped
- 1 red bell pepper, seeded & chopped
- ½ red onion, chopped fine
- 8 ¼ oz. pineapple tidbits, drain & reserve juice
- ¼ tsp salt, divided
- ½ tsp red pepper, divided
- 6 flounder filets
- ½ cup water

Directions:

1. In a medium bowl, combine mango, bell pepper, onion, pineapple, 1/8 teaspoon salt, and ¼ teaspoon pepper, mix well. Cover and refrigerate at least one hour.
2. Season fish with remaining salt and pepper and place in the cooking pot. Pour reserved pineapple juice and water over the fish.
3. Add the lid and set to sauté on med-high heat. Bring to a boil then reduce heat to low and cook 7-8 minutes or until fish flakes easily with a fork.

4. Transfer to fish to serving plates and top with mango salsa. Serve immediately.

Nutrition Info:

- Calories 200,Total Fat 4g,Total Carbs 17g,Protein 24g,Sodium 1092mg.

Flounder Veggie Soup

Servings: 10
Cooking Time: 20 Minutes

Ingredients:

- 2 cups water, divided
- 14 oz. chicken broth, low sodium
- 2 lbs. potatoes, peeled & cubed
- 1 onion, chopped
- 2 stalks celery, chopped
- 1 carrot, chopped
- 1 bay leaf
- 2 12 oz. cans evaporated milk, fat free
- 4 tbsp. butter
- 1 lb. flounder filets, cut in 1/2-inch pieces
- ½ tsp thyme
- ¼ tsp salt
- ¼ tsp pepper

Directions:

1. Add 1 ½ cups water, broth, potatoes, onion, celery, carrot, and the bay leaf to the cooking pot. Stir to mix.
2. Add the lid and set to pressure cooker on high. Set the timer for 8 minutes. When the timer goes off, use quick release to remove the lid.
3. Set cooker to sauté on med-low. Stir in milk, butter, fish, thyme, salt and pepper and bring to a boil.
4. In a small bowl, whisk together remaining water and cornstarch until smooth. Add to the soup and cook, stirring, until thickened. Discard the bay leaf and serve.

Nutrition Info:

- Calories 213,Total Fat 6g,Total Carbs 25g,Protein 14g,Sodium 649mg.

Cajun Salmon With Lemon

Servings: 1
Cooking Time: 10 Min

Ingredients:

- 1 salmon fillet
- Juice of ½ lemon
- 2 lemon wedges
- 1 tbsp Cajun seasoning /15g
- 1 tbsp chopped parsley; for garnishing /15g
- ¼ tsp brown sugar /1.25g

Directions:

1. Meanwhile, combine the sugar and lemon and coat the salmon with this mixture thoroughly. Coat the salmon with the Cajun seasoning as well.
2. Place a parchment paper into the Ninja Foodi, close the crisping lid and cook the salmon for 7 minutes on Air Crisp mode at 350 °F or 177°C. If you use a thicker fillet, cook no more than 6 minutes. Serve with lemon wedges and chopped parsley.

Creamy Crab Soup

Servings: 4
Cooking Time: 45 Min

Ingredients:

- 2 lb. Crabmeat Lumps /900g
- 2 celery stalk; diced
- 1 white onion; chopped
- ¾ cup heavy cream /188ml
- ½ cup Half and Half cream /125ml
- 1 ½ cup chicken broth /375ml
- ¾ cup Muscadet /98g
- 6 tbsp butter /90g
- 6 tbsp flour /90g
- 3 tsp Worcestershire sauce /15ml
- 3 tsp old bay Seasoning /15ml
- 2 tsp Hot sauce /10ml
- 3 tsp minced garlic /15g
- Salt to taste
- Lemon juice to serve
- Chopped dill to serve

Directions:

1. Melt the butter on Sear/Sauté mode, and mix in the all-purpose flour, in a fast motion to make a rue. Add celery, onion, and garlic.
2. Stir and cook until soft and crispy; for 3 minutes. While stirring, gradually add the half and half cream, heavy cream, and broth.
3. Let simmer for 2 minutes. Add Worcestershire sauce, old bay seasoning, Muscadet, and hot sauce. Stir and let simmer for 15 minutes. Add the crabmeat and mix it well into the sauce.
4. Close the crisping lid and cook on Broil mode for 10 minutes to soften the meat.
5. Dish into serving bowls, garnish with dill and drizzle squirts of lemon juice over. Serve with a side of garlic crusted bread.

Sweet Sour Fish

Servings: 4
Cooking Time: 6 Minutes

Ingredients:

- 1-pound fish chunks
- 1 tablespoon vinegar
- 2 drops liquid stevia
- 1/4 cup butter
- Black pepper and salt to taste

Directions:

1. Select "Sauté" mode on your Ninja Foodi.
2. Stir in butter and melt it.
3. Add fish chunks, sauté for 3 minutes.
4. Stir in stevia, salt, pepper, stir it.
5. Close the crisping lid.
6. Cook on "Air Crisp" mode for 3 minutes to 360°F.
7. Serve and enjoy.

Nutrition Info:

- Calories: 274g; Fat: 15g; Carbohydrates: 2g; Protein: 33g

Easy Clam Chowder

Servings: 6

Cooking Time: 3 Hours

Ingredients:

- 5 slices bacon, chopped
- 2 cloves garlic, chopped fine
- ½ onion, chopped
- ½ tsp thyme
- 1 cup chicken broth, low sodium
- 4 oz. cream cheese
- 18 oz. clams, chopped & drained
- 1 bay leaf
- 3 cups cauliflower, separated in florets
- 1 cup almond milk, unsweetened
- 1 cup heavy cream
- 2 tbsp. fresh parsley, chopped

Directions:

1. Add the bacon to the cooking pot and set to sauté on med-high heat. Cook until crisp, transfer to a paper-towel lined plate. Pour out all but 3 tablespoons of the fat.
2. Add the onion and garlic and cook 2-3 minutes until onion is translucent. Add the thyme and cook 1 minute more.
3. Add the broth, cream cheese, clams, bay leaf, and cauliflower, mix until combined. Add the lid and set to slow cook on low. Cook 2-3 hours until cauliflower is tender. Stir in the milk and cream and cook until heated through.
4. Ladle into bowls and top with bacon and parsley. Serve warm.

Nutrition Info:

- Calories 377,Total Fat 24g,Total Carbs 13g,Protein 27g,Sodium 468mg.

Clam Fritters

Servings: 4

Cooking Time: 10 Minutes

Ingredients:

- Nonstick cooking spray
- 1 1/3 cups flour
- 2 tsp baking powder
- 1 tsp Old Bay seasoning
- ¼ tsp cayenne pepper
- ¼ tsp salt
- ¼ tsp pepper
- 13 oz. clams, chopped
- 3 tbsp. clam juice
- 1 tbsp. lemon juice
- 2 eggs
- 1 ½ tbsp. chives, chopped
- 2 tbsp. milk

Directions:

1. Spray the fryer basket with cooking spray and add it to the cooking pot.
2. In a large bowl, combine flour, baking powder, Old Bay, cayenne pepper, salt, and pepper, mix well.
3. In a medium bowl, combine clams, clam juice, lemon juice, eggs, chives, and milk, mix well. Add the liquid ingredients to the dry ingredients and mix until combined.
4. Drop by spoonful into the fryer basket, don't over crowd them. Add the tender-crisp lid and set to air fry on 400°F. Cook 8-10 minutes until golden brown, turning over halfway through cooking time.

Nutrition Info:

- Calories 276,Total Fat 4g,Total Carbs 37g,Protein 21g,Sodium 911mg.

Tuna Zoodle Bake

Servings: 4

Cooking Time: 20 Minutes

Ingredients:

- Nonstick cooking spray
- 2 zucchini, cut in noodles with a spiralizer
- 1tsp olive oil
- ¼ cup onion, chopped fine
- 6 oz. tuna, drained
- ½ tbsp. tomato paste
- ½ cup tomatoes, diced & drained
- ¼ cup skim milk
- ½ tsp thyme
- ¼ tsp salt
- ¼ tsp pepper
- 1/8 cup parmesan cheese, fat free
- 1/4 cup cheddar cheese, reduced fat, grated

Directions:

1. Spray an 8x8-inch baking pan with cooking spray.
2. Place the zucchini in an even layer in the prepared pan.
3. Add the oil to the cooking pot and set to sauté on med-high heat. Once the oil is hot, add the onion and cook 2 minutes, or until soft.
4. Stir in the tuna and tomato paste and cook 1 minute more. Add the tomatoes, milk, thyme, salt, and pepper and bring to a low simmer. Stir in parmesan cheese and cook until it melts.
5. Pour the tuna mixture over the zucchini and sprinkle cheddar cheese over the top. Wipe out the pat and place the baking pan in it.

6. Add the tender-crisp lid and set to bake on 400°F. Bake 15 minutes until cheese is melted and bubbly. Serve.

Nutrition Info:

- Calories 80,Total Fat 3g,Total Carbs 2g,Protein 11g,Sodium 371mg.

Arroz Con Cod

Servings: 4
Cooking Time: 30 Minutes

Ingredients:

- ¼ cup olive oil
- 2 tbsp. garlic, chopped
- ½ cup red onion, chopped
- ½ cup red bell pepper, chopped
- ½ cup green bell pepper, chopped
- 2 cups long grain rice
- 3 tbsp. tomato paste
- 2 tsp turmeric
- 2 tbsp. cumin
- ½ tsp salt
- ¼ tsp pepper
- 4 cups chicken broth
- 1 bay leaf
- 1 lb. cod, cut in bite-size pieces
- ½ cup peas, cooked
- 4 tbsp. pimento, chopped
- 4 tsp cilantro, chopped

Directions:

1. Add the oil to the cooking pot and set to sauté on med-high.
2. Add the garlic, onion, and peppers, and cook, stirring frequently for 2 minutes.
3. Stir in rice, tomato paste, and seasonings, and cook another 2 minutes.
4. Add the broth and bay leaf and bring to a boil. Reduce heat, cover, and let simmer 5 minutes.
5. Add the fish, recover the pot and cook 15-20 minutes until all the liquid is absorbed. Turn off the cooker and let sit for 5 minutes.
6. To serve: spoon onto plates and top with cooked peas, pimento and cilantro.

Nutrition Info:

- Calories 282,Total Fat 15g,Total Carbs 35g,Protein 4g,Sodium 1249mg.

Salmon Florentine

Servings: 4
Cooking Time: 15 Minutes

Ingredients:

- 2 tbsp. olive oil, divided
- 4 salmon filets
- ½ tsp salt
- ¼ tsp pepper
- 4 cloves garlic, chopped fine
- 10 oz. fresh spinach
- ½ tbsp. lemon juice
- ¼ tsp basil

Directions:

1. Add 1 tablespoon oil to the cooking pot and set to sauté on medium heat.
2. Season salmon with salt and pepper and add to the pot. Cook 8-10 minutes or until fish flakes easily with a fork, turning over halfway through cooking time. Transfer to a plate.
3. Add remaining oil and let heat up. Add remaining ingredients and cook 2-3 minutes until spinach is wilted.
4. Place fish on serving plates and top with spinach mixture. Serve immediately.

Nutrition Info:

- Calories 436,Total Fat 30g,Total Carbs 4g,Protein 37g,Sodium 448mg.

Tuscan Cod

Servings:4
Cooking Time: 32 Minutes

Ingredients:

- 2 tablespoons canola oil, divided
- 1½ pounds baby red potatoes, cut into ½-inch pieces
- 2½ teaspoons kosher salt, divided
- 1 teaspoon freshly ground black pepper, divided
- 1 cup panko bread crumbs
- 6 tablespoons unsalted butter, divided
- 2 teaspoons poultry seasoning
- Juice of 1 lemon
- 1 medium onion, thinly sliced
- 1½ cups cherry tomatoes, halved
- 4 garlic cloves, quartered lengthwise
- ⅓ cup Kalamata olives, roughly chopped
- 4 fresh cod fillets
- 1 teaspoon fresh mint, finely chopped
- 1 lemon, cut into wedges

Directions:

1. Select SEAR/SAUTÉ and set to HI. Select START/STOP to begin. Let preheat for 5 minutes.
2. Add 1 tablespoon of oil and the potatoes. Season with 1½ teaspoons of salt and ½ teaspoon of pepper. Sauté for about 15 minutes, stirring occasionally, until the potatoes are golden brown.
3. While potatoes are cooking, combine the bread crumbs, 4 tablespoons of butter, poultry seasoning, the remaining 1 teaspoon of salt and ½ teaspoon of pepper, and lemon juice in a medium bowl. Stir well.
4. Once the potatoes are browned, carefully remove them from the pot and set aside. Add the remaining 1 tablespoon of oil, then the onion. Sauté for 2 to 3 minutes, until the onions are lightly browned. Add the tomatoes, garlic, and

olives and cook for about 2 minutes more, stirring occasionally. Return the potatoes to the pot, stir. Select START/STOP to pause cooking. Close crisping lid to retain heat.

5. Coat the cod on both sides with the remaining 2 tablespoons of butter. Evenly distribute the breadcrumb mixture on top of the cod, pressing the crumbs down firmly.

6. Open lid and place the Reversible Rack in the pot over the potato mixture, making sure it is the higher position. Place the cod fillets on the rack, bread-side up. Close crisping lid.

7. Select BAKE/ROAST, set temperature to 375°F, and set time to 12 minutes. Select START/STOP to begin.

8. When cooking is complete, leave the cod in the pot with the crisping lid closed for 5 minutes to rest before serving. After resting, the internal temperature of the cod should be at least 145°F and the bread crumbs should be golden brown. Serve with potato mixture and garnish with chopped mint and lemon wedges.

Nutrition Info:

- Calories: 583,Total Fat: 28g,Sodium: 815mg,Carbohydrates: 48g,Protein: 37g.

Spanish Steamed Clams

Servings: 6

Cooking Time: 20 Minutes

Ingredients:

- 3 tbsp. olive oil
- 1 onion, chopped fine
- 3 oz. prosciutto, chopped
- ¼ cup dry sherry
- 36 littleneck clams

Directions:

1. Add the oil to the cooking pot and set to sauté on med-high heat.
2. Add the onion and cook, stirring, 1 minutes. Reduce heat to low, add the lid and cook 10-15 minutes until onion is soft.
3. Stir in remaining ingredients and increase heat to medium. Add the lid and cook 5 minutes, or until the clams open.
4. Discard any unopened clams and serve immediately.

Nutrition Info:

- Calories 166,Total Fat 9g,Total Carbs 5g,Protein 15g,Sodium 657mg.

Shrimp & Sausage Gumbo

Servings: 8

Cooking Time: 1 Hour 30 Minutes

Ingredients:

- ½ cup peanut oil
- ½ cup flour
- 1 green bell pepper, chopped
- 1 onion, chopped
- 3 stalks celery, chopped
- 4 cloves garlic, chopped fine
- 1 tbsp. Cajun seasoning
- 1 quart chicken broth, low sodium
- 1 cup water
- 2 tsp Worcestershire sauce
- ¼ tsp pepper
- ½ tsp salt
- 12 oz. smoked andouille sausage, sliced ¼-inch thick
- 2 lbs. shrimp, peeled & deveined
- 3 green onions, chopped
- Hot sauce to taste

Directions:

1. Add the oil to the cooking pot and set to sauté on medium heat. Whisk in the flour until smooth. Cook, stirring until roux is a golden brown. Reduce heat to med-low and cook 20-30 minutes until roux is a deep brown.
2. Add the bell pepper, onion, and celery and increase heat to med-high. Cook, stirring frequently about 5 minutes. Add the garlic and cook 2 minutes more. Stir in Cajun seasoning.
3. Stirring constantly, slowly add the broth and water. Bring to a simmer and add the Worcestershire, pepper, and salt. Reduce heat to medium and simmer 30 minutes.
4. Add the sausage and cook until heated through, about 5 minutes. Add the shrimp and cook until they turn pink, about 5 minutes. Serve garnished with green onions and hot sauce to taste over cooked rice.

Nutrition Info:

- Calories 111,Total Fat 7g,Total Carbs 4g,Protein 8g,Sodium 207mg.

Spaghetti With Scallops And Arugula

Servings: 4

Cooking Time: 50 Min

Ingredients:

- 1¼ pounds scallops, peeled and deveined /562.5g
- 10 ounces spaghetti /300g
- 2 large garlic cloves, minced; divided
- 6 cups arugula /780g
- ¼ cup white wine /62.5ml
- 2½ cups water /625ml
- ⅓ cup tomato puree /88ml
- 1 tbsp lemon juice /15ml
- 1 tbsp melted butter /15ml
- ½ tsp red chili flakes or to taste /2.5g
- 1 tsp grated lemon zest /5g
- 1½ tsp s salt; divided /7.5g

Directions:

1. Arrange the scallops in the Crisping Basket. Season with ½ tsp salt, melted butter, and 1 minced garlic clove. Toss to coat and put the basket in the inner pot.

2. Close the crisping lid; choose Air Crisp, adjust the temperature to 400°F or 205°C and the cook time to 6 minutes.
3. Press Start. After 3 minutes, open the lid and use tongs to turn the scallops. Close the lid and resume cooking. Remove onto a plate and set aside.
4. On the pot, choose Sear/Sauté and adjust to High. Press Start to preheat the pot. Pour in the white wine and simmer for 1 to 2 minutes until reduced by half.
5. Add the spaghetti, water, remaining salt, garlic, puréed tomato, and chili flakes. Stir to combine.
6. Lock the pressure lid into place and set to Seal. Choose Pressure; adjust the pressure to High and the cook time to 5 minutes. Press Start.
7. After cooking, perform a quick pressure release and carefully open the lid. Stir in the lemon zest, juice, and arugula until wilted and soft. Add the scallops and heat through for a few minutes. Serve immediately.

Tilapia & Tamari Garlic Mushrooms

Servings: 4
Cooking Time: 10 Minutes
Ingredients:

- 2 tbsp. sesame oil, divided
- 2 cloves garlic, chopped fine
- 2 cups mushrooms, sliced
- 4 tilapia fillets
- ½ tsp salt
- ¼ tsp pepper
- 1 tbsp. fresh lime juice
- 1 tbsp. tamari
- ¼ cup cilantro, chopped

Directions:

1. Add 1 tablespoon oil to the cooking pot and set to sauté on med-high heat.
2. Add the garlic and mushrooms and cook, stirring occasionally, 2-3 minutes.
3. Add the rack to the pot and top with a sheet of foil. Place the fish on the foil and brush with the remaining oil. Season with salt and pepper and drizzle lime juice over the tops.
4. Add the tender-crisp lid and set to roast on 350°F. Cook 5 minutes or until fish flakes with a fork and the liquid from the mushrooms has evaporated.
5. Transfer fish to serving plates. Stir the tamari into the mushrooms and spoon over fish. Garnish with cilantro and serve.

Nutrition Info:

- Calories 298,Total Fat 12g,Total Carbs 2g,Protein 44g,Sodium 610mg.

Spicy Shrimp Pasta With Vodka Sauce

Servings:6
Cooking Time: 11 Minutes
Ingredients:

- 2 tablespoons extra-virgin olive oil
- 2 tablespoons minced garlic
- 1 teaspoon crushed red pepper flakes
- 1 small red onion, diced
- Kosher salt
- Freshly ground black pepper
- ¾ cup vodka
- 2¾ cups vegetable stock
- 1 can crushed tomatoes
- 1 box penne pasta
- 1 pound frozen shrimp, peeled and deveined
- 1 package cream cheese, cubed
- 4 cups shredded mozzarella cheese

Directions:

1. Select SEAR/SAUTÉ and set to MD:HI. Select START/STOP to begin. Let preheat for 5 minutes.
2. Add the olive oil, garlic, and crushed red pepper flakes. Cook until garlic is golden brown, about 1 minute. Add the onions and season with salt and pepper and cook until translucent, about 2 minutes.
3. Stir in the vodka, vegetable stock, crushed tomatoes, penne pasta, and frozen shrimp. Assemble pressure lid, making sure the pressure release valve is in the SEAL position.
4. Select PRESSURE and set temperature to HI. Set time to 6 minutes. Select START/STOP to begin.
5. When pressure cooking is complete, quick release the pressure by turning the pressure release valve to the VENT position. Carefully remove lid when unit has finished releasing pressure.
6. Stir in the cream cheese until it has melted. Layer the mozzarella on top of the pasta. Close crisping lid.
7. Select AIR CRISP, set temperature to 400°F, and set time to 5 minutes. Select START/STOP to begin.
8. When cooking is complete, open lid and serve.

Nutrition Info:

- Calories: 789,Total Fat: 35g,Sodium: 1302mg,Carbohydrates: 63g,Protein: 47g.

Basil Lemon Shrimp & Asparagus

Servings: 4
Cooking Time: 10 Minutes

Ingredients:

- 3 tbsp. water, divided
- 2 cloves garlic, chopped fine
- 2 tbsp. onion, chopped fine
- ½ tsp fresh ginger, grated
- ½ tsp salt
- ¼ tsp pepper
- ¼ tsp red pepper flakes
- 1 tbsp. fresh lemon juice
- 1 lb. asparagus, trimmed & cut in 1-inch pieces
- 1 lb. medium shrimp, peeled, deveined, tails removed
- 1 tsp lemon zest
- 3 tbsp. fresh basil, chopped

Directions:

1. Add 2 tablespoons water, garlic, and onion to the cooking pot and set to sauté on medium heat. Cook 1 minute, stirring.
2. Add remaining water, ginger, salt, pepper, red pepper flakes, lemon juice, and asparagus, stir to combine. Add the lid and cook 2-3 minutes until asparagus starts to turn bright green.
3. Add the shrimp and stir. Recover and cook another 3-5 minutes or until shrimp are pink and asparagus is fork-tender.
4. Stir in the lemon zest and basil and serve.

Nutrition Info:

- Calories 110,Total Fat 1g,Total Carbs 7g,Protein 18g,Sodium 645mg.

Seafood Chowder

Servings: 4
Cooking Time: 5 Hours

Ingredients:

- 2 cups clam juice
- 3 cups cauliflower, separated into florets
- 1 cup onion, sliced
- ½ cup celery, sliced
- 1/8 tsp saffron, crushed
- 2 cups skim milk, divided
- 8 oz. haddock filet, cut in 1-inch pieces
- 8 oz. cod filet, cut in 1-inch pieces
- ½ cup shrimp, peeled & deveined
- 1 tbsp. cornstarch
- Salt & white pepper, to taste
- 2 slices bacon, cooked crisp & crumbled

Directions:

1. Add the clam juice, vegetables, and saffron to the cooking pot and stir to mix.
2. Add the lid and set to slow cook on high. Cook 4-5 hours, stirring in 1 ½ cups milk in the last 30 minutes. Add the seafood in the last 15 minutes.
3. In a medium bowl, whisk together remaining milk and cornstarch until smooth. Stir into the chowder and continue cooking another 2-3 minutes until it thickens. Season with salt and pepper and serve topped with bacon.

Nutrition Info:

- Calories 245,Total Fat 7g,Total Carbs 15g,Protein 31g,Sodium 761mg.

Spicy "grilled" Catfish

Servings: 4
Cooking Time: 10 Minutes

Ingredients:

- Nonstick cooking spray
- 1 tbsp. fresh basil, chopped
- 1 tsp crushed red pepper flakes
- 1 tsp garlic powder
- ½ tsp salt
- ½ tsp pepper
- 4 catfish fillets
- 2 tbsp. olive oil

Directions:

1. Spray the rack with cooking spray and add to the cooking pot.
2. In a small bowl, combine all the spices and mix well.
3. Pat the fish dry with a paper towel. Rub both sides of the fish with the oil and coat with the seasoning mix.
4. Place the fish on the rack and add the tender-crisp lid. Set to roast on 350°F. Cook 7-9 minutes until fish flakes with a fork, turning over halfway through cooking time. Serve immediately.

Nutrition Info:

- Calories 211,Total Fat 11g,Total Carbs 0g,Protein 26g,Sodium 359mg.

Awesome Shrimp Roast

Servings: 2
Cooking Time: 7 Minutes

Ingredients:

- 3 tablespoons chipotle in adobo sauce, minced
- ¼ teaspoon salt
- 1/4 cup BBQ sauce
- ½ orange, juiced
- ½ pound large shrimps

Directions:

1. Preheat Ninja Foodi by pressing the "Bake/Roast" mode and setting it to "400 °F" and timer to 7 minutes.
2. Let it preheat until you hear a beep.
3. Set shrimps over Grill Grate and lock lid, cook until the timer runs out.
4. Serve and enjoy.

Nutrition Info:

- Calories: 173; Fat: 2g; Carbohydrates: 21g; Protein: 17g

Mustard And Apricot-glazed Salmon With Smashed Potatoes

Servings:4
Cooking Time: 25 Minutes
Ingredients:

- 20 ounces baby potatoes, whole
- 1½ cups water
- 4 frozen skinless salmon fillets
- ¼ cup apricot preserves
- 2 teaspoons Dijon mustard
- 2 tablespoons extra-virgin olive oil
- ½ teaspoon kosher salt
- ½ teaspoon freshly ground black pepper

Directions:

1. Place the potatoes and water in the pot. Put Reversible Rack in pot, making sure it is in the higher position. Place salmon on the rack. Assemble pressure lid, making sure the pressure release valve is in the SEAL position.
2. Select PRESSURE and set to HI. Set time to 5 minutes. Select START/STOP to begin.
3. Mix together the apricot preserves and mustard in a small bowl.
4. When pressure cooking is complete, quick release the pressure by turning the pressure release valve to the VENT position. Carefully remove lid when unit has finished releasing pressure.
5. Carefully remove rack with salmon. Remove potatoes from pot and drain. Place the potatoes on a cutting board and, using the back of a knife, carefully press down to flatten each. Drizzle the flattened potatoes with the olive oil and season with salt and pepper.
6. Place Cook & Crisp Basket in the pot. Place the potatoes into the basket and close crisping lid.
7. Select AIR CRISP, set temperature to 390°F, and set time to 15 minutes. Select START/STOP to begin.
8. After 8 minutes, open lid, and using silicone-tipped tongs, gently flip the potatoes. Lower basket back into pot and close lid to resume cooking.
9. When cooking is complete, remove basket from pot. Return the rack with the salmon to the pot, making sure the rack is in the higher position. Gently brush the salmon with the apricot and mustard mixture.
10. Close crisping lid. Select BROIL and set time to 5 minutes. Select START/STOP to begin.
11. When cooking is complete, remove salmon and serve immediately with the potatoes.

Nutrition Info:

- Calories: 359,Total Fat: 11g,Sodium: 711mg,Carbohydrates: 36g,Protein: 31g.

Haddock With Sanfaina

Servings: 4
Cooking Time: 40 Min
Ingredients:

- 4 haddock fillets
- 1 can diced tomatoes, drained /435g
- ½ small onion; sliced
- 1 small jalapeño pepper, seeded and minced
- 2 large garlic cloves, minced
- 1 eggplant; cubed
- 1 bell pepper; chopped
- 1 bay leaf
- ⅓ cup sliced green olives /44g
- ¼ cup chopped fresh chervil; divided /32.5g
- 3 tbsps olive oil /45ml
- 3 tbsps capers; divided/45g
- ½ tsp dried basil /2.5g
- ¼ tsp salt /1.25g

Directions:

1. Season the fish on both sides with salt, place in the refrigerator, and make the sauce. Press Sear/Sauté and set to Medium. Press Start. Melt the butter until no longer foaming. Add onion, eggplant, bell pepper, jalapeño, and garlic; sauté for 5 minutes.
2. Stir in the tomatoes, bay leaf, basil, olives, half of the chervil, and half of the capers. Remove the fish from the refrigerator and lay on the vegetables in the pot.
3. Seal the pressure lid, choose Pressure; adjust the pressure to Low and the cook time to 3 minutes; press Start. After cooking, do a quick pressure release and carefully open the lid. Remove and discard the bay leaf.
4. Transfer the fish to a serving platter and spoon the sauce over. Sprinkle with the remaining chervil and capers. Serve.

Mediterranean Cod

Servings: 4
Cooking Time: 20 Min
Ingredients:

- 4 fillets cod
- 1 bunch fresh thyme sprigs
- 1 pound cherry tomatoes, halved /450g
- 1 clove garlic, pressed
- 1 cup white rice /130g
- 2 cups water /500ml
- 1 cup Kalamata olives /130g
- 2 tbsp pickled capers /30g
- 1 tbsp olive oil; divided /15ml
- 1 tsp olive oil /15ml
- 1 pinch ground black pepper
- 3 pinches salt

Directions:

1. Line a parchment paper to the steamer basket of your Foodi. Place about half the tomatoes in a single layer on the paper. Sprinkle with thyme, reserving some for garnish. Arrange cod fillets on the top of tomatoes. Sprinkle with a little bit of olive oil.
2. Spread the garlic, pepper, salt, and remaining tomatoes over the fish. In the pot, mix rice and water. Lay a trivet over the rice and water. Lower steamer basket onto the trivet.
3. Seal the pressure lid, choose Pressure, set to High, and set the timer to 7 minutes. Press Start. When ready, release the pressure quickly.
4. Remove the steamer basket and trivet from the pot. Use a fork to fluff rice. Plate the fish fillets and apply a garnish of olives, reserved thyme, pepper, remaining olive oil, and capers. Serve with rice.

Caribbean Catfish With Mango Salsa

Servings: 4
Cooking Time: 10 Minutes
Ingredients:

- 1 red pepper, roasted & chopped
- 1 mango, peeled & chopped
- 1 orange, peeled & chopped
- ¼ cup cilantro, chopped fine
- ¼ cup green onion, chopped fine
- 1 tsp jalapeno, chopped
- 1 tbsp. olive oil
- 1 tsp salt, divided
- ½ tsp pepper, divided
- ½ cup panko bread crumbs
- ½ cup coconut, shredded
- 4 catfish fillets
- Nonstick cooking spray

Directions:

1. In a medium bowl, combine red pepper, mango, orange, cilantro, green onion, jalapeno, olive oil, ¼ tsp salt, and ¼ tsp pepper. Cover and let sit until ready to use.
2. In a shallow dish, stir together bread crumbs and coconut until combined.
3. Season catfish with salt and pepper. Dredge in bread crumbs coating both sides thoroughly.
4. Spray the fryer basket with cooking spray. Lay the catfish in the basket in a single layer. Add the tender-crisp lid and set to air fry on 375°F. Cook fish 8-10 minutes per side until golden brown and fish flakes easily with a fork.
5. Transfer fish to serving plates and top with mango salsa. Serve immediately.

Nutrition Info:

- Calories 357,Total Fat 12g,Total Carbs 34g,Protein 30g,Sodium 534mg.

Salmon With Balsamic-glazed Brussels Sprouts

Servings:2
Cooking Time: 57 Minutes
Ingredients:

- 2 cups brown rice
- 2½ cups water
- 2 salmon fillets
- 4 tablespoons everything bagel seasoning, divided
- 1 pound Brussels sprouts, ends trimmed, cut in half
- 1 tablespoon olive oil
- 2 tablespoons balsamic glaze

Directions:

1. Place the rice and water in the cooking pot. Assemble the pressure lid, making sure the pressure release valve is in the SEAL position.
2. Select PRESSURE and set to HI. Set the time to 30 minutes. Select START/STOP to begin.
3. Meanwhile, season both sides of the salmon fillets with the everything bagel seasoning, using one tablespoon per fillet. Set aside.
4. When pressure cooking is complete, allow the pressure to release naturally for 10 minutes. After 10 minutes, quick release any remaining pressure by moving the pressure release valve to the VENT position. Carefully remove the lid when the unit has finished releasing pressure.
5. Season both sides of each salmon fillet with one tablespoon of the everything bagel seasoning.
6. In a medium bowl, combine the Brussels sprouts and olive oil. Toss to coat, and then sprinkle with one tablespoon of the everything bagel seasoning. Toss again to ensure Brussels sprouts are coated.
7. Place the Cook & Crisp Basket into the cooking pot. Close the crisping lid. Select AIR CRISP, set the temperature to 390°F, and set the time to 16 minutes. Select START/STOP to begin. Allow to preheat for 5 minutes, then add the sprouts to the Cook & Crisp Basket. Close the crisping lid to begin cooking.
8. After 8 minutes, open the crisping lid, lift the basket, and shake the sprouts. Lower the basket back into the pot and close the lid to resume cooking another 8 minutes or until the Brussels sprouts reach your desired crispiness.
9. Once timer is complete, transfer the sprouts to a bowl and toss with remaining tablespoon of seasoning and the balsamic glaze.
10. Close the crisping lid. Select AIR CRISP, set the temperature to 390°F, and set the time to 11 minutes. Select START/STOP to begin. Allow to preheat for 5 minutes, then add the salmon fillets to the Cook & Crisp basket. Close the lid to begin cooking.
11. Once timer is complete, remove fillets from basket and serve alongside sprouts and rice.

Nutrition Info:

- Calories: 1028,Total Fat: 30g,Sodium: 1440mg,Carbohydrates: 154g,Protein: 55g.

Coconut Shrimp With Pineapple Rice

Servings:4
Cooking Time: 45 Minutes
Ingredients:

- 2 tablespoons canola oil
- 1 can diced pineapple
- 1 yellow onion, diced
- 1 cup long-grain white rice
- 1½ cups chicken stock
- ½ cup freshly squeezed lime juice
- ¾ cup all-purpose flour
- 1 tablespoon kosher salt
- ½ teaspoon freshly ground black pepper
- 2 large eggs
- ½ cup coconut flakes
- ½ cup plain panko bread crumbs
- 10 ounces, deveined shrimp, tails removed
- Cooking spray

Directions:

1. Select SEAR/SAUTÉ and set temperature to HI. Select START/STOP to begin. Let preheat for 5 minutes.
2. Add the oil and heat for 1 minute. Add the pineapple and onion. Cook, stirring frequently, for about 8 minutes, or until the onion is translucent.
3. Add the rice, chicken stock, and lime juice. Assemble pressure lid, making sure the pressure release valve is in the SEAL position.
4. Select PRESSURE and set to HI. Set time to 2 minutes. Select START/STOP to begin.
5. When pressure cooking is complete, allow press to naturally release for 10 minutes. After 10 minutes, quick release remaining pressure by turning the pressure release valve to the VENT position. Carefully remove lid when unit has finished releasing pressure.
6. Transfer the rice mixture to a bowl and cover to keep warm. Clean the cooking pot and return to the unit.
7. Create a batter station with three medium bowls. In the first bowl, mix together the flour, salt and pepper. In the second bowl, whisk the eggs. In the third bowl, combine the coconut flakes and bread crumbs. Dip each shrimp into the flour mixture. Next dip it in the egg. Finally, coat in the coconut mixture, shaking off excess as needed. Once all the shrimp are battered, spray them with cooking spray.
8. Place Cook & Crisp Basket into pot. Place the shrimp in basket and close crisping lid.
9. Select AIR CRISP, set temperature to 390°F, and set time to 10 minutes. Select START/STOP to begin.
10. After 5 minutes, open lid, then lift basket and shake the shrimp. Lower basket back into the pot and close the lid to continue cooking until the shrimp reach your desired crispiness.
11. When cooking is complete, serve the shrimp on top of the rice.

Nutrition Info:

- Calories: 601,Total Fat: 15g,Sodium: 784mg,Carbohydrates: 88g,Protein: 28g.

Crab Bisque

Servings: 6
Cooking Time: 15 Minutes
Ingredients:

- 3 tbsp. butter
- 1 carrot, chopped fine
- 2 stalks celery, chopped fine
- 2 tbsp. flour
- 1 clove garlic, chopped fine
- 1 tbsp. fresh parsley, chopped
- 2 cups chicken broth, low sodium
- ½ cup sherry
- ¼ tsp pepper
- 18 oz. lump crab meat
- 2 cups half and half

Directions:

1. Add the butter to the cooking pot and set to sauté on medium heat.
2. Once the butter has melted, add the carrots and celery and cook 5-7 minutes until vegetables start to soften.
3. Sprinkle in the flour and cook, stirring, one minute. Add remaining ingredients, except crab and cream, and stir to combine.
4. Bring to a boil and cook one minute. Reduce heat to low and stir in crab and cream. Cook, stirring until bisque is heated through. Serve immediately.

Nutrition Info:

- Calories 200,Total Fat 8g,Total Carbs 12g,Protein 18g,Sodium 770mg.

Cod Cornflakes Nuggets

Servings: 4
Cooking Time: 25 Min
Ingredients:

- 1 ¼ lb. cod fillets, cut into chunks /662.5g
- 1 egg
- 1 cup cornflakes /130g
- ½ cup flour /65g
- 1 tbsp olive oil/15ml
- 1 tbsp water /15ml
- Salt and pepper, to taste

Directions:

1. Add the oil and cornflakes in a food processor, and process until crumbed. Season the fish chunks with salt and pepper.

2. Beat the egg along with 1 tbsp or 15ml water. Dredge the chunks in flour first, then dip in the egg, and coat with cornflakes. Arrange on a lined sheet. Close the crisping lid and cook at 350 °F or 177°C for 15 minutes on Air Crisp mode.

Cod On Lentils

Servings: 4
Cooking Time: 65 Min
Ingredients:

- 4 cod fillets
- 1 lemon, juiced
- 1 yellow bell pepper; diced
- 1 red bell pepper; diced
- 4 cups vegetable broth /1000ml
- 1 cup panko breadcrumbs /130g
- ¼ cup minced fresh cilantro /32.5g
- 2 cups lentils, soaked /260g
- 1 tbsp olive oil /15ml
- 4 tbsps melted butter /60ml
- 1 tsp lemon zest /5g
- 1 tsp salt /5g

Directions:

1. Choose Sear/Sauté on the pot and set to Medium High. Choose Start/Stop to preheat the pot. Combine the oil, lentils, yellow and red bell peppers in the preheated pot and cook for 1 minute. Mix in the vegetable broth.
2. Seal the pressure lid, choose Pressure, set to High, and set the time to 6 minutes. Choose Start/Stop.
3. In a small bowl, combine the breadcrumbs, butter, cilantro, lemon zest, lemon juice, and salt. Spoon the breadcrumb mixture evenly on the cod fillet.
4. When cooking ended, perform a quick pressure release, and carefully open the pressure lid.
5. Fix the reversible rack in the pot, which will be over the lentils. Lay the cod fillets on the rack.
6. Close the crisping lid. Choose Air Crisp, set the temperature to 350°F or 177°C, and set the time to 12 minutes; press Start/Stop.
7. When ready, share the lentils into four serving plates, and top with salmon.

Swordfish With Caper Sauce

Servings: 4
Cooking Time: 8 Minutes
Ingredients:

- 4 swordfish steaks, about 1-inch thick
- 4 tablespoons unsalted butter
- 1 lemon, sliced into 8 slices
- 1 tablespoon lemon juice
- 1 tablespoon olive oil
- 2 tablespoons capers, drained
- Sea salt, to taste
- Black pepper, to taste

Directions:

1. Take a large shallow bowl and whisk together the lemon juice and oil.
2. Season with swordfish steaks with black pepper and salt on each side, place in the oil mixture.
3. Turn to coat both sides and refrigerate for 15 minutes.
4. Preheat Ninja Foodi by pressing the "GRILL" option and setting it to "MAX" and timer to 8 minutes.
5. Let it preheat until you hear a beep.
6. Set the swordfish over the grill grate, Lock and secure the Ninja Foodi's lid and cook for 9 minutes.
7. Then turn off the heat.
8. Enjoy.

Nutrition Info:

- Calories: 472; Fat: 31g; Carbohydrates: 2g; Protein: 48g

Simple Salmon & Asparagus

Servings: 4
Cooking Time: 15 Minutes
Ingredients:

- 4 salmon filets
- 1 tsp rosemary
- ½ tsp pepper, divided
- 14 oz. vegetable broth, low sodium
- 1 tbsp. lemon juice
- ½ lb. asparagus, trimmed & cut in 2-inch pieces

Directions:

1. Season the fish with rosemary and ¼ teaspoon pepper and add to cooking pot.
2. In a small bowl, whisk together broth, lemon juice, and remaining pepper until smooth. Pour over fish.
3. Add the lid and set to sauté on medium heat. Once mixture reaches a boil, reduce heat to low and simmer 5 minutes.
4. Add the asparagus around the salmon, recover, and cook another 5 minutes until asparagus is fork-tender and fish flakes easily. Serve immediately..

Nutrition Info:

- Calories 163,Total Fat 5g,Total Carbs 3g,Protein 25g,Sodium 454mg.

Crabmeat With Broccoli Risotto

Servings: 4

Cooking Time: 80 Min

Ingredients:

- 1 pound broccoli, cut into florets and chopped into 1-inch pieces /450g
- 8 ounces lump crabmeat /240g
- 1 small onion; chopped (about ½ cup) /65g
- 2 cups vegetable stock /500ml
- ⅓ cup grated Pecorino Romano cheese/44g
- 1 cup short grain rice /130g
- ⅓ cup white wine /88ml
- 1 tbsp olive oil /15ml
- 1 tsp salt; divided /5g
- 2 tbsps ghee /30g

Directions:

1. Preheat your Foodi by closing the crisping lid. Choose Air Crisp; adjust the temperature to 375°F or 191°C and the time to 2 minutes. Press Start. Add the broccoli in the crisping basket and drizzle with the olive oil. Season with ½ tsp of salt and toss.
2. Put the basket in the inner pot. Close the crisping lid; choose Air Crisp, adjust the temperature to 375°F or 191°C and the cook time to 10 minutes. Press Start.
3. After 5 minutes, open the lid and stir the broccoli, then resume cooking. When done cooking, take out the basket and set aside.
4. Choose Sear/Sauté and adjust to Medium. Press Start and melt the ghee. Add and sauté the onion for 5 minutes until softened.
5. Stir in the rice and cook for 1 minute. Add the wine and cook for 2 to 3 minutes, stirring frequently, until the liquid has almost completely evaporated.
6. Pour in vegetable stock and the remaining salt. Stir to combine. Seal the pressure lid, choose Pressure, adjust the pressure to High, and the cook time to 8 minutes. Press Start.
7. After cooking, perform a quick pressure release and carefully open the pressure lid. Gently stir in the crabmeat, and cheese. Taste and adjust the seasoning. Serve immediately.

Vegan & Vegetable

Creamy Polenta & Mushrooms

Servings: 2

Cooking Time: 40 Minutes

Ingredients:

- 3 tbsp. olive oil
- 1 lb. assorted mushrooms, rinsed & chopped
- 1 clove garlic, chopped fine
- 1 tsp salt, divided
- 3/8 tsp pepper, divided
- 2 ½ cups water, divided
- 3 tbsp. butter
- 1 ½ tbsp. fresh lemon juice
- 1 tbsp. fresh parsley, chopped
- ½ cup stone-ground white grits
- 1/8 cup heavy cream
- 3 tbsp. parmesan cheese, grated, divided
- ¼ cup mascarpone

Directions:

1. Add oil to the cooking pot and set to sauté on medium heat.
2. Add mushrooms, garlic, ½ teaspoon salt, and ¼ teaspoon pepper and cook, stirring occasionally, until mushrooms are nicely browned and liquid has evaporated, about 6-8 minutes.
3. Add ¼ cup water, butter, lemon juice, and parsley and cook, stirring, until butter melts. Cook 1-2 minutes. Transfer to a large bowl and keep warm.
4. Add the remaining water to the pot and increase heat to med-high. Bring just to a boil.
5. Whisk in grits slowly until combined. Reduce heat to med-low and simmer, stirring occasionally, about 30 minutes, or until liquid is absorbed. Turn off the heat.
6. Stir in cream, 1 tablespoon cheese, and remaining salt and pepper and mix well. Ladle polenta onto serving plates. Top with mushrooms, mascarpone, and remaining parmesan cheese. Serve immediately.

Nutrition Info:

- Calories 102,Total Fat 7g,Total Carbs 8g,Protein 2g,Sodium 215mg.

Bok Choy And Zoddle Soup

Servings: 6
Cooking Time: 35 Min
Ingredients:

- 1 lb. baby bok choy, stems removed /450g
- 2 zucchinis, spiralized
- 6 oz. Shitake mushrooms, stems removed and sliced to a 2-inch thickness /180g
- 2-inch ginger; chopped
- 2 cloves garlic, peeled
- 3 carrots, peeled and sliced diagonally
- 2 sweet onion; chopped
- 6 cups water /1500ml
- 2 tbsp sesame oil /30ml
- 2 tbsp soy sauce /30ml
- 2 tbsp chili paste /30g
- Salt to taste
- Sesame seeds to garnish
- Chopped green onion to garnish

Directions:

1. In a food processor, add the chili paste, ginger, onion, and garlic; and process them until they are pureed. Turn on the Ninja foodi and select Sear/Sauté mode to High.
2. Pour in the sesame oil, once it has heated add the onion puree and cook for 3 minutes while stirring constantly to prevent burning. Add the water, mushrooms, soy sauce, and carrots.
3. Close the lid, secure the pressure valve, and select Pressure mode on High pressure for 5 minutes. Press Start/Stop.
4. Once the timer has ended, do a quick pressure release and open the lid. Add the zucchini noodles and bok choy, and stir to ensure that they are well submerged in the liquid.
5. Adjust the taste with salt, cover the pot with the crisping lid, and let the vegetables cook for 10 minutes on Broil mode.
6. Use a soup spoon to dish the soup with veggies into soup bowls. Sprinkle with green onions and sesame seeds. Serve as a complete meal.

Minty Radishes

Servings: 4
Cooking Time: 15 Minutes
Ingredients:

- 1-pound radishes, halved
- black pepper and salt
- 2 tablespoons balsamic vinegar
- 2 tablespoon mint, chopped
- 2 tablespoons olive oil

Directions:

1. In your Ninja Foodi's basket, combine the radishes with the vinegar and the other ingredients.
2. Cook on Air Crisp at 380 °F for 15 minutes.
3. Divide the radishes between plates and serve.

Nutrition Info:

- Calories: 170; Fat: 4.5g; Carbohydrates: 7.4g; Protein: 4.6g

Whole Roasted Cabbage With White Wine Cream Sauce

Servings:8
Cooking Time: 32 Minutes
Ingredients:

- 1 head green cabbage
- ½ cup, plus 1 tablespoon water
- 1 tablespoon extra-virgin olive oil
- Kosher salt
- Freshly ground black pepper
- 2 cups white wine
- ¼ cup minced red onion
- 1 cup heavy (whipping) cream
- ¼ cup minced fresh dill
- ¼ cup minced fresh parsley
- 2 tablespoons whole-grain mustard
- 1 tablespoon cornstarch

Directions:

1. Place the cabbage and ½ cup of water, stem-side down, in the pot.
2. With a knife cut an X into the top of the cabbage cutting all the way through to the bottom through the core. Assemble pressure lid, making sure the pressure release valve is in the SEAL position.
3. Select PRESSURE and set temperature to HI. Set time to 15 minutes. Select START/STOP to begin.
4. When pressure cooking is complete, quick release the pressure by turning the pressure release valve to the VENT position. Carefully remove lid when unit has finished releasing pressure.
5. Brush the cabbage with the olive oil and season with salt and pepper. Close crisping lid.
6. Select AIR CRISP, set temperature to 390°F, and set time to 12 minutes. Select START/STOP to begin.
7. Once cooking is complete, open lid, lift out the cabbage, wrap with foil, and set aside. Leave any remaining water in the pot.
8. Select SEAR/SAUTÉ. Set temperature to HI. Select START/STOP to begin.
9. Add the white wine and onion and stir, scraping any brown bits off the bottom of the pot. Stir in the cream, dill, parsley, and mustard. Let simmer for 5 minutes.
10. In a small bowl, whisk together the cornstarch and the remaining 1 tablespoon of water until smooth. Stir it into the mixture in the pot. Cook until the sauce has thickened and coats the back of a spoon, about 2 minutes.
11. Pour half of the sauce over the cabbage. Cut the cabbage into 8 pieces and serve with remaining sauce.

Nutrition Info:

- Calories: 206,Total Fat: 14g,Sodium: 129mg,Carbohydrates: 10g,Protein: 3g.

Creamy Carrot Soup

Servings: 4
Cooking Time: 15 Minutes

Ingredients:

- 3 ½ cups chicken broth, low sodium
- 5 carrots, peeled & cut in 1-inch pieces
- 1 large parsnip, peeled & cut in 1-inch pieces
- 1 potato, peeled & cut in 1-inch pieces
- 1 onion, chopped
- 2 ½ cups skim milk
- ¼ tsp thyme
- ¼ tsp pepper

Directions:

1. Add the broth, carrots, parsnip, potato, and onion to the cooking pot and toss to mix.
2. Add the lid and set to pressure cook on high. Set the timer for 8 minutes. When timer goes off, use natural release to remove the pressure.
3. Use an immersion blender to process the vegetables until almost smooth.
4. Set to sauté on medium heat. Stir in remaining ingredients and cook 6-8 minutes or until heated through. Ladle into bowls and serve.

Nutrition Info:

- Calories 226,Total Fat 2g,Total Carbs 42g,Protein 13g,Sodium 206mg.

Zucchini Cream Soup

Servings: 6
Cooking Time: 40 Minutes

Ingredients:

- Nonstick cooking spray
- 1 cup onion, chopped
- ½ red bell pepper, chopped
- 3 cloves garlic, chopped fine
- 1 ½ lb. zucchini, cut in ½-inch cubes
- 28 oz. vegetable broth, low sodium
- 1 tbsp. fresh dill, chopped
- ½ tsp salt
- ¼ tsp pepper
- 1 cup skim milk
- 3 tbsp. cornstarch

Directions:

1. Spray the cooking pot with cooking spray. Set to sauté on med-high heat.
2. Add onion, bell pepper, and garlic and cook 4-5 minutes, stirring frequently, until soft.
3. Add zucchini, broth, dill, salt, and pepper and bring to a boil. Reduce heat to low, cover and cook 25-30 minutes until zucchini is soft.
4. In a small bowl, whisk together milk and cornstarch until smooth. Stir into soup and cook another 2-3 minutes until thickened. Serve.

Nutrition Info:

- Calories 72,Total Fat 1g,Total Carbs 14g,Protein 5g,Sodium 764mg.

Green Squash Gruyere

Servings: 4
Cooking Time: 70 Min

Ingredients:

- 1 large green squash; sliced
- 2 cups tomato sauce /500ml
- 1 cup shredded mozzarella cheese /130g
- 1½ cups panko breadcrumbs /195g
- ⅓ cup grated Gruyere cheese /44g
- 3 tbsps melted unsalted butter /45ml
- 2 tsp s salt /10g

Directions:

1. Season the squash slices on both sides with salt and place the slices on a wire rack to drain liquid for 5 to 10 minutes. In a bowl, combine the melted butter, breadcrumbs, and Gruyere cheese and set aside.
2. Rinse the squash slices with water and blot dry with paper towel. After, arrange the squash in the inner pot in a single layer as much as possible and pour the tomato sauce over the slices.
3. Seal the pressure lid, choose Pressure, set to High, and the time to 5 minutes. Press Start to commence cooking. When the timer has read to the end, perform a quick pressure release. Sprinkle the squash slices with the mozzarella cheese.
4. Close the crisping lid. Choose Bake/Roast; adjust the temperature to 375°F or 191°C and the cook time to 2 minutes. Press Start to broil.
5. After, carefully open the lid and sprinkle the squash with the breadcrumb mixture. Close the crisping lid again, choose Bake/Roast, adjust the temperature to 375°F, and the cook time to 8 minutes. Press Start to continue broiling. Serve immediately.

Artichoke & Spinach Casserole

Servings: 6
Cooking Time: 30 Minutes

Ingredients:

- Nonstick cooking spray
- 2 tsp olive oil
- ½ cup onion, chopped
- 3 cloves garlic, chopped fine
- 1 cup quinoa, cooked
- 14 oz. artichoke hearts, drained & chopped
- 10 oz. spinach, thawed & chopped
- ¾ cup mozzarella cheese, grated, divided
- ½ tsp nutmeg
- ¼ tsp pepper
- 2 eggs
- ¾ cup plain Greek yogurt

Directions:

1. Spray cooking pot with cooking spray.
2. Add oil and set to sauté on medium heat.
3. Add onion and garlic and cook, stirring frequently, 3-5 minutes until onion is soft. Turn off heat.
4. In a large bowl, combine quinoa, artichokes, spinach, ½ cup mozzarella, nutmeg, and pepper, mix well.
5. In a medium bowl, whisk together egg and yogurt and stir into quinoa mixture. Sprinkle remaining cheese over the top.
6. Add the tender-crisp lid and set to bake on 375°F. Bake 25-30 minutes until heated through and cheese is melted and starting to brown. Serve.

Nutrition Info:

- Calories 160,Total Fat 4g,Total Carbs 19g,Protein 14g,Sodium 216mg.

Garganelli With Cheese And Mushrooms

Servings: 4
Cooking Time: 60 Min

Ingredients:

- 1 large egg
- 8 ounces garganelli /240g
- 8 ounces Swiss cheese, shredded /240g
- 1 recipe sautéed mushrooms
- 1 can full fat evaporated milk /360ml
- 1½ cups panko breadcrumbs /195g
- 1¼ cups water /312.5ml
- 2 tbsps chopped fresh cilantro /30g
- 3 tbsps sour cream /45ml
- 3 tbsps melted unsalted butter /45ml
- 3 tbsps grated Cheddar cheese /45g
- 1½ tsp s salt /7.5g
- 1½ tsp s arrowroot starch /7.5g

Directions:

1. Pour the garganelli into the inner pot, add half of the evaporated milk, the water, and salt. Seal the pressure lid, choose Pressure, set to High and the time to 4 minutes. Press Start.
2. In a bowl, whisk the remaining milk with the egg. In another bowl, combine the arrowroot starch with the Swiss cheese.
3. When the pasta has cooked, perform a natural pressure release for 3 minutes, then a quick pressure release and carefully open the lid. Pour in the milk-egg mixture and a large handful of the starch mixture. Stir to melt the cheese and then add the remaining cheese in 3 or 4 batches while stirring to melt. Mix in the mushrooms, cilantro, and sour cream.
4. In a bowl, mix the breadcrumbs, melted butter, and cheddar cheese. Then, sprinkle the mixture evenly over the pasta. Close the crisping lid. Choose Broil and adjust the time to 5 minutes. Press Start to begin crisping.
5. When done, the top should be brown and crispy, otherwise broil further for 3 minutes, and serve immediately.

Hot & Sour Soup

Servings: 5
Cooking Time: 20 Minutes

Ingredients:

- 3 ½ cups chicken broth, low sodium, divided
- ½ lb. firm tofu, cut in 1-inch cubes
- ¼ lb. mushrooms, sliced
- 3 tbsp. soy sauce, low sodium
- 3 tbsp. vinegar
- 1 tsp ginger
- ½ tsp pepper
- 2 tbsp. cornstarch
- 1 egg, lightly beaten
- ½ cup fresh bean sprouts
- ½ tsp sesame oil

Directions:

1. Add 3 ¼ cups broth, tofu, mushrooms, soy sauce, vinegar, ginger, and pepper to the cooking pot and stir well.
2. Set to sauté on medium heat and bring to a boil.
3. In a small bowl, whisk together remaining broth and cornstarch until smooth. Reduce heat to low and whisk in cornstarch mixture until thickened.
4. Slowly stir in egg to form egg "ribbons". Add bean sprouts and simmer 1-2 minutes or until heated through. Stir in sesame oil and serve immediately.
5. Slowly stir in egg to form egg strands. Add bean sprouts and simmer 1 to 2 minutes, or until heated through, stirring occasionally.

Nutrition Info:

- Calories 123,Total Fat 6g,Total Carbs 8g,Protein 11g,Sodium 978mg.

Tofu & Carrot Toss

Servings: 4
Cooking Time: 20 Minutes
Ingredients:

- 1 tbsp. coconut oil
- 1 lb. carrots, grated
- 1 lb. extra firm tofu, drained, pressed & crumbled
- 1/3 cup soy sauce
- 1/3 cup sesame seeds
- 1 tsp dark sesame oil
- 1/4 cup cilantro, chopped

Directions:

1. Add oil to the cooking pot and set to sauté on med-high heat.
2. Add carrots and cook 15 minutes, stirring occasionally.
3. Add tofu and cook until carrots are tender, about 5 minutes. Stir in soy sauce and sesame seeds and cook 1 minute more, stirring constantly.
4. Turn the heat off and stir in sesame oil and cilantro. Serve over rice.

Nutrition Info:

- Calories 279,Total Fat 20g,Total Carbs 16g,Protein 17g,Sodium 851mg.

Zucchinis Spinach Fry

Servings: 4
Cooking Time: 17 Minutes
Ingredients:

- 2 zucchinis, sliced
- 1-pound baby spinach
- ½ cup tomato sauce
- Black pepper and salt
- 1 tablespoon avocado oil
- 1 red onion, chopped
- 1 tablespoon sweet paprika
- ½ teaspoon garlic powder
- ½ teaspoon chilli powder

Directions:

1. Set the Foodi on Sauté, stir in the oil, heat it up, add the onion and sauté for 2 minutes.
2. Add the zucchinis, spinach, and the other ingredients Put the Ninja Foodi's lid on and cook on High for 15 minutes.
3. Release the pressure quickly for 5 minutes, divide everything between plates and serve.

Nutrition Info:

- Calories: 130; Fat: 5.5g; Carbohydrates: 3.3g; Protein: 1g

Curried Vegetables

Servings: 6
Cooking Time: 10 Minutes
Ingredients:

- 1 ½ tbsp. olive oil
- 1 ½ cups onion, chopped
- 1 ½ tbsp. fresh ginger, grated
- 1 ½ tbsp. garlic, chopped fine
- 4 ½ carrots, peeled & chopped
- 1 ½ red bell peppers, sliced in thin strips
- 1 ½ orange bell peppers, sliced in thin strips
- 4 cups coconut milk, unsweetened
- 1 ½ cups kale, ribs removed & chopped
- ¾ cup water
- 3 tbsp. curry powder

Directions:

1. Add oil to the cooking pot and set to sauté on med-high heat.
2. Add the onion and cook until translucent, about 3-4 minutes. Add ginger and garlic and cook 1 minute more.
3. Stir in carrots and bell peppers and cook until peppers are tender, about 3-4 minutes.
4. Stir in coconut milk, kale, water and curry paste until combined.
5. Add the lid and set to pressure cook on high. Set timer for 2 minutes. Once timer goes off, use quick release to remove the pressure. Stir well and serve.

Nutrition Info:

- Calories 323,Total Fat 27g,Total Carbs 20g,Protein 4g,Sodium 57mg.

Stuffed Mushrooms

Servings: 4
Cooking Time: 40 Min
Ingredients:

- 10 large white mushrooms, stems removed
- 1 red bell pepper, seeded and chopped
- 1 small onion; chopped
- 1 green onion; chopped
- ¼ cup roasted red bell peppers; chopped /32.5g
- ¼ cup grated Parmesan cheese /32.5g
- ½ cup water/125ml
- 1 tbsp butter /15g
- ½ tsp dried oregano /2.5g
- Salt and black pepper to taste

Directions:

1. Turn on the Ninja Foodi and select Sear/Sauté mode on Medium. Put in the butter to melt and add the roasted and fresh peppers, green onion, onion, oregano, salt, and pepper. Use a spoon to mix and cook for 2 minutes.
2. Spoon the bell pepper mixture into the mushrooms and use a paper towel to wipe the pot and place the stuffed mushrooms in it, 5 at a time. Pour in water.
3. Close the lid, secure the pressure valve, and select pressure mode on High pressure for 5 minutes. Press Start/Stop. Once the timer has ended, do a quick pressure release and open the lid.

4. Sprinkle with parmesan cheese and close the crisping lid. Select Bake/Roast, adjust the temperature to 380°F or 194°C and the time to 2 minutes and press Start/Stop button.
5. Use a set of tongs to remove the stuffed mushrooms onto a plate and repeat the cooking process for the remaining mushrooms. Serve hot with a side of steamed green veggies and a sauce.

Balsamic Cabbage With Endives

Servings: 4
Cooking Time: 15 Minutes
Ingredients:

- 1 green cabbage head, shredded
- 2 endives, trimmed and sliced lengthwise
- Black pepper and salt to the taste
- 1 tablespoon olive oil
- 2 shallots, chopped
- ½ cup chicken stock
- 1 tablespoon sweet paprika
- 1 tablespoon balsamic vinegar

Directions:
1. Set the Foodi on Sauté mode, stir in the oil, heat it up, add the shallots and sauté for 2 minutes.
2. Add the cabbage, the endives and the other ingredients.
3. Put the Ninja Foodi's lid on and cook on High for 13 minutes.
4. Release the pressure quickly for 5 minutes, divide the mix between plates and serve.

Nutrition Info:
- Calories: 120; Fat: 2g; Carbohydrates: 3.3g; Protein: 4

Garlic Bread Pizza

Servings:6
Cooking Time: 10 Minutes
Ingredients:

- 6 slices frozen garlic bread or Texas Toast
- ¾ cup tomato-basil sauce or your favorite tomato sauce
- 6 slices mozzarella cheese

Directions:
1. Insert Cook & Crisp Basket in pot. Close crisping lid. Select AIR CRISP, set temperature to 390°F, and set time to 5 minutes. Select START/STOP to begin preheating.
2. Once unit has preheated, place three of the garlic bread slices in the basket, and top with half the sauce and 3 slices of cheese. Close crisping lid.
3. Select AIR CRISP, set temperature to 375°F, and set time to 5 minutes. Select START/STOP to begin.
4. When cooking is complete, remove the pizzas from the basket. Repeat steps 2 and 3 with the remaining slices of garlic bread, sauce, and cheese.

Nutrition Info:
- Calories: 192,Total Fat: 7g,Sodium: 548mg,Carbohydrates: 21g,Protein: 10g.

Caramelized Sweet Potatoes

Servings: 4
Cooking Time: 20 Minutes
Ingredients:

- 1 cup water
- 2 large sweet potatoes
- 2 tbsp. butter
- ½ tsp salt
- ¼ tsp pepper

Directions:
1. Add the trivet and water to the cooking pot.
2. Prick the potatoes with a fork and place on the trivet. Add the lid and set to pressure cook on high. Set timer for 15 minutes. Once timer goes off, use natural release to remove the pressure.
3. Transfer potatoes to a cutting board and slice ½-inch thick.
4. Remove the trivet and add butter to the pot. Set to sauté on med-high heat.
5. Add the potatoes and cook, turning occasionally, until potatoes are nicely browned on both sides. Season with salt and pepper and serve.

Nutrition Info:
- Calories 107,Total Fat 6g,Total Carbs 14g,Protein 1g,Sodium 227mg.

Pasta Primavera

Servings:6
Cooking Time: 18 Minutes
Ingredients:

- ½ red onion, sliced
- 1 carrot, thinly sliced
- 1 head broccoli, cut into florets
- 1 red bell pepper, thinly sliced
- 1 yellow squash, halved lengthwise and sliced into half moons
- 1 zucchini, halved lengthwise and sliced into half moons
- ¼ cup extra-virgin olive oil
- ½ teaspoon dried basil
- ½ teaspoon dried oregano
- ½ teaspoon dried parsley
- ¼ teaspoon dried rosemary
- ¼ teaspoon crushed red pepper flakes
- 1 box penne pasta
- 4 cups water
- 2 tablespoons freshly squeezed lemon juice
- ½ cup grated Parmesan cheese, divided

Directions:
1. Place Cook & Crisp Basket in pot. Close crisping lid. Select AIR CRISP, set temperature to 390°F, and set time to 5 minutes. Select START/STOP to begin preheating.

2. In a large bowl, combine the red onion, carrot, broccoli, bell pepper, yellow squash, zucchini, olive oil, basil, oregano, parsley, rosemary, and red pepper flakes, and toss to combine.
3. Once unit has preheated, add the vegetable mixture to the basket. Close lid.
4. Select AIR CRISP, set temperature to 390°F, and set time to 15 minutes. Select START/STOP to begin.
5. When cooking is complete, remove the vegetables and basket, and set aside.
6. Add the pasta and water. Assemble pressure lid, making sure the pressure release valve is in the SEAL position.
7. Select PRESSURE and set to HI. Set time to 3 minutes. Select START/STOP to begin.
8. When pressure cooking is complete, allow pressure to naturally release for 10 minutes. After 10 minutes, quick release remaining pressure by moving the pressure release valve to the VENT position. Carefully remove lid when unit has finished releasing pressure.
9. Add vegetables to pasta. Add the lemon juice and ¼ cup of Parmesan cheese and stir. Serve and top with remaining cheese.

Nutrition Info:

- Calories: 388,Total Fat: 12g,Sodium: 127mg,Carbohydrates: 60g,Protein: 15g.

Veggie Mash With Parmesan

Servings: 6
Cooking Time: 15 Min

Ingredients:

- 3 pounds Yukon Gold potatoes, cut into 1-inch pieces /1350g
- 1 garlic clove, minced
- 1 cup Parmesan cheese, shredded /130g
- ¼ cup butter, melted /32.5ml
- 1 ½ cups cauliflower, broken into florets /195g
- 1 carrot; chopped
- ¼ cup milk /62.5ml
- 1 tsp salt /5g
- Fresh parsley for garnish

Directions:

1. Into your pot, add veggies, salt and cover with enough water. Seal the pressure lid, choose Pressure, set to High, and set the timer to 10 minutes. Press Start. When ready, release the pressure quickly.
2. Drain the vegetables and mash them with a potato masher; add garlic, butter and milk, and whisk until everything is well incorporated. Serve topped with parmesan cheese and chopped parsley.

Pumpkin Soup

Servings: 8
Cooking Time: 8 Hours

Ingredients:

- 15 oz. pumpkin
- 1 cup celery, chopped
- ½ cup carrots, chopped fine
- ½ cup onion, chopped fine
- ¼ tsp salt
- ½ tsp oregano
- ½ tsp rosemary
- ¼ tsp red pepper
- ¼ tsp ginger
- 28 oz. vegetable broth
- ¼ cup whipped cream
- 3 tbsp. pumpkin seeds, toasted

Directions:

1. Add all ingredients, except whipped cream and pumpkin seeds, to the cooking pot, mix well.
2. Add the lid and set to slow cook on low. Cook 6-8 hours.
3. Stir in whipped cream until thoroughly combined. Ladle into bowls and top with pumpkin seeds. Serve.

Nutrition Info:

- Calories 78,Total Fat 5g,Total Carbs 8g,Protein 3g,Sodium 500mg.

Cheesy Squash Tart

Servings: 8
Cooking Time: 45 Minutes

Ingredients:

- 1 spaghetti squash
- 2 tbsp. olive oil
- 2 eggs
- 1/3 cup + 2 tbsp. parmesan cheese, divided
- 1 cup ricotta cheese, fat free
- 1 clove garlic, chopped fine
- 2 tsp Italian seasoning
- ¼ tsp salt
- 1 cup light spaghetti sauce
- ½ cup mozzarella cheese, low fat, grated

Directions:

1. Place enough water in the cooking pot to reach 1-inch up sides. Add the squash, whole. Add the lid and set to pressure cook on high. Set timer for 13 minutes.
2. When timer goes off, use natural release to remove the pressure. Squash should be tender. Transfer to a cutting board and let cool 15-20 minutes.
3. Add the rack to the cooking pot. Spray an 8-inch deep-dish pie plate with cooking spray.
4. In a large bowl, combine oil, eggs, and 1/3 cup parmesan cheese, mix well.
5. Cut the squash in half lengthwise and remove the seeds. Use a fork to scrape out the flesh and add it to the egg mixture, mix well.
6. Pour the squash mixture into the prepared pie dish and press on the bottom and up sides to form a "crust".

7. In a small bowl, combine the ricotta, garlic, Italian seasoning, and salt and mix well. Spread evenly in the crust and top with spaghetti sauce.
8. Place the dish on the rack and add the tender-crisp lid. Set to bake on 325°F. Bake 25 minutes. Open the lid and sprinkle the remaining cheese over the top. Bake another 5 minutes or until the cheese melts. Let tart rest 10 minutes before serving.

Nutrition Info:

- Calories 170,Total Fat 9g,Total Carbs 13g,Protein 10g,Sodium 277mg.

Warming Harvest Soup

Servings: 6
Cooking Time: 20 Minutes

Ingredients:

- 3 tbsp. butter, unsalted
- ½ cup onion, chopped
- 2 sprigs thyme, stems removed
- 2 lb. butternut squash, peeled & cut in 1-inch pieces
- 1 tsp sugar
- ½ tsp salt
- 4 cups water
- 2 tbsp. milk

Directions:

1. Add butter to the cooking pot and set to sauté on medium heat.
2. Once butter has melted, add onion and thyme and cook until onion is soft, about 5 minutes.
3. Add squash, sugar, and salt and cook, stirring occasionally 3 minutes. Stir in water.
4. Add the lid and set to pressure cook on high. Set the timer for 10 minutes. When the timer goes off, use quick release to remove the pressure.
5. Transfer soup to a blender in batches and process until smooth. Return the soup back to the pot.
6. Set back to sauté on medium heat. Stir in milk and cook 3-5 minutes until heated through. Serve.

Nutrition Info:

- Calories 129,Total Fat 6g,Total Carbs 19g,Protein 2g,Sodium 206mg.

Mushroom Risotto With Swiss Chard

Servings: 4
Cooking Time: 60 Min

Ingredients:

- 1 small bunch Swiss chard; chopped
- ½ cup sautéed mushrooms /65g
- ½ cup caramelized onions /65g
- ⅓ cup white wine /88ml
- 2 cups vegetable stock /500ml
- ⅓ cup grated Pecorino Romano cheese /44g
- 1 cup short grain rice /130g
- 3 tbsps ghee; divided /45g
- ½ tsp salt /2.5g

Directions:

1. Press Sear/Sauté and adjust to Medium. Press Start to preheat the inner pot. Melt 2 tbsps of ghee and sauté the Swiss chard for 5 minutes until wilted. Spoon into a bowl and set aside.
2. Use a paper towel to wipe out any remaining liquid in the pot and melt the remaining ghee. Stir in the rice and cook for about 1 minute.
3. Add the white wine and cook for 2 to 3 minutes, with occasional stirring until the wine has evaporated. Add in stock and salt; stir to combine.
4. Seal the pressure lid, choose Pressure; adjust the pressure to High and the cook time to 8 minutes; press Start. When the timer is done reading, perform a quick pressure release and carefully open the lid.
5. Stir in the mushrooms, swiss chard, and onions and let the risotto heat for 1 minute. Mix the cheese into the rice to melt, and adjust the taste with salt.Spoon the risotto into serving bowls and serve immediately.

Cauliflower Cakes

Servings: 6
Cooking Time: 15 Minutes

Ingredients:

- 1 cup water
- 1 head cauliflower, cut in florets
- ¼ cup onion, chopped
- ½ cup cheddar cheese, low fat, grated
- ½ cup panko bread crumbs
- 2 eggs, lightly beaten
- ½ tsp salt
- ¼ tsp cayenne pepper
- Nonstick cooking spray

Directions:

1. Add water, cauliflower and onion to the cooking pot. Add the lid and set to pressure cook on high. Set the timer for 6 minutes. When the timer goes off, use quick release to remove the pressure. Drain and add the vegetables to a large bowl.
2. Mash the cauliflower with an electric mixer beating until smooth.
3. Stir in remaining ingredients. Form into 12 patties.
4. Spray the fryer basket with cooking spray. Place the patties in a single layer in the basket. Add the tender-crisp lid and set to air fry on 375°F. Cook cauliflower 4-5 minutes per side until golden brown. Serve immediately.

Nutrition Info:

- Calories 102,Total Fat 3g,Total Carbs 12g,Protein 8g,Sodium 395mg.

Creamy Kale

Servings: 4
Cooking Time: 15 Minutes

Ingredients:

- 1 tablespoon lemon juice
- 2 tablespoons balsamic vinegar
- 1-pound kale, torn
- 1 tablespoon ginger, grated
- 1 garlic clove, minced
- 2 tablespoons olive oil
- 1 cup heavy cream
- A pinch of black pepper and salt
- 2 tablespoons chives, chopped

Directions:

1. Set the Foodi on Sauté mode, stir in the oil, heat it up, add the garlic and the ginger and sauté for 2 minutes.
2. Stir in the kale, lemon juice and the other ingredients.
3. Put the Ninja Foodi's lid on and cook on High for 13 minutes.
4. Release the pressure quickly for 5 minutes, divide between plates and serve.

Nutrition Info:

- Calories: 130; Fat: 2g; Carbohydrates: 3.4g; Protein: 2g

Colorful Vegetable Medley

Servings: 4
Cooking Time: 15 Min

Ingredients:

- 16 asparagus, trimmed
- 1 small head broccoli, broken into florets
- 1 small head cauliflower, broken into florets
- 5 ounces green beans /150g
- 2 carrots, peeled and cut on bias into 1/4-inch rounds
- 1 cup water /250ml
- salt to taste

Directions:

1. Into the pot, add water and set trivet on top of water and place steamer basket on top of the trivet. In an even layer, spread green beans, broccoli, cauliflower, asparagus, and carrots in the steamer basket.
2. Seal the pressure lid, choose Pressure, set to High, and set the timer to 3 minutes on High. When ready, release the pressure quickly. Remove steamer basket from cooker and add salt to vegetables for seasoning. Serve immediately.

Spicy Salmon With Wild Rice

Servings: 4
Cooking Time: 50 Min

Ingredients:

- 1 cup wild rice /130g
- 1 cup vegetable stock /250ml
- 2 limes, juiced
- 2 jalapeño peppers, seeded and diced
- 4 garlic cloves, minced
- 4 skinless salmon fillets
- A bunch of asparagus, trimmed and cut diagonally
- 2 tbsps chopped fresh parsley /30g
- 3 tbsps olive oil; divided /45ml
- 2 tbsps honey /30ml
- 1 tsp sweet paprika /5g
- 1 tsp salt /5g
- 1 tsp freshly ground black pepper /5g

Directions:

1. Pour the brown rice and vegetable stock in the pot; stir to combine. Put the reversible rack in the pot in the higher position and lay the salmon fillets on the rack.
2. Seal the pressure lid, choose Pressure, set to High, and set the time to 2 minutes; press Start. In a bowl, toss the broccoli with 1 tbsp of olive oil and season with the salt and black pepper. In another bowl, evenly combine the remaining oil, the lime juice, honey, paprika, jalapeño, garlic, and parsley.
3. When done cooking, do a quick pressure release, and carefully open the pressure lid.
4. Pat the salmon dry with a paper towel and coat the fish with the honey sauce while reserving a little for garnishing.
5. Arrange the asparagus around the salmon. Close the crisping lid; choose Broil and set the time to 7 minutes. Choose Start/Stop.
6. When ready, remove the salmon from the rack. Dish the salmon with asparagus and rice. Garnish with parsley and remaining sauce. Serve immediately.

Risotto And Roasted Bell Peppers

Servings: 4
Cooking Time: 80 Min

Ingredients:

- 4 mixed bell peppers, seeds removed and chopped diagonally
- 1 garlic clove, minced
- 2 cups carnaroli rice /260g
- 1½ cups grated Parmesan cheese, plus more for garnish /195g
- 5 cups vegetable stock /1250ml
- ¼ cup freshly squeezed lemon juice /62.5ml
- 2 tbsps ghee; divided /30g
- 2 tbsps unsalted butter /30g
- 1 tsp grated lemon zest /15g
- 2 tsp s salt; divided /10g
- 1 tsp freshly ground black pepper /5g

Directions:

1. On the pot, choose Sear/Sauté and set to Medium High. Choose Start/Stop to preheat the pot. Melt the ghee and cook the garlic until fragrant, about 1 minute.

2. Then, pour the stock, lemon juice, lemon zest, and rice into the pot. Sprinkle with 1 tsp of salt and stir to combine well.
3. Seal the pressure lid, hit Pressure, set to High, and the timer to 7 minutes; press Start. While the rice cooks, in a bowl, toss the peppers with the remaining ghee, salt, and black pepper.
4. When the timer has ended, do a natural pressure release for 10 minutes, then a quick pressure release. Stir the butter into the rice until properly mixed.
5. Then, put the reversible rack inside the pot in the higher position, which will be over the risotto. Arrange the bell peppers on the rack.
6. Close the crisping lid. Choose Broil and set the time to 8 minutes; press Start/Stop.
7. When done cooking, take out the rack from the pot. Stir the Parmesan cheese into the risotto. To serve, spoon the risotto into serving plates, top with the bell peppers and garnish with extra Parmesan. Serve immediately.

Quinoa Pesto Bowls With Veggies

Servings: 2
Cooking Time: 30 Min

Ingredients:

- 1 cup quinoa, rinsed /130g
- 1 cup broccoli florets /130g
- ¼ cup pesto sauce /62.5ml
- 2 cups water /500ml
- ½ pound Brussels sprouts /225g
- 2 eggs
- 1 small beet, peeled and cubed
- 1 carrot, peeled and chopped
- 1 avocado, thinly sliced
- lemon wedges; for serving
- salt and ground black pepper to taste

Directions:

1. In the pot, mix water, salt, quinoa and pepper. Set the reversible rack to the pot over quinoa. To the reversible rack, add eggs, Brussels sprouts, broccoli, beet cubes, carrots, pepper and salt.
2. Seal the pressure lid, choose Pressure, set to High, and set the timer to 1 minute. Press Start. Release pressure naturally for 10 minutes, then release any remaining pressure quickly.
3. Remove reversible rack from the pot and set the eggs to a bowl of ice water. Peel and halve the eggs. Use a fork to fluff quinoa.
4. Separate quinoa, broccoli, avocado, carrots, beet, Brussels sprouts, eggs, and a dollop of pesto into two bowls. Serve alongside a lemon wedge.

Cabbage With Bacon

Servings: 4
Cooking Time: 20 Minutes

Ingredients:

- 4 cups red cabbage, shredded
- ¼ cup veggie stock
- A pinch of black pepper and salt
- 1 tablespoon olive oil
- 1 cup canned tomatoes, crushed
- Zest of 1 lime, grated
- 2 ounces bacon, cooked and crumbled

Directions:

1. Put the reversible rack in the Foodi, add the baking pan inside and grease it with the oil.
2. Add the cabbage, the stock and the other ingredients into the pan.
3. Cook on Baking mode at 380 °F for 20 minutes.
4. Divide the mix between plates and serve.

Nutrition Info:

- Calories: 144; Fat: 3g; Carbohydrates: 4.5g; Protein: 4.4g

Eggplant Lasagna

Servings: 4
Cooking Time: 25 Min

Ingredients:

- 3 large eggplants; sliced in uniform ¼ inches
- ¼ cup Parmesan cheese, grated /32.5g
- 4 ¼ cups Marinara sauce /1062.5ml
- 1 ½ cups shredded Mozzarella cheese /195g
- Cooking spray
- Chopped fresh basil to garnish

Directions:

1. Open the pot and grease it with cooking spray. Arrange the eggplant slices in a single layer on the bottom of the pot and sprinkle some cheese all over it.
2. Arrange another layer of eggplant slices on the cheese, sprinkle this layer with cheese also, and repeat the layering of eggplant and cheese until both Ingredients are exhausted.
3. Lightly spray the eggplant with cooking spray and pour the marinara sauce all over it. Close the lid and pressure valve, and select Pressure mode on High pressure for 8 minutes. Press Start/Stop.
4. Once the timer has stopped, do a quick pressure release, and open the lid. Sprinkle with grated parmesan cheese, close the crisping lid and cook for 10 minutes on Bake/Roast mode on 380 °F or 194°C.
5. With two napkins in hand, gently remove the inner pot. Allow cooling for 10 minutes before serving. Garnish the lasagna with basil and serve warm as a side dish.

Rice Stuffed Zucchini Boats

Servings: 4
Cooking Time: 55 Min

Ingredients:

- 2 small zucchini
- ½ cup chopped toasted cashew nuts /65g
- ½ cup grated Parmesan cheese; divided /65g
- ½ cup cooked white short grain rice /65g
- ½ cup canned white beans, drained and rinsed /65g
- ½ cup chopped tomatoes /65g
- 2 tbsps melted butter; divided /30ml
- ½ tsp salt /2.5g
- ½ tsp freshly ground black pepper /2.5g

Directions:

1. Cut each zucchini in half and then, cut in half lengthwise and scoop out the pulp. Chop the pulp roughly and place in a medium bowl. In the bowl, add the rice, beans, tomatoes, cashew nuts, ¼ cup or 32.5g of Parmesan cheese, 1 tbsp or 15mlof melted butter, the salt, and black pepper. Combine the mixture well but not to break the beans.
2. Put the Crisping Basket in the pot. Close the crisping lid, choose Air Crisp, set the temperature to 400°F, and the time to 5 minutes.
3. Spoon the mixed Ingredients into the zucchini boats and arrange the stuffed zucchinis in a single layer in the preheated basket. Close the crisping lid. Choose Air Crisp, set the temperature to 400°F or 205°C, and the time to 15 minutes. Choose Start/Stop to begin cooking.
4. After 15 minutes, sprinkle the zucchini boats with the remaining Parmesan cheese and butter.
5. Close the crisping lid. Choose Broil, set the time to 5 minutes, and choose Start/Stop to broil.
6. When done cooking, ensure it is as crisp as you desire, otherwise broil for a few more minutes. Remove the zucchinis onto a plate, allow cooling for about a minute, and serve.

Crème De La Broc

Servings: 6
Cooking Time: 25 Min

Ingredients:

- 1 ½ cups grated yellow and white Cheddar cheese + extra for topping /195g
- 1 ½ oz. cream cheese /195g
- 1 medium Red onion; chopped
- 3 cloves garlic, minced
- 4 cups chopped broccoli florets, only the bushy tops/520g
- 3 cups heavy cream /750ml
- 3 cups vegetable broth /750ml
- 4 tbsp butter /60g
- 4 tbsp flour /60g
- 1 tsp Italian Seasoning /5g
- Salt and black pepper to taste

Directions:

1. Select Sear/Sauté mode, adjust to High and melt the butter once the pot is ready. Add the flour and use a spoon to stir until it clumps up. Gradually pour in the heavy cream while stirring until white sauce forms. Fetch out the butter sauce into a bowl and set aside.
2. Press Stop and add the onions, garlic, broth, broccoli, Italian seasoning, and cream cheese. Use a wooden spoon to stir the mixture.
3. Seal the lid, and select Pressure mode on High pressure for 12 minutes. Press Start/Stop. Once the timer has ended, do a quick pressure release.
4. Add in butter sauce and cheddar cheese, salt, and pepper. Close the crisping lid and cook on Broil mode for 3 minutes. Dish the soup into serving bowls, top it with extra cheese, to serve.

Cauliflower Enchiladas

Servings:5
Cooking Time: 25 Minutes

Ingredients:

- 2 tablespoons canola oil
- 1 large head cauliflower, cut into 1-inch florets
- 2 teaspoons ground cumin
- 1 teaspoon ground chili pepper
- 2 teaspoons kosher salt
- ½ teaspoon freshly ground black pepper
- 1 can diced tomatoes, drained
- 5 flour tortillas
- 1 can red enchilada sauce
- 1½ cups shredded Mexican blend cheese
- ½ cup chopped cilantro, for garnish

Directions:

1. In a medium bowl, toss together the oil, cauliflower, cumin, chili pepper, salt, and black pepper. Place the cauliflower in the Cook & Crisp Basket and place the basket in pot. Close crisping lid.
2. Select AIR CRISP, set temperature to 390°F, and set time to 15 minutes. Select START/STOP to begin.
3. After 8 minutes, open lid, then lift the basket and shake the cauliflower. Lower basket back into pot and close lid. Continue cooking, until the cauliflower reaches your desired crispiness.
4. When cooking is complete, remove basket from pot. Place the cauliflower in a bowl and mix with the tomatoes.
5. Lay the tortillas on a work surface. Divide the cauliflower-
6. tomato mixture between the tortillas and roll them up. Place the filled tortillas seam-side down in the pot. Pour the enchilada sauce on top.
7. Close crisping lid. Select BROIL and set time to 10 minutes. Select START/STOP to begin.

8. After 5 minutes, open lid and add the cheese on top. Close lid and continue cooking until cheese is golden brown.
9. When cooking is complete, add cilantro and serve.

Nutrition Info:

- Calories: 315,Total Fat: 19g,Sodium: 822mg,Carbohydrates: 28g,Protein: 13g.

Cheese Crusted Carrot Casserole

Servings: 6
Cooking Time: 40 Minutes

Ingredients:

- 1 ¼ lb. carrots, sliced
- Nonstick cooking spray
- ½ cup light mayonnaise
- ¼ cup onion, chopped fine
- 1 tsp horseradish
- ¼ cup cheddar cheese, reduced fat, grated
- 1 tbsp. whole wheat bread crumbs

Directions:

1. Add the carrots to the cooking pot with enough water to cover them. Set to sauté on high and bring to a boil. Reduce heat to med-low and simmer 7-9 minutes until carrots are tender-crisp. Drain.
2. Spray the cooking pot with cooking spray.
3. In a small bowl, combine mayonnaise, onion, and horseradish, mix well.
4. Return carrots to the cooking pot and spread mayonnaise mixture over the top. Sprinkle the cheese and bread crumbs over the top.
5. Add the tender-crisp lid and set to bake on 350°F. Bake 25-30 minutes until top is golden brown. Serve.

Nutrition Info:

- Calories 121,Total Fat 7g,Total Carbs 12g,Protein 2g,Sodium 245mg.

Veggie Lover's Pizza

Servings:1
Cooking Time: 8 Minutes

Ingredients:

- 1 store-bought pizza dough, rolled into an 8-inch circle
- ¼ cup traditional pizza sauce
- 1 teaspoon minced garlic
- ⅔ cup shredded mozzarella cheese
- ¼ cup chopped green bell pepper
- ¼ cup sliced mushrooms
- Crushed red pepper flakes, for garnish

Directions:

1. Select BAKE/ROAST, set the temperature to 400°F, and set time to 5 minutes to preheat. Select START/STOP to begin.
2. Place the rolled dough in the Ninja Cook & Crisp Basket. Spread the pizza sauce over the crust, leaving about a 1-inch border uncovered. Sprinkle on the garlic, top with the mozzarella cheese, and evenly distribute the green bell pepper and mushrooms over the pizza.
3. Place the Cook & Crisp Basket into the pot and close the crisping lid.
4. Select BAKE/ROAST, set the temperature to 400°F, and set the time to 8 minutes. Select START/STOP to begin.
5. When cooking is complete, carefully open the lid and remove the pizza. Serve, garnished with red pepper flakes, if using.

Nutrition Info:

- Calories: 636,Total Fat: 20g,Sodium: 1150mg,Carbohydrates: 95g,Protein: 33g.

Quinoa Stuffed Butternut Squash

Servings:4
Cooking Time: 13 Minutes

Ingredients:

- 2 tablespoons extra-virgin olive oil
- 1 tablespoon minced garlic
- 1 small shallot, minced
- Kosher salt
- Freshly ground black pepper
- ½ cup dried cranberries
- 1 cup tri-colored quinoa
- 2¾ cups water, divided
- 2 cups roughly chopped kale
- 1 small butternut squash, top trimmed, halved lengthwise
- 1 tablespoon freshly squeezed orange juice
- Zest of 1 orange
- 1 jar pine nuts
- 1 can chickpeas, rinsed and drained

Directions:

1. Select SEAR/SAUTÉ and set to HI. Select START/STOP to begin. Let preheat for 5 minutes.
2. Add the olive oil, garlic, shallot, salt, and pepper. Cook until garlic and shallot have softened and turned golden brown, about 2 minutes.
3. Stir in the cranberries, quinoa, and 1¼ cups of water. Assemble pressure lid, making sure the pressure release valve is in the SEAL position.
4. Select PRESSURE and set to HI. Set time to 2 minutes. Select START/STOP to begin.
5. When pressure cooking is complete, allow pressure to naturally release for 10 minutes. After 10 minutes, quick release remaining pressure by turning the pressure release valve to the VENT position. Carefully remove lid when the unit has finished releasing pressure.
6. Place the quinoa in a large bowl. Stir in the kale. Cover the bowl with aluminum foil and set aside.
7. Pour the remaining 1½ cups of water into the pot. Place the butternut squash cut-side up on the Reversible Rack, then lower it into the pot. Assemble pressure lid, making sure the pressure release valve is in the SEAL position.

8. Select PRESSURE and set to HI. Set the time to 8 minutes. Select START/STOP to begin.

9. Mix the orange juice, orange zest, pine nuts, and chickpeas into the quinoa mixture.

10. When pressure cooking is complete, quick release the pressure by turning the pressure release valve to the VENT position. Carefully remove lid when unit has finished releasing pressure.

11. Carefully remove rack from pot. Using a spoon slightly hollow out the squash. Spoon the quinoa mixture into the squash. Cut in half and serve.

Nutrition Info:

- Calories: 563,Total Fat: 21g,Sodium: 66mg,Carbohydrates: 83g,Protein: 16g.

Spanish Rice

Servings: 4

Cooking Time: 50 Min

Ingredients:

- 1 small onion; chopped
- 1 can pinto beans, drained and rinsed /480g
- 2 garlic cloves, minced
- 1 banana pepper, seeded and chopped
- ¼ cup stewed tomatoes /32.5g
- ½ cup vegetable stock /125ml
- 1 cup jasmine rice /130g
- ⅓ cup red salsa /88g
- 3 tbsps ghee /45g
- 1 tbsp chopped fresh parsley /15g
- 1 tsp Mexican Seasoning Mix /5g
- 1 tsp salt /5g

Directions:

1. On your Foodi, choose Sear/Sauté and adjust to Medium. Press Start to preheat the inner pot. Add the ghee to melt until no longer foaming and cook the onion, garlic, and banana pepper in the ghee. Cook for 2 minutes or until fragrant.
2. Stir in the rice, salsa, tomato sauce, vegetable stock, Mexican seasoning, pinto beans, and salt. Seal the pressure lid, choose Pressure and adjust the pressure to High and the cook time to 6 minutes; press Start.
3. After cooking, do a natural pressure release for 10 minutes. Stir in the parsley, dish the rice, and serve.

Mashed Broccoli With Cream Cheese

Servings: 4

Cooking Time: 12 Min

Ingredients:

- 3 heads broccoli; chopped
- 2 cloves garlic, crushed
- 6 oz. cream cheese /180g
- 2 cups water /500ml
- 2 tbsp butter, unsalted /30g
- Salt and black pepper to taste

Directions:

1. Turn on the Ninja Foodi and select Sear/Sauté mode, adjust to High. Drop in the butter, once it melts add the garlic and cook for 30 seconds while stirring frequently to prevent the garlic from burning.
2. Then, add the broccoli, water, salt, and pepper. Close the lid, secure the pressure valve, and select Pressure mode on High pressure for 5 minutes. Press Start/Stop.
3. Once the timer has ended, do a quick pressure release and use a stick blender to mash the Ingredients until smooth to your desired consistency and well combined.
4. Stir in Cream cheese. Adjust the taste with salt and pepper. Close the crisping lid and cook for 2 minutes on Broil mode. Serve warm.

Okra Stew

Servings: 4

Cooking Time: 12 Minutes

Ingredients:

- 1-pound okra, trimmed
- 2 leeks, sliced
- Black pepper and salt to the taste
- 1 cup tomato sauce
- ¼ cup pine nuts, toasted
- 1 tablespoon cilantro, chopped

Directions:

1. In your Ninja Foodi, mix the okra with the leeks and the other ingredients except the cilantro.
2. Put the Ninja Foodi's lid on and cook on High for 12 minutes.
3. Release the pressure quickly for 5 minutes, divide the okra mix into bowls and serve with the cilantro sprinkled on top.

Nutrition Info:

- Calories: 146; Fat: 3g; Carbohydrates: 4g; Protein: 3g

Eggplant With Kale

Servings: 4

Cooking Time: 15 Minutes

Ingredients:

- Juice of 1 lime
- 1-pound eggplant, roughly cubed
- 1 cup kale, torn
- A pinch of black pepper and salt
- ½ teaspoon chilli powder
- ½ cup chicken stock
- 3 tablespoons olive oil

Directions:

1. Set the Foodi on Sauté mode, stir in the oil, heat it up, add the eggplant and sauté for 2 minutes.
2. Stir in the kale and the rest of the ingredients.

3. Put the Ninja Foodi's lid on and cook on and cook on High for 13 minutes.
4. Release the pressure quickly for 5 minutes, divide the mix between plates and serve.

Nutrition Info:

- Calories: 110; Fat: 3g; Carbohydrates: 4.3g; Protein: 1.1g

Baked Cajun Turnips

Servings: 4
Cooking Time: 85 Min

Ingredients:

- 4 small turnips, scrubbed clean
- 4 green onions; chopped; divided
- ¼ cup whipping cream /62.5ml
- ¼ cup sour cream /62.5ml
- ½ cup chopped roasted red bell pepper /65g
- 1½ cups shredded Monterey Jack cheese /195g
- ⅓ cup grated Parmesan cheese /44g
- 1 tsp Cajun seasoning mix /5g

Directions:

1. Pour 1 cup of water into the inner pot. Put the reversible rack in the pot and place the turnips on top. Seal the pressure lid, choose Pressure, adjust the pressure to High, and the cook time to 10 minutes; press Start. After cooking, perform a natural pressure release for 5 minutes.
2. Remove the turnips to a cutting board and allow cooling. Slice off a ½-inch piece from the top and the longer side of each turnip. Scoop the pulp into a bowl, including the flesh from the sliced tops making sure not to rip the skin of the turnip apart.
3. In the bowl with the pulp, add the whipping cream and sour cream and use a potato mash to break the pulp and mix the Ingredients until fairly smooth. Stir in the roasted bell pepper, Cajun seasoning, and Monterey Jack cheese. Fetch out 2 tbsps of green onions and stir the remaining into the mashed turnips.
4. Next, fill the turnip skins with the mashed mixture and sprinkle with the Parmesan. Pour the water into the inner pot and return the pot to the base.
5. Put the Crisping basket into the pot. Close the crisping lid; choose Air Crisp, adjust the temperature to 375°F or 191°C, and the time to 2 minutes. Press Start.
6. When the timer is done, open the lid and put the turnips in the basket. Close the crisping lid; choose Air Crisp, adjust the temperature to 375°F or 191°C, and the cook time to 15 minutes. Press Start. Cool for a few minutes and garnish with the reserved onions.

Red Beans And Rice

Servings: 4
Cooking Time: 1 Hr

Ingredients:

- 1 cup red beans, rinsed and stones removed /130g
- ½ cup rice, rinsed /65g
- 1 ½ cup vegetable broth /375ml
- 1 onion; diced
- 1 red bell pepper; diced
- 1 stalk celery; diced
- 1 tbsp fresh thyme leaves, or to taste /15g
- 2 tbsps olive oil /30ml
- ½ tsp cayenne pepper /2.5g
- water as needed
- salt and freshly ground black pepper to taste

Directions:

1. Into the pot, add beans and water to cover about 1-inch. Seal the pressure lid, choose Pressure, set to High, and set the timer to 1 minute. Press Start. When ready, release the pressure quickly. Drain the beans and set aside. Rinse and pat dry the inner pot.
2. Return inner pot to pressure cooker, add oil to the pot and press Sear/Sauté. Add onion to the oil and cook for 3 minutes until soft. Add celery and pepper and cook for 1 to 2 minutes until fragrant. Add garlic and cook for 30 seconds until soft; add rice.
3. Transfer the beans back into inner pot and top with broth. Stir black pepper, thyme, cayenne pepper, and salt into mixture. Seal the pressure lid, choose Pressure, set to High, and set the timer to 15 minutes. Press Start.
4. When ready, release pressure quickly. Add more thyme, black pepper and salt as desired.

Tomato Galette

Servings:4
Cooking Time: 40 Minutes

Ingredients:

- ½ pound mixed tomatoes, cut into ¼-inch slices
- 3 inches of leek, thinly sliced
- 2 garlic cloves, diced
- Kosher salt
- 1 store-bought refrigerated pie crust
- 2 tablespoons bread crumbs
- 4 tablespoons shredded Parmesan cheese, divided
- 4 tablespoons shredded mozzarella, divided
- 1 egg, beaten
- Freshly ground black pepper

Directions:

1. Place the tomatoes, leeks, and garlic into large bowl. Sprinkle with salt and set aside for at least 5 minutes to draw out the juices from the vegetables.
2. Strain the excess juice off the tomato mixture and pat down the vegetables with paper towels.
3. Unroll the pie crust and place it in the Ninja Multi-Purpose Pan or a 1½-quart round ceramic baking dish and form it to the bottom of the pan. Lay the extra dough loosely on the sides of the pan.

4. Sprinkle the bread crumbs in a thin layer on the pie crust bottom, then scatter 3 tablespoons each of Parmesan and mozzarella cheese on top. Place the tomato mixture in a heap in the middle of the dough and top with the remaining 1 tablespoon each of Parmesan and mozzarella cheese.
5. Fold the edges of the crust over the tomatoes and brush with the egg.
6. Close crisping lid. Select BAKE/ROAST, set temperature to 350°F, and set time to 45 minutes. Select START/STOP to begin. Let preheat for 5 minutes.
7. Place pan on the Reversible Rack, making sure the rack is in the lower position. Cover galette loosely with aluminum foil (do not seal the pan).
8. Once unit has preheated, open lid and carefully place the rack with pan in the pot. Close crisping lid.
9. After 20 minutes, open lid and remove the foil. Close lid and continue cooking.
10. When cooking is complete, remove rack with pan and set aside to let cool. Cut into slices, season with pepper, and serve.

Nutrition Info:

- Calories: 288,Total Fat: 15g,Sodium: 409mg,Carbohydrates: 31g,Protein: 9g.

Potato Filled Bread Rolls

Servings: 4
Cooking Time: 25 Min

Ingredients:

- 8 slices of bread
- 2 green chilies, deseeded; chopped
- 5 large potatoes, boiled, mashed
- 2 sprigs curry leaf
- 1 medium onion; chopped
- 1 tbsp olive oil /15ml
- ½ tsp mustard seeds /2.5g
- ½ tsp turmeric /2.5g
- Salt, to taste

Directions:

1. Combine the olive oil, onion, curry leaves, and mustard seed, in the Ninja Foodi basket. Cook for 5 minutes. Mix the onion mixture with the mashed potatoes, chilies, turmeric, and some salt. Divide the dough into 8 equal pieces.
2. Trim the sides of the bread, and wet it with some water. Make sure to get rid of the excess water. Take one wet bread slice in your palm and place one of the potato pieces in the center.
3. Roll the bread over the filling, sealing the edges. Place the rolls onto a prepared baking dish, close the crisping lid and cook for 12 minutes on Air Crisp at 350 °F or 177°C.

Veggie Lasagna

Servings: 4
Cooking Time: 35 Minutes

Ingredients:

- Nonstick cooking spray
- 2 Portobello mushrooms, sliced ¼-inch thick
- 1 eggplant, cut lengthwise in 6 slices
- 1 yellow squash, cut lengthwise in 4 slices
- 1 red bell pepper, cut in ½-inch strips
- ½ tsp garlic powder
- ½ tsp salt
- ½ tsp black pepper
- ½ cup ricotta cheese, fat free, divided
- 2 tbsp. fresh basil, chopped, divided
- ¾ cup mozzarella cheese, grated fine, divided
- ¼ cup tomato sauce

Directions:

1. Spray the cooking pot and rack with cooking spray.
2. Place a single layer of vegetables in the cooking pot. Add the rack and place remaining vegetables on it. Season vegetables with garlic powder, salt, and pepper.
3. Add the tender-crisp lid and set to roast on 425°F. Cook vegetables 15-20 minutes until tender, stirring halfway through cooking time. Transfer to a large plate.
4. Spray an 8x8-inch baking pan with cooking spray.
5. Line the bottom of the pan with 3 slices of eggplant. Spread ¼ cup ricotta cheese, 1 tablespoon basil, and ¼ cup mozzarella over eggplant.
6. Layer with remaining vegetables, then remaining ricotta, basil and ¼ cup mozzarella on top. End with 3 slices of eggplant and pour tomato sauce over then sprinkle remaining cheese over the top.
7. Add the rack back to the cooking pot and place the lasagna on it. Add the tender-crisp lid and set to bake on 350°F. Bake 15-20 minutes until cheese is melted and lasagna is heated through, serve.

Nutrition Info:

- Calories 145,Total Fat 3g,Total Carbs 18g,Protein 14g,Sodium 490mg.

Hawaiian Tofu

Servings: 6
Cooking Time: 3 Hours
Ingredients:

- 1 package extra firm tofu, cubed
- ¼ cup fresh pineapple, cubed
- ¼ cup tamari, low sodium
- 1 tbsp. sesame oil
- 1 tbsp. olive oil
- 1 tbsp. brown rice vinegar
- 2 cloves garlic, chopped
- 2 tsp fresh ginger, chopped
- 4 cups zucchini, chopped
- ¼ cup sesame seeds

Directions:

1. Add the tofu to the cooking pot.
2. Add the pineapple, soy sauce, sesame oil, olive oil, vinegar, garlic, and ginger to a food processor or blender. Process until smooth. Pour over tofu.
3. Add the lid and set to slow cook on low. Cook 3 hours, stirring occasionally.
4. During the last 15 minutes of cooking time, add the zucchini and sesame seeds to the pot and stir to combine. Serve over quinoa or rice.

Nutrition Info:

- Calories 164,Total Fat 13g,Total Carbs 5g,Protein 10g,Sodium 680mg.

Sesame Radish

Servings: 4
Cooking Time: 15 Minutes
Ingredients:

- 2 leeks, sliced
- ½ pound radishes, sliced
- 2 scallions, chopped
- 2 tablespoons black sesame seeds
- 1/3 cup chicken stock
- 1 tablespoon ginger, grated
- 1 tablespoon chives, minced

Directions:

1. In your Ninja Foodi, combine the leeks with the radishes and the other ingredients.
2. Put the Ninja Foodi's lid on and cook on High for 15 minutes more.
3. Release the pressure quickly for 5 minutes, divide everything between plates and serve.

Nutrition Info:

- Calories: 112; Fat: 2g; Carbohydrates: 4.2g; Protein: 2g

Pomegranate Radish Mix

Servings: 4
Cooking Time: 8 Minutes
Ingredients:

- 1-pound radishes, roughly cubed
- Black pepper and salt to the taste
- 2 garlic cloves, minced
- ½ cup chicken stock
- 2 tablespoons pomegranate juice
- ¼ cup pomegranate seeds

Directions:

1. In your Ninja Foodi, combine the radishes with the stock and the other ingredients.
2. Put the Ninja Foodi's lid on and cook on High for 8 minutes.
3. Release the pressure quickly for 5 minutes, divide everything between plates and serve.

Nutrition Info:

- Calories: 133; Fat: 2.3g; Carbohydrates: 2.4g; Protein: 2g

Radish Apples Salad

Servings: 4
Cooking Time: 15 Minutes
Ingredients:

- 1-pound radishes, roughly cubed
- 2 apples, cored and cut into wedges
- ¼ cup chicken stock
- 2 spring onions, chopped
- 3 tablespoons tomato paste
- Juice of 1 lime
- Cooking spray
- 1 tablespoon cilantro, chopped

Directions:

1. In your Ninja Foodi, combine the radishes with the apples and the other ingredients.
2. Put the Ninja Foodi's lid on and cook on High for 15 minutes.
3. Release the pressure quickly for 5 minutes, divide everything between plates and serve.

Nutrition Info:

- Calories: 122; Fat: 5g; Carbohydrates: 4.5g; Protein: 3g

Snacks, Appetizers & Sides

Almond Lover's Bars

Servings: 20
Cooking Time: 30 Minutes
Ingredients:

- 2 cups almond flour, sifted
- 1 ½ cups flour
- 1 tsp baking powder
- ½ tsp salt
- 10 tbsp. butter, soft
- 1 cup sugar
- 2 eggs
- 2 tsp vanilla
- 1 tbsp. powdered sugar

Directions:

1. Line an 8-inch square baking dish with parchment paper.
2. In a medium bowl, whisk together both flours, baking powder, and salt.
3. In a large bowl, beat butter and sugar until creamy.
4. Beat in eggs and vanilla. Then stir in dry ingredients until combined. Press firmly in prepared pan.
5. Place the rack in the cooking pot and place the pan on it. Add the tender-crisp lid and set to bake on 325°F. Bake 25-30 minutes until lightly browned and the bars pass the toothpick test.
6. Let cool before cutting into bars. Sprinkle with powdered sugar before serving.

Nutrition Info:

- Calories 207,Total Fat 11g,Total Carbs 23g,Protein 3g,Sodium 83mg.

Popcorn Chicken

Servings: 4
Cooking Time: 15 Minutes
Ingredients:

- Nonstick cooking spray
- 1 cup cornflakes, crushed
- ½ cup Bisquick baking mix, reduced fat
- ½ tsp garlic powder
- ½ tsp salt
- ¼ tsp pepper
- ½ tsp paprika
- ¾ lb. chicken breasts, boneless, skinless & cut in 1-inch pieces

Directions:

1. Lightly spray fryer basket with cooking spray.
2. In a large Ziploc bag, combine cornflakes, baking mix, garlic powder, salt, pepper, and paprika, shake to mix.
3. Add chicken and shake to coat.
4. Place chicken in basket in single layer, spray lightly with cooking spray.
5. Add the tender-crisp lid and set to air fry on 400°F. Cook chicken 12-15 minutes until crispy on the outside and no longer pink on the inside, turning over halfway through cooking time. Serve immediately.

Nutrition Info:

- Calories 179,Total Fat 3g,Total Carbs 17g,Protein 21g,Sodium 596mg.

Herby Fish Skewers

Servings: 4
Cooking Time: 75 Min
Ingredients:

- 1 pound cod loin, boneless, skinless; cubed /450g
- 2 garlic cloves, grated
- 1 lemon, juiced and zested
- 1 lemon, cut in wedges to serve
- 3 tbsp olive oil /45ml
- 1 tsp dill; chopped /5g
- 1 tsp parsley; chopped /5g
- Salt to taste

Directions:

1. In a bowl, combine the olive oil, garlic, dill, parsley, salt, and lemon juice. Stir in the cod and place in the fridge to marinate for 1 hour. Thread the cod pieces onto halved skewers.
2. Arrange into the oiled Ninja Foodi basket; close the crisping lid and cook for 10 minutes at 390 °F or 199°C. Flip them over halfway through cooking. When ready, remove to a serving platter, scatter lemon zest and serve with wedges.

Crispy Delicata Squash

Servings:4
Cooking Time: 15 Minutes
Ingredients:

- 1 large delicata squash, seeds removed and sliced
- 1 tablespoon extra-virgin olive oil
- ¼ teaspoon sea salt

Directions:

1. Place Cook & Crisp Basket in pot. Close crisping lid. Select AIR CRISP, set temperature to 390°F, and set time to 5 minutes. Select START/STOP to begin preheating.
2. In a large bowl, toss the squash with the olive oil and season with salt.
3. Once unit has preheated, place the squash in the basket. Close crisping lid.
4. Select AIR CRISP, set temperature to 390°F, and set time to 15 minutes. Select START/STOP to begin.

5. After 7 minutes, open the lid, then lift the basket and shake the squash. Lower the basket back into pot. Close lid and continue cooking until the squash achieves your desired crispiness.

Nutrition Info:

- Calories: 75,Total Fat: 4g,Sodium: 117mg,Carbohydrates: 10g,Protein: 2g.

Teriyaki Chicken Wings

Servings: 6
Cooking Time: 30 Min

Ingredients:

- 2 lb. chicken wings /900g
- 1 cup teriyaki sauce /250ml
- 1 tbsp honey /15ml
- 2 tbsp cornstarch 30g
- 2 tbsp cold water /30ml
- 1 tsp finely ground black pepper /5g
- 1 tsp sesame seeds /5g

Directions:

1. In the pot, combine honey, teriyaki sauce and black pepper until the honey dissolves completely; toss in chicken to coat. Seal the pressure lid, choose Pressure, set to High, and set the timer to 10 minutes. Press Start.
2. When ready, release the pressure quickly. Transfer chicken wings to a platter. Mix cold water with the cornstarch.
3. Press Sear/Sauté and stir in cornstarch slurry into the sauce and cook for 3 to 5 minutes until thickened. Top the chicken with thickened sauce. Add a garnish of sesame seeds, and serve.

Glazed Walnuts

Servings: 4
Cooking Time: 4 Minutes

Ingredients:

- ⅓ cup of water
- 6 ounces walnuts
- 5 tablespoon Erythritol
- ½ teaspoon ground ginger
- 3tablespoons psyllium husk powder

Directions:

1. Combine Erythritol and water together in a mixing bowl.
2. Add ground ginger and stir the mixture until the erythritol is dissolved.
3. Transfer the walnuts to the Ninja Foodi's insert and add sweet liquid.
4. Close the Ninja Foodi's lid and cook the dish in the "Pressure" mode for 4 minutes.
5. Remove the walnuts from the Ninja Foodi's insert.
6. Dip the walnuts in the Psyllium husk powder and serve.

Nutrition Info:

- Calories: 286; Fat: 25.1g; Carbohydrates: 10.4g; Protein: 10.3g

Enchilada Bites

Servings: 12
Cooking Time: 25 Minutes

Ingredients:

- ½ lb. ground turkey
- ¾ cup mild red enchilada sauce
- ½ cup black beans, drained & rinsed
- ½ tsp cumin
- 1 tbsp. cilantro, chopped
- Nonstick cooking spray
- 6 whole wheat tortillas, 6-inch
- 1 cup cheddar cheese, reduced fat, grated fine

Directions:

1. Add turkey to the cooking pot and set cooker to sauté on medium heat. Cook 8-10 minutes until no longer pink.
2. Add enchilada sauce, beans, cumin, and cilantro, stir to mix. Reduce heat to low and simmer 5 minutes. Transfer to a bowl.
3. Lightly spray fryer basket with cooking spray.
4. Spray both sides of the tortillas. Spread 2 tablespoons turkey mixture over each tortilla and top with 4 teaspoons cheese. Roll up tightly and secure with a toothpick. Cut each roll in half and place them in a single layer in the basket.
5. Add the tender-crisp lid and set to air fryer on 375°F. Bake 8-10 minutes, or until cheese has melted. Cut each roll in half and serve.

Nutrition Info:

- Calories 135,Total Fat 4g,Total Carbs 15g,Protein 9g,Sodium 465mg.

Loaded Potato Skins

Servings:4
Cooking Time: 45 Minutes

Ingredients:

- 2 large Russet potatoes, cleaned
- 1 tablespoon extra-virgin olive oil
- Kosher salt
- Freshly ground black pepper
- ¾ cup shredded sharp Cheddar cheese
- 3 tablespoons unsalted butter
- ¼ cup milk
- ¼ cup sour cream, plus more for serving
- 1 bunch chives, sliced
- 4 slices of ham, cubed

Directions:

1. Using a fork, poke holes in each potato. Rub each potato with the olive oil and season the skin with salt and pepper. Place the potatoes on the Reversible Rack in the lower position and place in the pot. Close the crisping lid.
2. Select AIR CRISP, set temperature to 390°F, and set time to 35 minutes. Select START/STOP to begin.
3. When cooking is complete, open lid and use tongs to transfer the potatoes to a cutting board.

4. Cut the potatoes in half lengthwise. Using a spoon, scoop out the flesh into a large bowl, leaving about ¼ inch of flesh on the skins. Set aside.
5. Sprinkle the hollowed-out potato skins with ¼ cup of cheese and place them back in the pot on the rack. Close crisping lid.
6. Select BROIL and set time to 5 minutes. Select START/STOP to begin.
7. Add the butter, milk, and sour cream to the bowl with the flesh. Season with salt and pepper and mash together. Use a spatula to fold in ¼ cup of cheese, one-quarter of the chives, and ham into the potato mixture.
8. When cooking is complete, open lid. Using tongs, carefully transfer the potato skins to the cutting board. Evenly distribute the mashed potato mixture into each potato skin and top with the remaining ¼ cup of cheese. Return the loaded potato skins to the rack. Close crisping lid.
9. Select BROIL and set time to 5 minutes. Select START/STOP to begin.
10. When cooking is complete, open lid. Carefully remove the potatoes. Cut them in half and garnish with the remaining chives. Serve with additional sour cream, if desired.

Nutrition Info:

- Calories: 402,Total Fat: 24g,Sodium: 561mg,Carbohydrates: 32g,Protein: 14g.

Crispy Chicken Skin

Servings: 7
Cooking Time: 10 Minutes

Ingredients:

- 1 teaspoon red chili flakes
- 1 teaspoon black pepper
- 1 teaspoon salt
- 9 ounces of chicken skin
- 2 tablespoons butter
- 1 teaspoon olive oil
- 1 teaspoon paprika

Directions:

1. Combine the black pepper, chilli flakes, and paprika together.
2. Stir the mixture and combine it with the chicken skin.
3. Let the mixture rest for 5 minutes. Set the Ninja Foodi's insert to" Sauté" mode.
4. Add the butter to the Ninja Foodi's insert and melt it.
5. Add the chicken skin and sauté it for 10 minutes, stirring frequently.
6. Once the chicken skin gets crunchy, remove it from the Ninja Foodi's insert.
7. Place the chicken skin on the paper towel and drain.
8. Serve warm.

Nutrition Info:

- Calories: 134; Fat: 11.5g; Carbohydrates: 0.98g; Protein: 7g

Crispy Sesame Shrimp

Servings: 10
Cooking Time: 10 Minutes

Ingredients:

- 1 cup flour
- ¼ tsp salt
- ¼ tsp cayenne pepper
- ¾ cup club soda
- Nonstick cooking spray
- 1 lb. medium shrimp, peel & devein
- 2 tsp sesame seeds

Directions:

1. In a medium bowl, combine flour, salt, and pepper.
2. Whisk in club soda until combined.
3. Spray fryer basket with cooking spray.
4. Dip shrimp, one at a time, in the batter and place in basket in a single layer. Sprinkle with sesame seeds.
5. Add tender-crisp lid and set cooker to air fryer function on 400°F. Cook shrimp 8-10 minutes or until golden brown. Serve immediately.

Nutrition Info:

- Calories 81,Total Fat 1g,Total Carbs 10g,Protein 7g,Sodium 319mg.

Strawberry Snack Bars

Servings: 16
Cooking Time: 30 Minutes

Ingredients:

- Butter flavored cooking spray
- 1 cup butter, soft
- 2 oz. stevia
- 1 tbsp. sour cream, reduced fat
- 1 egg
- 1 cup flour
- 1 cup whole wheat flour
- 1 cup strawberry jam, sugar free
- 1 tbsp. brown sugar
- 2 tbsp. walnuts, chopped

Directions:

1. Spray an 8-inch square pan with cooking spray.
2. In a medium bowl, beat butter and Stevia until creamy.
3. Beat in sour cream and egg until combined.
4. Stir in both flours, ½ cup at a time, until mixture forms a soft dough.
5. Press half the dough in the bottom of the prepared pan. Spread the jam over the top. Then spread the other half of the dough gently over the top. Sprinkle the brown sugar and nuts over the top.
6. Place the rack in the cooking pot and place the pan on it. Add the tender-crisp lid and set to bake on 375°F. Bake 25-30 minutes until bubbly and golden brown.
7. Transfer to wire rack to cool before cutting.

Nutrition Info:

- Calories 195,Total Fat 13g,Total Carbs 22g,Protein 3g,Sodium 97mg.

Artichoke Bites

Servings: 8
Cooking Time: 70 Min
Ingredients:

- ¼ cup frozen chopped kale /32.5g
- ¼ cup finely chopped artichoke hearts /32.5g
- ¼ cup goat cheese /32.5g
- ¼ cup ricotta cheese /32.5g
- 4 sheets frozen phyllo dough, thawed
- 1 lemon, zested
- 1 large egg white
- 1 tbsp olive oil /15ml
- 2 tbsps grated Parmesan cheese /30ml
- 1 tsp dried basil /5g
- ½ tsp salt /2.5g
- ½ tsp freshly ground black pepper /2.5g

Directions:

1. In a bowl, mix the kale, artichoke hearts, ricotta cheese, parmesan cheese, goat cheese, egg white, basil, lemon zest, salt, and pepper. Put the Crisping Basket in the pot. Close the crisping lid, choose Air Crisp, set the temperature to 375°F or 191°C, and the time to 5 minutes; press Start/Stop.
2. Then, place a phyllo sheet on a clean flat surface. Brush with olive oil, place a second phyllo sheet on the first, and brush with oil. Continue layering to form a pile of four oiled sheets.
3. Working from the short side, cut the phyllo sheets into 8 strips. Cut the strips in half to form 16 strips.
4. Spoon 1 tbsp of filling onto one short side of every strip. Fold a corner to cover the filling to make a triangle; continue repeatedly folding to the end of the strip, creating a triangle-shaped phyllo packet. Repeat the process with the other phyllo bites.
5. Open the crisping lid and place half of the pastry in the basket in a single layer. Close the lid, Choose Air Crisp, set the temperature to 350°F or 177°C, and the timer to 12 minutes; press Start/Stop.
6. After 6 minutes, open the lid, and flip the bites. Return the basket to the pot and close the lid to continue baking. When ready, take out the bites into a plate. Serve warm.

Zucchini Egg Tots

Servings: 8
Cooking Time: 9 Minutes
Ingredients:

- 2 medium zucchinis
- 1 egg
- 1 teaspoon salt
- ½ teaspoon baking soda
- 1 teaspoon lemon juice
- 1 teaspoon basil
- 1 tablespoon oregano
- ⅓ cup oatmeal flour
- 1 tablespoon olive oil
- 1 teaspoon minced garlic
- 1 tablespoon butter

Directions:

1. Wash the zucchini and grate it. Beat the egg in a suitable mixing bowl and blend it using a whisk.
2. Add the baking soda, lemon juice, basil, oregano, and flour to the egg mixture.
3. Stir it carefully until smooth. Combine the grated zucchini and egg mixture together.
4. Knead the dough until smooth. Mix olive oil with minced garlic together.
5. Set the Ninja Foodi's insert to" Sauté" mode.
6. Add butter and transfer the mixture to the Ninja Foodi's insert. Melt the mixture.
7. Make the small tots from the zucchini dough and place them in the melted butter mixture.
8. Sauté the dish for 3 minutes on each side.
9. Once the zucchini tots are cooked, remove them from the Ninja Foodi's insert and serve.

Nutrition Info:

- Calories: 64; Fat: 4.4g; Carbohydrates: 4.35g; Protein: 2g

Crispy Spiced Cauliflower Bites

Servings: 12
Cooking Time: 15 Minutes
Ingredients:

- Nonstick cooking spray
- 1 egg
- 1 tbsp. water
- 1 cup whole wheat panko bread crumbs
- 1 tbsp. garlic powder
- ½ tsp onion powder
- 1 tbsp. fresh parsley, chopped
- 6 cups cauliflower florets
- ¼ cup light mayonnaise
- 2 tbsp. sweet chili sauce
- 2 tbsp. hot sauce

Directions:

1. Lightly spray the fryer basket with cooking spray and place in the cooking pot.
2. In a small bowl, whisk together egg and water.
3. In a separate small bowl, stir together bread crumbs, garlic powder, onion powder, and parsley.
4. Dip each floret first in egg then in bread crumbs. Place in fryer basket, in batches.
5. Add the tender-crisp lid and set to air fry on 400°F. Bake cauliflower 15 minutes or until golden brown and crispy.

6. In a small bowl, whisk together mayonnaise, chili sauce, and hot sauce. When all the cauliflower is done, drizzle sauce over the top and serve.

Nutrition Info:

- Calories 77,Total Fat 3g,Total Carbs 11g,Protein 3g,Sodium 177mg.

South Of The Border Corn Dip

Servings: 8

Cooking Time: 2 Hours

Ingredients:

- 33 oz. corn with chilies
- 10 oz. tomatoes & green chilies, diced
- 8 oz. cream cheese, cubed
- ½ cup cheddar cheese, grated
- ¼ cup green onions, chopped
- ½ tsp garlic, diced fine
- ½ tsp chili powder

Directions:

1. Place all ingredients in the cooking pot and stir to mix.
2. Add the lid and set to slow cooking function on low heat. Set timer for 2 hours. Stir occasionally.
3. Dip is done when all the cheese is melted and it's bubbly. Stir well, then transfer to serving bowl and serve warm.

Nutrition Info:

- Calories 225,Total Fat 13g,Total Carbs 24g,Protein 7g,Sodium 710mg.

Turkey Scotch Eggs

Servings: 6

Cooking Time: 20 Min

Ingredients:

- 10 oz. ground turkey /300g
- 4 eggs, soft boiled, peeled
- 2 garlic cloves, minced
- 2 eggs, lightly beaten
- 1 white onion; chopped
- ½ cup flour /65g
- ½ cup breadcrumbs /65g
- 1 tsp dried mixed herbs /5g
- Salt and pepper to taste
- Cooking spray

Directions:

1. Mix together the onion, garlic, salt, and pepper. Shape into 4 balls. Wrap the turkey mixture around each egg, and ensure the eggs are well covered.
2. Dust each egg ball in flour, then dip in the beaten eggs and finally roll in the crumbs, until coated. Spray with cooking spray.
3. Lay the eggs into your Ninja Foodi's basket. Set the temperature to 390 °F or 199°C, close the crisping lid and cook for 15 minutes. After 8 minutes, turn the eggs. Slice in half and serve warm.

Potato Samosas

Servings:4

Cooking Time: 31 Minutes

Ingredients:

- 2 tablespoons canola oil
- 4 cups Russet potatoes, peeled and cut into ½-inch cubes
- 1 small yellow onion, diced
- 1 cup frozen peas
- 1½ teaspoons kosher salt
- 2½ teaspoons curry powder
- 1 cup vegetable stock
- 1 (½ package) frozen puff pastry sheet, thawed
- 1 egg beaten with 1 teaspoon water

Directions:

1. Select SEAR/SAUTÉ and set temperature to HI. Select START/STOP to begin. Let preheat for 5 minutes.
2. Add the oil and let heat for 1 minute. Add the potatoes, onions, and peas and cook, stirring frequently, about 10 minutes. Add the salt and curry powder and stir to coat the vegetables with it. Add the vegetable stock. Assemble pressure lid, making sure the pressure release valve is in the SEAL position.
3. Select PRESSURE and set to LO. Set time to 1 minute. Select START/STOP to begin.
4. When pressure cooking is complete, quick release the pressure by turning the pressure release valve to the VENT position. Carefully remove the lid when the unit has finished releasing pressure.
5. Transfer the potato mixture to a medium bowl. Let fully cool, about 15 minutes.
6. Lay out the puff pastry sheet on a cutting board. Using a rolling pin, roll out the sheet into a 12-by-10-inch rectangle. Cut it in 4 strips lengthwise, then cut the strips into thirds for a total of 12 squares.
7. Place 2 tablespoons of potato mixture in center of a pastry square. Brush the egg wash onto edges, and then fold one corner to another to create a triangle. Use a fork to seal edges together. Repeat with the remaining potato mixture and pastry squares.
8. Insert Cook & Crisp Basket into unit. Close crisping lid. Select AIR CRISP, set temperature to 390°F, and set time to 20 minutes. Select START/STOP to begin. Let preheat for 5 minutes.
9. Once unit has preheated, working in batches, place 3 samosas in the basket. Close lid to begin cooking.
10. After 5 minutes, open lid and use silicone-tipped tongs to remove the samosas. Repeat with the remaining batches of samosas.
11. Once all samosas are cooked, serve immediately.

Nutrition Info:

- Calories: 449,Total Fat: 24g,Sodium: 639mg,Carbohydrates: 53g,Protein: 10g.

Garlicky Tomato

Servings: 5
Cooking Time: 5 Minutes
Ingredients:

- 5 tomatoes
- ¼ cup chives, chopped
- ⅓ cup garlic clove, minced
- ½ teaspoon salt
- ½ teaspoon black pepper
- 1 tablespoon olive oil
- 7 ounces Parmesan cheese

Directions:

1. Wash the tomatoes and slice them into thick slices.
2. Place the sliced tomatoes in the Ninja Foodi's insert.
3. Combine the grated cheese and minced garlic and stir the mixture.
4. Sprinkle the tomato slices with chives, black pepper, and salt.
5. Then sprinkle the sliced tomatoes with the cheese mixture.
6. Close the Ninja Foodi's lid and cook the dish in the "Pressure" mode for 5 minutes.
7. Once done, remove the tomatoes carefully and serve.

Nutrition Info:

- Calories: 224; Fat: 14g; Carbohydrates: 12.55g; Protein: 13g

Cheesy Jalapeno Boats

Servings: 12
Cooking Time: 25 Minutes
Ingredients:

- 8 oz. cream cheese, reduced fat, soft
- 1 cup cheddar cheese, reduced fat, grated
- 1 tsp garlic powder
- 2 eggs
- 2 tbsp. skim milk
- 1 cup panko bread crumbs
- ½ tsp paprika
- ½ tsp chili powder
- ½ tsp salt
- ¼ tsp pepper
- 12 jalapeno peppers, halved lengthwise, stems & seeds removed

Directions:

1. Place the rack in the cooking pot and line with parchment paper.
2. In a medium bowl, beat together cream cheese, cheddar, and garlic powder.
3. In a small bowl, whisk together eggs and milk.
4. In a shallow dish, stir together bread crumbs, paprika, chili powder, salt, and pepper.
5. Spread a tablespoon of cheese mixture in each jalapeno. Dip in egg mixture then coat with bread crumbs. Place on the parchment paper.
6. Add the tender-crisp lid and set to bake on 350°F. Cook 20-25 minutes or until golden brown. Serve immediately.
7. Bake 30 to 35 minutes, or until golden.

Nutrition Info:

- Calories 107,Total Fat 5g,Total Carbs 9g,Protein 6g,Sodium 326mg.

Mexican Street Corn

Servings:3
Cooking Time: 14 Minutes
Ingredients:

- 3 ears corn, husked, rinsed, and dried
- Olive oil spray
- ¼ cup sour cream
- ¼ cup mayonnaise
- ¼ cup crumbled cotija cheese, plus more for garnish
- 1 teaspoon freshly squeezed lime juice
- ½ teaspoon garlic powder
- ¼ teaspoon chili powder, plus more as needed
- Fresh cilantro leaves, for garnish
- ½ teaspoon salt
- ½ teaspoon freshly ground black pepper

Directions:

1. Select AIR CRISP, set the temperature to 400°F, and set the time to 5 minutes to preheat. Select START/STOP to begin.
2. Lightly mist the corn with olive oil and place the corn in the Cook & Crisp Basket. Close the crisping lid.
3. Select AIR CRISP, set the temperature to 400°F, and set the time to 12 minutes. Select START/STOP to begin. After 7 minutes, flip the corn. Close the crisping lid and cook for 5 minutes more.
4. While the corn cooks, in a small bowl, stir together the sour cream, mayonnaise, cotija cheese, lime juice, garlic powder, and chili powder until blended.
5. When cooking is complete, carefully remove the corn and brush or spoon the sauce onto it. Sprinkle with cilantro, cotija cheese, and more chili powder.
6. If desired, return the corn to the basket. Close the crisping lid. Select BROIL and set the time for 2 minutes. Select START/STOP to begin.
7. Serve hot, seasoned with salt and pepper, as needed.

Nutrition Info:

- Calories: 280,Total Fat: 15g,Sodium: 701mg,Carbohydrates: 35g,Protein: 7g.

Cheesy Tangy Arancini

Servings: 6
Cooking Time: 105 Min

Ingredients:

- ½ cup olive oil, plus 1 tbsp /140ml
- 2 large eggs
- 2 garlic cloves, minced
- 1 small white onion; diced
- ½ cup apple cider vinegar /125ml
- 2 cups short grain rice /260g
- 2 cups fresh panko bread crumbs /260g
- 5 cups chicken stock /1250ml
- 1½ cups grated Parmesan cheese, plus more for garnish /195g
- 1 cup chopped green beans /130g
- 1 tsp salt /5g
- 1tsp freshly ground black pepper /5g

Directions:

1. Choose Sear/Sauté on the pot and set to Medium High. Choose Start/Stop to preheat the pot. Add 1 tbsp of oil and the onion, cook the onion until translucent, add the garlic and cook further for 2 minutes or until the garlic starts getting fragrant.
2. Stir in the stock, vinegar, and rice. Seal the pressure lid, choose pressure, set to High, and set the time to 7 minutes; press Start.
3. After cooking, perform a natural pressure release for 10 minutes, then a quick pressure release and carefully open the pressure lid.
4. Stir in the Parmesan cheese, green beans, salt, and pepper to mash the rice until a risotto forms. Spoon the mixture into a bowl and set aside to cool completely.
5. Clean the pot and in a bowl, combine the breadcrumbs and the remaining olive oil. In another bowl, lightly beat the eggs.
6. Form 12 balls out of the risotto or as many as you can get. Dip each into the beaten eggs, and coat in the breadcrumb mixture.
7. Put half of the rice balls in the Crisping Basket in a single layer. Close the crisping lid, hit Air Crisp, set the temperature to 400°F or 205°C, and set the time to 10 minutes; press Start. Leave to cool before serving.

Pork Shank

Servings: 6
Cooking Time: 45 Minutes

Ingredients:

- 1-pound pork shank
- ½ cup parsley, chopped
- 4 garlic cloves
- 1 teaspoon salt
- ½ teaspoon paprika
- 2 tablespoons olive oil
- 1 teaspoon cilantro, chopped
- 1 tablespoon celery
- 1 carrot, grated
- 1 cup of water
- 1 red onion, chopped
- ⅓ cup wine
- 2 tablespoons lemon juice

Directions:

1. Chop the parsley and slice the garlic cloves.
2. Combine the vegetables together and add salt, paprika, cilantro, wine, and lemon juice and stir the mixture.
3. Combine the pork shank and marinade together and leave the mixture.
4. Combine the sliced onion and grated carrot together.
5. Add celery and blend well. Add the vegetables to the pork shank mixture and stir using your hands.
6. Place the meat in the Ninja Foodi's insert and add water.
7. Close the Ninja Foodi's lid, and set the Ninja Foodi to" Pressure."
8. Cook for 45 minutes. Once done, remove the meat from the Ninja Foodi's insert and chill the dish well.
9. Slice the pork shank and serve.

Nutrition Info:

- Calories: 242; Fat: 19.8g; Carbohydrates: 5.38g; Protein: 11g

Caribbean Chicken Skewers

Servings: 8
Cooking Time: 30 Minutes

Ingredients:

- 2 tsp jerk seasoning
- 1 lime, juiced
- 1 tbsp. extra virgin olive oil
- 1 lb. chicken, boneless, skinless & cut in 1-inch cubes
- 1 red onion, cut in 1-inch pieces
- 1 cup cherry tomatoes
- 1 cup fresh pineapple, cut in 1-inch cubes
- 1 very ripe plantain, peel on, sliced
- ½ tsp salt
- ½ tsp pepper
- Nonstick cooking spray

Directions:

1. If using wood skewers, soak them in water for 30 minutes.
2. In a large bowl, combine jerk seasoning, lime juice, and olive oil.
3. Add the chicken, onions, and tomatoes and toss to coat. Cover and refrigerate 20 minutes.
4. Thread skewers with chicken, onion, tomatoes, pineapple, and plantains, leaving a little space at both ends. Sprinkle skewers with salt and pepper.
5. Lightly spray the rack with cooking spray and place in the cooking pot. Place the skewers on top.

6. Add the tender-crisp lid and set to air fry on 400°F. Cook skewers 25-30 minutes until chicken is cooked through. Baste with marinade and turn over halfway through cooking time. Serve.

Nutrition Info:

- Calories 127,Total Fat 3g,Total Carbs 11g,Protein 13g,Sodium 173mg.

Mexican Bean Dip

Servings: 12

Cooking Time: 10 Minutes

Ingredients:

- 2 15 ½ oz. cans pinto beans, rinsed & drained, divided
- 1 cup salsa, divided
- 1 tsp olive oil
- 1 onion, chopped fine
- 1 green bell pepper, chopped fine
- 3 cloves garlic, chopped fine
- 1 tbsp. coriander
- 2 tsp cumin
- ¾ tsp salt
- ½ cup cheddar cheese, grated
- 1 tomato, chopped

Directions:

1. Add 1 can of beans and ¼ cup salsa to food processor and pulse until smooth.
2. Add oil to the cooker and set to sauté function on medium heat.
3. Once oil is hot, add onion, bell pepper, and garlic and cook until tender, about 5-7 minutes.
4. Stir in blended bean mixture, remaining can of beans, and seasonings. Bring to a boil, stirring frequently.
5. Reduce heat to low and simmer 5 minutes, stirring frequently.
6. Pour into a serving bowl and top with cheese and tomato. Serve immediately.

Nutrition Info:

- Calories 128,Total Fat 3g,Total Carbs 19g,Protein 7g,Sodium 491mg.

Apple Pecan Cookie Bars

Servings: 12

Cooking Time: 20 Minutes

Ingredients:

- Nonstick cooking spray
- 2/3 cup sugar
- 2 egg whites
- ½ tsp vanilla
- ½ cup flour
- 1 tsp baking powder
- 2 cups Granny Smith apples, chopped
- ¼ cup pecans, chopped

Directions:

1. Lightly spray an 8-inch baking pan with cooking spray.
2. In a large bowl, whisk together egg whites, sugar, and vanilla until frothy.
3. Whisk in flour and baking powder until combined.
4. Fold in apples and nuts and pour into pan.
5. Place the rack in the cooking pot and place the pan on it. Add the tender-crisp lid and set to air fry on 350°F. Bake 18-20 minutes or until the cookies pass the toothpick test.
6. Let cool before cutting and serving.

Nutrition Info:

- Calories 90,Total Fat 2g,Total Carbs 18g,Protein 1g,Sodium 10mg.

Honey Mustard Hot Dogs

Servings: 4

Cooking Time: 22 Min

Ingredients:

- 20 Hot Dogs, cut into 4 pieces
- ¼ cup honey /62.5ml
- ¼ cup red wine vinegar /62.5ml
- ½ cup tomato puree /125ml
- ¼ cup water /62.5ml
- 1½ tsp soy sauce /7.5ml
- 1 tsp Dijon mustard /5g
- Salt and black pepper to taste

Directions:

1. Add the tomato puree, red wine vinegar, honey, soy sauce, Dijon mustard, salt, and black pepper in a medium bowl. Mix them with a spoon.
2. Put sausage weenies in the crisp basket, and close the crisping lid. Select Air Crisp mode. Set the temperature to 370 °F or 188°C and the timer to 4 minutes. Press Start/Stop. At the 2-minute mark, turn the sausages.
3. Once ready, open the lid and pour the sweet sauce over the sausage weenies.
4. Close the pressure lid, secure the pressure valve, and select Pressure mode on High for 3 minutes. Press Start/Stop. Once the timer has ended, do a quick pressure release. Serve and enjoy.

Roasted Veggie Dip

Servings: 10

Cooking Time: 15 Minutes

Ingredients:

- Nonstick cooking spray
- 3 zucchini, sliced
- 1 red bell pepper, sliced
- 1 red onion, sliced
- 2 cloves garlic, peeled

Directions:

1. Place the rack in the cooking pot and select air fry function on 400°F.
2. Spray a baking dish with cooking spray. Spread vegetables in the pan and spray them with cooking spray.

3. Place on the rack and add the tender-crisp lid. Bake 15 minutes or until vegetables are tender.
4. Transfer to a food processor or blender and pulse 30-60 seconds or until smooth. Spoon into serving dish and serve warm or cold.

Nutrition Info:

- Calories 10,Total Fat 1g,Total Carbs 2g,Protein 0g,Sodium 1mg.

Rosemary Potato Fries

Servings: 4
Cooking Time: 30 Min

Ingredients:

- 4 russet potatoes, cut into sticks
- 2 garlic cloves, crushed
- 2 tbsp butter, melted /30ml
- 1 tsp fresh rosemary; chopped /5g
- Salt and pepper, to taste

Directions:

1. Add butter, garlic, salt, and pepper to a bowl; toss until the sticks are well-coated. Lay the potato sticks into the Ninja Foodi's basket. Close the crisping lid and cook for 15 minutes at 370 °F or 188°C. Shake the potatoes every 5 minutes.
2. Once ready, check to ensure the fries are golden and crispy all over if not, return them to cook for a few minutes.
3. Divide standing up between metal cups lined with nonstick baking paper, and serve sprinkled with rosemary.

Shallot Pepper Pancakes

Servings: 8
Cooking Time: 15 Minutes

Ingredients:

- 8 ounces shallot, chopped
- 2 tablespoons chives, chopped
- 1 red onion, chopped
- 1 cup coconut flour
- 2 egg
- ¼ cup sour cream
- 1 teaspoon baking soda
- 1 tablespoon lemon juice
- 1 teaspoon salt
- 1 teaspoon cilantro, chopped
- ½ teaspoon basil
- 1 tablespoon olive oil
- 1 bell pepper, chopped

Directions:

1. Chop the shallot and chives and combine them into a mixing bowl.
2. Whisk the eggs in a another bowl and add baking soda and lemon juice.
3. Stir the mixture and add the cream, salt, cilantro, basil, and coconut flour.
4. Blend the mixture well until smooth.
5. Add the vegetables to the egg mixture.
6. Stir it to the batter that forms. Set the Ninja Foodi's insert to" Sauté" mode.
7. Pour the olive oil in the Ninja Foodi's insert and preheat it.
8. Ladle the batter and cook the pancakes for 2 minutes on each side.
9. Keep the pancakes under aluminium foil to keep them warm until all the pancakes are cooked.
10. Serve the pancakes while warm.

Nutrition Info:

- Calories: 138; Fat: 6g; Carbohydrates: 7.6g; Protein: 4.7g

Spicy Glazed Pecans

Servings: 12
Cooking Time: 30 Minutes

Ingredients:

- Nonstick cooking spray
- 6 cups pecan halves
- 6 tbsp. butter, melted
- ¼ cup Worcestershire sauce
- 2 tbsp. hot sauce
- 1 tbsp. soy sauce
- 1 tbsp. hot curry powder
- 1 tbsp. chili powder

Directions:

1. Lightly spray the fryer basket with cooking spray.
2. In a large bowl, combine all ingredients and toss well to coat the pecans.
3. Add half the mixture to the fryer basket and place in the cooking pot. Add the tender-crisp lid and set to air fry on 250°F. Cook 20 minutes. Shake the basket and cook 10 minutes more.
4. Transfer cooked nuts to a baking sheet lined with parchment paper and spread out to cool. Repeat with remaining nut mixture. Serve warm or room temperature.

Nutrition Info:

- Calories 402,Total Fat 41g,Total Carbs 9g,Protein 5g,Sodium 220mg.

Chicken And Vegetable Egg Rolls

Servings:16
Cooking Time: 10 Minutes Per Batch

Ingredients:

- 2 tablespoons sherry
- 2 tablespoons soy sauce
- 2 tablespoons beef broth
- 2 tablespoons cornstarch
- ½ teaspoon salt
- ½ teaspoon granulated sugar
- ½ teaspoon ground ginger

- 3 tablespoons canola oil
- 8 scallions, chopped
- ½ cup chopped mushrooms
- 3 cups shredded cabbage
- ½ cup shredded carrot
- ½ cup bean sprouts, washed
- 2 cups chopped cooked chicken
- 1 package egg rolls wrappers
- 1 egg, beaten
- Cooking spray
- Hot mustard, for dipping
- Sweet and sour sauce, for dipping

Directions:

1. In a small bowl, stir together the sherry, soy sauce, beef broth, cornstarch, salt, sugar, and ginger until combined and the sugar dissolves. Set aside.
2. Select SEAR/SAUTÉ and set temperature to HI. Select START/STOP to begin and allow to preheat for 5 minutes.
3. Add the canola oil to the cooking pot and allow to heat for 1 minute. Add the scallions and mushrooms and sauté for 2 to 3 minutes, stirring well, until the vegetables just begin to soften.
4. Add the cabbage, carrot, and bean sprouts, stirring to incorporate well. Decrease the temperature to MD:LO. Cook the vegetables for about 7 minutes, until cabbage and carrots are softened.
5. Stir in the chicken. Add the sauce and cook, stirring constantly, until the sauce thickens the filling, about 3 minutes. Select START/STOP to end the function. Transfer the filling to a bowl to cool. Wash the pot and return it to the cooker.
6. Place the Cook & Crisp Basket in the Foodi pot.
7. Select AIR CRISP, set the temperature to 390°F, and set the time to 5 minutes to preheat. Select START/STOP to begin.
8. Working one at a time, using a small silicone spatula, moisten the 4 sides of an egg roll wrapper with the beaten egg. Place 3 tablespoons of the filling on the center of the egg roll wrapper. Fold an edge over the mixture and tuck it under the point. Fold the edges in and continue rolling. Press the end point over the top of the roll to seal. Continue with the remaining wrappers and filling.
9. Place 3 egg rolls in the basket, making sure they don't touch each other. Coat the egg rolls in on cooking spray, then close the crisping lid.
10. Select AIR CRISP, set the temperature to 390°F, and set the time to 10 minutes. After 5 minutes, open the crisping lid, flip the egg rolls, and spritz the other side with cooking spray. Close the crisping lid and cook for the remaining 5 minutes.
11. Using tongs, carefully transfer the egg rolls to a wire rack to cool for least 6 minutes before serving.
12. Repeat step 8 with the remaining egg rolls. Keep in mind that the unit is already hot, which may decrease the cooking time. Monitor closely for doneness.
13. Serve with the hot mustard and sweet and sour sauce for dipping.

Nutrition Info:

- Calories: 166,Total Fat: 6g,Sodium: 364mg,Carbohydrates: 20g,Protein: 9g.

Gingered Butternut Squash

Servings: 6

Cooking Time: 15 Minutes

Ingredients:

- 8 cups butternut squash, peeled, seeded, & cut in 1-inch cubes
- 1 cup water
- ½ tsp salt
- 4 tbsp. butter
- ¼ cup half n half
- 3 tbsp. honey
- ½ tsp ginger
- ¼ tsp cinnamon

Directions:

1. Add the squash, water, and salt to the cooking pot, stir.
2. Add the lid and select pressure cooking on high. Set timer for 12 minutes. When the timer goes off, use quick release to remove the lid.
3. Drain the squash and place in a large bowl.
4. Add remaining ingredients. Set cooker to saute on medium heat. Cook until butter melts, stirring occasionally
5. Once the butter melts, pour the sauce over the squash and mash with a potato masher. Serve.

Nutrition Info:

- Calories 198,Total Fat 9g,Total Carbs 31g,Protein 2g,Sodium 267mg.

Cheesy Bacon Brussel Sprouts

Servings: 6

Cooking Time: 15 Minutes

Ingredients:

- Nonstick cooking spray
- 3 slices turkey bacon, chopped
- 2 tsp olive oil
- 1 lb. Brussels sprouts, trimmed & cut in half
- 2 cloves garlic, diced fine
- ¼ cup water
- 3 oz. goat cheese, soft
- 2 tbsp. skim milk
- 1 tbsp. parmesan cheese
- ¼ tsp salt
- ¼ tsp pepper
- 1 tsp paprika

Directions:

1. Spray the cooking pot with cooking spray. Set to sauté on med-high heat.
2. Add bacon and cook until crisp, transfer to paper-towel line plate.
3. Add oil and let it get hot. Add Brussel sprouts and cook, stirring frequently, 5 minutes or until they start to brown.
4. Add water, cover and cook another 5 minutes or until fork-tender. Drain any water from the pot.
5. Add goat cheese, milk, parmesan, salt, and pepper. Cook, stirring frequently, until cheese has melted.
6. Stir in bacon and cook until heated through. Sprinkle with paprika and serve.

Nutrition Info:

- Calories 106,Total Fat 6g,Total Carbs 8g,Protein 7g,Sodium 274mg.

Sweet Potato Skins

Servings: 4
Cooking Time: 20 Minutes

Ingredients:

- 2 sweet potatoes, baked & halved lengthwise
- 1 tsp olive oil
- 2 cloves garlic, diced fine
- 1 tbsp. fresh lime juice
- 2 cups baby spinach
- ½ cup chicken, cooked & shredded
- 1 tsp oregano
- 1 tsp cumin
- 2 tsp chili powder
- ½ cup mozzarella cheese, grated
- ¼ cup cilantro, chopped

Directions:

1. Scoop out the center of the potatoes, leaving some on the side to help keep the shape.
2. Set the cooker to sauté on med-high heat and add the oil.
3. Once the oil is hot, add garlic, lime juice, and spinach. Cook 2-3 minutes until spinach is wilted.
4. In a large bowl, mash the sweet potato centers until almost smooth.
5. Stir in chicken, oregano, cumin, and chili powder. Stir in spinach until combined.
6. Place the rack in the cooking pot and top with parchment paper.
7. Spoon the potato mixture into the skins and top with cheese. Place on the rack.
8. Add the tender-crisp lid and set to bake on 400°F. Bake 15-20 minutes until cheese is melted and lightly browned. Let cool slightly then cut each skin in 4 pieces and serve garnished with cilantro.

Nutrition Info:

- Calories 132,Total Fat 2g,Total Carbs 20g,Protein 9g,Sodium 155mg.

Asian Chicken Nuggets

Servings: X
Cooking Time: 20 Minutes

Ingredients:

- 1 lb. chicken breasts, boneless, skinless & cut in 1-inch pieces
- 1 tsp salt
- ½ tsp pepper
- 2 eggs
- 1 cup Panko bread crumbs
- ¼ cup lite soy sauce
- ¼ cup honey
- 4 cloves garlic, diced fine
- 2 tbsp. hoisin sauce
- 1 tablespoon freshly grated ginger
- 1 tablespoon Sriracha
- 2 green onions, sliced thin
- 2 tsp sesame seeds

Directions:

1. Place the rack in the cooking pot and top with a sheet of parchment paper.
2. Sprinkle the chicken with salt and pepper.
3. In a shallow dish, beat the eggs.
4. Place the bread crumbs in a separate shallow dish. Working in batches, dip the chicken first in the eggs then bread crumbs, pressing to coat the chicken well.
5. Place the chicken on the parchment paper in a single layer. Add the tender-crisp lid and select air fry on 400 °F. Bake the chicken 10-15 minutes until golden brown and cooked through, turning over halfway through cooking time. Transfer to serving plate and keep warm.
6. Set the cooker to sauté on med-high heat. Add the soy sauce, honey, garlic, hoisin, ginger, and Sriracha, stir to combine. Cook, stirring frequently, until sauce thickens, about 2 minutes.
7. Add chicken and toss to coat. Serve immediately garnished with green onions and sesame seeds.

Nutrition Info:

- Calories 304,Total Fat 7g,Total Carbs 27g,Protein 32g,Sodium 1149mg.

Louisiana Crab Dip

Servings:8
Cooking Time: 50 Minutes

Ingredients:

- 2 tablespoons unsalted butter
- 3 garlic cloves, minced
- ½ cup mayonnaise
- 1 pound whipped or room temperature cream cheese
- 2 teaspoons Worcestershire sauce
- 3 teaspoons hot sauce
- 3 teaspoons freshly squeezed lemon juice

- 2 teaspoons Creole seasoning
- ¾ cup Parmesan cheese
- 1 pound lump crab meat

Directions:

1. Select SEAR/SAUTÉ and set to MED. Select START/STOP to begin. Let preheat for 3 minutes.
2. Add the butter and garlic and sauté for 2 minutes.
3. Add the mayonnaise, cream cheese, Worcestershire sauce, hot sauce, lemon juice, Creole seasoning, and Parmesan cheese. Stir well.
4. Add the crab meat and lightly fold to incorporate. Close crisping lid.
5. Select BAKE/ROAST, set temperature to 350°F, and set time to 40 minutes. Select START/STOP to begin
6. When cooking is complete, open lid. Let cool for 10 minutes before serving.

Nutrition Info:

- Calories: 391,Total Fat: 39g,Sodium: 976mg,Carbohydrates: 4g,Protein: 16g.

Apricot Snack Bars

Servings: 16

Cooking Time: 25 Minutes

Ingredients:

- Butter flavored cooking spray
- ¾ cup oats
- ¾ cup flour
- ¼ cup brown sugar
- ¾ tsp vanilla
- ¼ cup butter
- ¾ cup apricot preserves, sugar free

Directions:

1. Lightly spray an 8-inch baking pan with cooking spray. Place the rack in the cooking pot.
2. In a large bowl, combine oats, flour, sugar, and vanilla until combined.
3. With a pastry blender or a fork, cut the butter in until mixture is crumbly. Press half the mixture in the bottom of the pan.
4. Spread the preserves over the top of the oat mixture and sprinkle the remaining oat over the top, gently press down.
5. Place the pan on the rack and add the tender-crisp lid. Set to air fry on 350°F. Bake 25-30 minutes until golden brown and bubbly.
6. Transfer to a wire rack and let cool before cutting.

Nutrition Info:

- Calories 100,Total Fat 3g,Total Carbs 18g,Protein 2g,Sodium 3mg.

Chicken Pork Nuggets

Servings: 6

Cooking Time: 20 Minutes

Ingredients:

- 2 cups ground chicken
- ½ cup dill, chopped
- 1 egg
- 2 tablespoons pork rinds
- 1 tablespoon heavy cream
- ½ cup almond flour
- 3 tablespoons butter
- 1 tablespoon canola oil
- 1 teaspoon black pepper

Directions:

1. Beat the egg in a suitable mixing bowl.
2. Add the chopped dill and ground chicken. Blend the mixture until it is smooth.
3. Sprinkle the dish with black pepper and cream.
4. Blend the nugget mixture again. Form the nuggets from the meat mixture and dip them in the almond flour and pork rinds.
5. Sprinkle the Ninja Foodi's insert with the canola oil and butter.
6. Set the Ninja Foodi's insert to "Pressure" mode. Once the butter mixture starts to melt, add the nuggets.
7. Close the Ninja Foodi's lid and cook the dish for 20 minutes.
8. Once done, check if the nuggets are cooked and remove them from the Ninja Foodi's insert.
9. Drain on a paper towel and serve.

Nutrition Info:

- Calories: 217; Fat: 15.4g; Carbohydrates: 3.1g; Protein: 17.4 g

Fried Beef Dumplings

Servings: 8

Cooking Time: 45 Min

Ingredients:

- 8 ounces ground beef /240g
- 20 wonton wrappers
- 1 carrot, grated
- 1 large egg, beaten
- 1 garlic clove, minced
- ½ cup grated cabbage /65g
- 2 tbsps olive oil /30ml
- 2 tbsps coconut aminos /30g
- ½ tbsp melted ghee /7.5ml
- ½ tbsp ginger powder /7.5g
- ½ tsp salt /2.5g
- ½ tsp freshly ground black pepper/2.5g

Directions:

1. Put the Crisping Basket in the pot. Close the crisping lid, choose Air Crisp, set the temperature to 400°F or 205°C, and the time to 5 minutes; press Start/Stop. In a large bowl, mix the beef, cabbage, carrot, egg, garlic, coconut aminos, ghee, ginger, salt, and black pepper.

2. Put the wonton wrappers on a clean flat surface and spoon 1 tbsp of the beef mixture into the middle of each wrapper.
3. Run the edges of the wrapper with a little water; fold the wrapper to cover the filling into a semi-circle shape and pinch the edges to seal. Brush the dumplings with olive oil.
4. Lay the dumplings in the preheated basket, choose Air Crisp, set the temperature to 400°F or 205°C, and set the time to 12 minutes. Choose Start/Stop to begin frying.
5. After 6 minutes, open the lid, pull out the basket and shake the dumplings. Return the basket to the pot and close the lid to continue frying until the dumplings are crispy to your desire.

Crispy Cheesy Zucchini Bites

Servings: 6
Cooking Time: 10 Minutes

Ingredients:

- 2 zucchini, cut in 3/4-inch thick slices
- Nonstick cooking spray
- ½ cup panko bread crumbs
- 1 tbsp. parmesan cheese
- 1 tbsp. lite mayonnaise
- ½ tsp garlic powder
- ½ tsp onion powder
- ¼ tsp seasoned salt
- ¼ tsp pepper

Directions:

1. Pour enough water to cover the bottom of the cooking pot about 1 inch. Set to sauté on high heat and bring to a boil.
2. Add zucchini, reduce heat to low and simmer 3-5 minutes or just until tender. Drain and pat dry with paper towels.
3. Lightly spray the fryer basket with cooking spray and place it in the cooking pot.
4. In a small bowl, stir together bread crumbs, cheese, garlic powder, onion powder, salt, and pepper.
5. Spread one side of each zucchini slice with mayonnaise and place in a single layer in the basket. Sprinkle crumb mixture over top of each slice.
6. Add tender-crisp lid and set to air fry on 450°F. Bake 3-5 minutes, or until golden brown. Serve immediately.

Nutrition Info:

- Calories 48,Total Fat 1g,Total Carbs 7g,Protein 1g,Sodium 196mg.

Parmesan Stuffed Mushrooms

Servings: 5
Cooking Time: 15 Minutes

Ingredients:

- 1 lb. button mushrooms, wash & remove stems
- 2 tbsp. olive oil, divided
- ¼ cup parmesan cheese, fat free
- 2 cloves garlic, diced fine
- ¼ cup cream cheese, fat free, soft
- ¼ cup whole wheat panko bread crumbs

Directions:

1. Place the rack in the cooking pot and top with a piece of parchment paper.
2. Brush the mushrooms with 1 tablespoon oil.
3. In a small bowl, combine parmesan, garlic, and cream cheese until smooth. Spoon 1 teaspoon of the mixture into each mushroom. Place mushrooms on parchment paper.
4. In a separate small bowl, stir together bread crumbs and remaining oil. Sprinkle over tops of mushrooms.
5. Add the tender-crisp lid and select bake on 375°F. Cook mushrooms 15 minutes, or until tops are nicely browned and mushrooms are tender. Serve immediately.

Nutrition Info:

- Calories 121,Total Fat 6g,Total Carbs 10g,Protein 7g,Sodium 191mg.

Steak And Minty Cheese

Servings: 4
Cooking Time: 15 Min

Ingredients:

- 2 New York strip steaks
- 8 oz. halloumi cheese /240g
- 12 kalamata olives
- Juice and zest of 1 lemon
- Olive oil
- 2 tbsp chopped parsley /30g
- 2 tbsp chopped mint /30g
- Salt and pepper, to taste

Directions:

1. Season the steaks with salt and pepper, and gently brush with olive oil. Place into the Ninja Foodi, close the crisping lid and cook for 6 minutes (for medium rare) on Air Crisp mode at 350 °F or 177°C. When ready, remove to a plate and set aside.
2. Drizzle the cheese with olive oil and place it in the Ninja Foodi; cook for 4 minutes.
3. Remove to a serving platter and serve with sliced steaks and olives, sprinkled with herbs, and lemon zest and juice.

Jalapeno Meatballs

Servings: 8
Cooking Time: 10 Minutes

Ingredients:

- 1 lb. lean ground beef
- ¾ lb. ground pork
- ½ cup panko bread crumbs
- 1 egg, beaten
- 2 tbsp. jalapenos, diced fine
- 1¼ tsp cumin
- 1 onion, grated
- 28 oz. tomatoes, crushed

- ½ cup fresh cilantro, chopped fine
- 2 tsp garlic, diced fine
- 1 tsp red pepper flakes
- ½ tsp cinnamon

Directions:

1. In a large bowl, combine beef, pork, bread crumbs, egg, jalapeno, cumin, and cinnamon. Mix well then form into meatballs.
2. Add the onion, tomatoes, cilantro, garlic, and red pepper flakes to the cooking pot. Place the meatballs in the sauce.
3. Add the lid and select pressure cooking on low. Set the timer for 10 minutes. When the timer goes off, use quick release to remove the lid.
4. Transfer meatballs to serving plate and top with sauce. Serve immediately.

Nutrition Info:

- Calories 412,Total Fat 22g,Total Carbs 14g,Protein 38g,Sodium 320mg.

Broccoli Turmeric Tots

Servings: 8
Cooking Time: 8 Minutes

Ingredients:

- 1-pound broccoli
- 3 cups of water
- 1 teaspoon salt
- 1 egg
- 1 cup pork rind
- ½ teaspoon paprika
- 1 tablespoon turmeric
- ⅓ cup almond flour
- 2 tablespoons olive oil

Directions:

1. Wash the broccoli and chop it roughly.
2. Put the broccoli in the Ninja Foodi's insert and add water.
3. Set the Ninja Foodi's insert to "Steam" mode and steam the broccoli for 20 minutes.
4. Remove the broccoli from the Ninja Foodi's insert and let it cool.
5. Transfer the broccoli to a blender. Add egg, salt, paprika, turmeric, and almond flour.
6. Blend the mixture until smooth. Add pork rind and blend the broccoli mixture for 1 minute more.
7. Pour the olive oil in the Ninja Foodi's insert.
8. Form the medium tots from the broccoli mixture and transfer them to the Ninja Foodi's insert.
9. Set the Ninja Foodi's insert to "Sauté" mode and cook for 4 minutes on each side.
10. Once the dish is done, remove the broccoli tots from the Ninja Foodi's insert.
11. Allow them to rest before serving.

Nutrition Info:

- Calories: 147; Fat: 9.9g; Carbohydrates: 4.7g; Protein: 11.6g

Jalapeno Salsa

Servings: 10
Cooking Time: 7 Minutes

Ingredients:

- 8 ounces jalapeno pepper
- ¼ cup Erythritol
- 5 tablespoon water
- 2 tablespoons butter
- 1 teaspoon paprika

Directions:

1. Wash the jalapeno pepper and remove the seeds.
2. Slice it into thin circles. Sprinkle the sliced jalapeno pepper with paprika and Erythritol.
3. Put the butter and jalaeno mixture into the Ninja Foodi's insert and add water.
4. Set the Ninja Foodi's insert to" Sauté" mode.
5. Once the butter melts, add the sliced jalapeno in the Ninja Foodi's insert.
6. Close the Ninja Foodi's lid and sauté the dish for 7 minutes.
7. Once done, remove the dish from the Ninja Foodi's insert.
8. Cool it and serve.

Nutrition Info:

- Calories: 28; Fat: 2.5g; Carbohydrates: 7.5g; Protein: 0.4g

Asparagus Fries With Chipotle Dip

Servings: 4
Cooking Time: 10 Minutes

Ingredients:

- Nonstick cooking spray
- 1 lb. asparagus, ends trimmed
- 1/3 cup panko bread crumbs
- ¼ cup parmesan cheese
- ¼ tsp pepper
- ½ tsp salt, divided
- 1/8 tsp garlic powder
- 1/8 tsp cayenne pepper
- 3 tbsp. skim milk
- 1 cup Greek yogurt
- 1 tbsp. chipotle peppers, pureed
- 1 clove garlic, diced fine

Directions:

1. Lightly spray fryer basket with cooking spray.
2. In a small bowl, combine bread crumbs, parmesan, pepper, salt, garlic powder, and cayenne pepper, mix well.
3. Pour milk in a shallow dish.

4. Dip asparagus in the milk then dredge in crumb mixture, pressing crumbs to stick. Place asparagus in a single layer in the basket.
5. Place the basket in the cooking pot and add the tender-crisp lid. Select air fry on 425°F. Cook 8-10 minutes until golden brown, turning halfway through cooking time. Repeat with remaining asparagus.
6. In a small bowl, stir together yogurt, peppers, garlic, and remaining salt. Serve with fried asparagus for dipping.

Nutrition Info:

- Calories 133,Total Fat 5g,Total Carbs 16g,Protein 8g,Sodium 505mg.

Sweet Potato And Beetroot Chips

Servings:1
Cooking Time: 8 Hours

Ingredients:

- ½ small beet, peeled and cut into ⅛-inch slices
- ½ small sweet potato, peeled and cut into ⅛-inch slices
- ½ tablespoon extra-virgin olive oil
- ½ teaspoon sea salt

Directions:

1. In a large bowl, toss the beet slices with half the olive oil until evenly coated. Repeat, in a separate bowl, with the sweet potato slices and the rest of the olive oil (if you don't mind pink sweet potatoes, you can toss them together in one bowl). Season with salt.
2. Arrange the beet slices flat in a single layer in the bottom of the pot. Arrange the sweet potato slices flat in a single layer on the Reversible Rack in the lower position. Place rack in pot and close crisping lid.
3. Select DEHYDRATE, set temperature to 135°F, and set time to 8 hours. Select START/STOP to begin.
4. When dehydrating is complete, remove rack from pot. Transfer the beet and sweet potato chips to an airtight container.

Nutrition Info:

- Calories: 221,Total Fat: 7g,Sodium: 1057mg,Carbohydrates: 36g,Protein: 4g.

Cheesy Stuffed Mushroom

Servings: 7
Cooking Time: 7 Minutes

Ingredients:

- 12 ounces Parmesan cheese
- 7 mushroom caps
- 2 teaspoons minced garlic
- ¼ sour cream
- 1 teaspoon butter
- 1 teaspoon ground white pepper
- 2 teaspoons oregano

Directions:

1. Mix the minced garlic, sour cream, ground white pepper, and oregano, and stir the mixture.
2. Add grated parmesan to the minced garlic mixture.
3. Blend the mixture until smooth.
4. Stuff the mushrooms with the cheese mixture and place the dish in the Ninja Foodi's insert.
5. Set the Ninja Foodi's insert to "Pressure" mode, add butter, and close the Ninja Foodi's lid.
6. Cook the dish for 7 minutes.
7. Once done, remove it from the Ninja Foodi's insert, let it rest briefly, and serve.

Nutrition Info:

- Calories: 203; Fat: 7.6g; Carbohydrates: 8.35g; Protein: 8g

Chocolate Chip & Zucchini Snack Bars

Servings: 12
Cooking Time: 30 Minutes

Ingredients:

- Nonstick cooking spray
- 1 ¼ cup oat flour
- ¼ cup + 2 tbsp. coconut flour
- ¼ cup oats
- 1 ½ tsp baking powder
- ½ tsp baking soda
- ½ tsp cinnamon
- ¼ tsp salt
- 2 bananas, mashed
- 1 cup zucchini, grated
- ½ cup almond milk, unsweetened
- ¼ cup applesauce, unsweetened
- 2 tsp vanilla
- ¾ cup chocolate chips, sugar free

Directions:

1. Set to air fryer on 350°F. Lightly spray an 8-inch square baking pan with cooking spray.
2. In a large bowl, combine both flours, oats, baking powder, baking soda, cinnamon, and salt.
3. In a medium bowl, whisk together bananas, zucchini, milk, applesauce, and vanilla. Add to dry ingredients and mix just until combined.
4. Fold in chocolate chips and pour into prepared pan.
5. Add the rack to the cooking pot and place the pan on it. Add the tender-crisp lid and bake 30-35 minutes or until toothpick inserted in center comes out clean.
6. Let cool in pan 10 minutes then cut into 12 bars.
7. Preheat oven to 350F. Lightly grease a 9×9 baking pan with cooking spray or oil.

Nutrition Info:

- Calories 194,Total Fat 7g,Total Carbs 27g,Protein 5g,Sodium 168mg.

Spicy Turkey Meatballs

Servings: 8
Cooking Time: 15 Minutes
Ingredients:

- 1 lb. lean ground turkey
- 1 onion, chopped fine
- ¼ cup shredded wheat cereal, crushed
- 2 egg whites
- ½ tsp garlic powder
- ½ tsp salt
- ¼ tsp pepper
- Nonstick cooking spray
- ¼ cup jalapeno pepper jelly

Directions:

1. In a large bowl, combine all ingredients, except pepper jelly, and mix well. Form into 24 1-inch meatballs.
2. Lightly spray the fryer basket with cooking spray. Place meatballs in a single layer in the basket, these will need to be cooked in batches.
3. Add the basket to the cooking pot and secure the tender crisp lid. Set to air fry on 400°F. Cook meatballs 12-15 minutes, until no longer pink inside, turning halfway through cooking time.
4. Place the pepper jelly in a medium, microwave safe bowl. Microwave in 30 second intervals until the jelly is melted.
5. Toss cooked meatballs in the melted pepper jelly and serve immediately.
6. In a medium bowl, combine the turkey, onion, cereal, egg whites, garlic powder, salt, and black pepper. Shape into 24 one-inch meatballs.

Nutrition Info:

- Calories 113,Total Fat 5g,Total Carbs 6g,Protein 12g,Sodium 199mg.

Desserts

Mixed Berry Cobbler

Servings: 4
Cooking Time: 40 Min
Ingredients:

- 2 bags frozen mixed berries
- 1 cup sugar /130g
- 3 tbsps arrowroot starch /45g
- For the topping
- 1 cup self-rising flour /130g
- ⅔ cup crème fraiche, plus more as needed /177ml
- 1 tbsp melted unsalted butter /15ml
- 1 tbsp whipping cream /15ml
- 5 tbsps powdered sugar; divided /75g
- ¼ tsp cinnamon powder /1.25g

Directions:

1. To make the base, pour the blackberries into the inner pot along with the arrowroot starch and sugar. Mix to combine. Seal the pressure lid, choose Pressure; adjust the pressure to High and the cook time to 3 minutes; press Start. After cooking, perform a quick pressure release and carefully open the lid.
2. To make the topping, in a small bowl, whisk the flour, cinnamon powder, and 3 tbsps of sugar. In a separate small bowl, whisk the crème fraiche with the melted butter.
3. Pour the cream mixture on the dry ingredients and combine evenly. If the mixture is too dry, mix in 1 tbsp of crème fraiche at a time until the mixture is soft.
4. Spoon 2 to 3 tbsps of dough on top over the peaches and spread out slightly on top. Brush the topping with the whipping cream and sprinkle with the remaining sugar.
5. Close the crisping lid and Choose Bake/Roast; adjust the temperature to 325°F or 163°Cand the cook time to 12 minutes. Press Start. Check after 8 minutes; if the dough isn't cooking evenly, rotate the pot about 90 , and continue cooking.
6. When ready, the topping should be cooked through and lightly browned. Allow cooling before slicing. Serve warm.

Cherry Cheesecake

Servings:8
Cooking Time: 30 Minutes
Ingredients:

- 4 packages cream cheese, at room temperature
- 1 cup granulated sugar
- 3 tablespoons cornstarch
- 3 whole eggs
- 2 egg yolks
- ¼ cup heavy (whipping) cream
- 1 teaspoon kosher salt
- 1½ cups crushed graham crackers
- ½ cup unsalted butter, melted

- 1 cup water
- 1 can cherries in syrup

Directions:

1. In a large bowl, combine the cream cheese, sugar, cornstarch, eggs, egg yolks, cream, and salt. Use an electric mixer to mix until smooth and velvety.
2. In a medium bowl, combine the graham crackers and melted butter until it resembles wet sand.
3. Line the inside of the Ninja Multi-Purpose Pan or another 9-inch round baking dish with plastic wrap. Ensure the wrap is flush to the bottom of the dish and comes fully up the sides of the pan.
4. Place the graham cracker mixture in the center of the dish. Use a silicone-tipped spatula to press the mix outward. The mix should lay completely and evenly across the bottom of the dish.
5. Pour the cheesecake batter over the crust, then use the spatula to evenly smooth it out. Tightly wrap the top of the baking dish with a new piece of plastic wrap so that the cheesecake is completely covered.
6. Place the cheesecake on Reversible Rack, making sure it is in the lower steam position. Place rack with pan in pot. Pour the water into the pot. Assemble pressure lid, making sure the pressure release valve is in the SEAL position.
7. Select PRESSURE and set to HI. Set time to 30 minutes. Select START/STOP to begin.
8. When pressure cooking is complete, allow pressure to naturally release for 10 minutes. After 10 minutes, quick release remaining pressure by moving the pressure release valve to the VENT position. Carefully remove lid when unit has finished releasing pressure.
9. Remove top layer of plastic wrap from the cheesecake. Refrigerate the cheesecake to completely cool, at least 4 hours.
10. When ready to serve, remove the cheesecake from the refrigerator and place on a serving dish or cutting board. Use top edges of the remaining plastic wrap to remove cheesecake from the pan. Pull the plastic wrap out from underneath cheesecake. Top the cheesecake with the cherries in syrup as desired and serve.

Nutrition Info:

- Calories: 789,Total Fat: 58g,Sodium: 760mg,Carbohydrates: 57g,Protein: 13g.

Caramel Pecan Coffee Cake

Servings: 16

Cooking Time: 35 Minutes

Ingredients:

- Butter flavored cooking spray
- 3 cups almond flour, sifted
- 1 tsp baking powder
- 1 tsp baking soda
- ½ teaspoon salt
- ½ cup butter, softened
- ½ cup Stevia
- 3 eggs
- ½ cup almond milk, unsweetened
- 1 tsp vanilla
- ½ cup caramel sauce, sugar free, divided
- ½ cup pecans, chopped, divided

Directions:

1. Place the rack in the cooking pot. Spray a Bundt pan with cooking spray.
2. In a medium bowl, combine flour, baking powder, baking soda, and salt, mix well.
3. In a large bowl, beat butter and Stevia until fluffy.
4. Beat in eggs, milk, and vanilla. Stir in dry ingredients just until combined.
5. Pour half the batter in the prepared pan. Top with half the caramel sauce and half the pecans. Use a butter knife to lightly swirl sauce and nuts into the batter. Top with remaining batter.
6. Place the pan and on the rack and add the tender-crisp lid. Set to air fry on 325 °F. Bake 35-40 minutes or until coffee cake passes the toothpick test.
7. Let cool in pan 15 minutes, then invert onto serving plate. Drizzle with remaining caramel sauce and sprinkle with remaining nut. Serve.

Nutrition Info:

- Calories 119,Total Fat 9g,Total Carbs 15g,Protein 2g,Sodium 250mg.

Blackberry Crisp

Servings: 6

Cooking Time: 45 Minutes

Ingredients:

- 6 cups blackberries
- 2 tbsp. sugar, divided
- 1 tbsp. cornstarch
- 1 cup oats
- ½ cup almond flour
- ½ cup almonds, chopped
- 1 tsp cinnamon
- ¼ tsp salt
- ¼ cup coconut oil, melted

Directions:

1. Add the rack to the cooking pot. Spray an 8-inch baking dish with cooking spray.
2. In a large bowl, add the blackberries, 1 tablespoon sugar, and cornstarch, toss to coat. Pour into prepared dish.
3. In the same bowl, combine oats, flour, nuts, cinnamon, salt, coconut oil, and remaining sugar, mix well. Pour over berries.
4. Place the dish on the rack. Add the tender-crisp lid and set to bake on 350°F. Bake 30-35 minutes or until top is golden brown. Transfer to wire rack to cool before serving.

Nutrition Info:

- Calories 282,Total Fat 13g,Total Carbs 38g,Protein 6g,Sodium 100mg.

Strawberry Crumble

Servings: 5
Cooking Time: 2 Hours
Ingredients:

- 1 cup almond flour
- 2 tablespoons butter, melted
- 10 drops liquid stevia
- 4 cups fresh strawberries, hulled and sliced
- 1 tablespoon butter, chopped

Directions:

1. Lightly, grease the Ninja Foodi's insert.
2. In a suitable, stir in the flour, melted butter and stevia and mix until a crumbly mixture form.
3. In the pot of the prepared Ninja Foodi, place the strawberry slices and dot with chopped butter.
4. Spread the flour mixture on top evenly
5. Close the Ninja Foodi's lid with a crisping lid and select "Slow Cooker".
6. Set on "Low" for 2 hours.
7. Press the "Start/Stop" button to initiate cooking.
8. Place the pan onto a wire rack to cool slightly.
9. Serve warm.

Nutrition Info:

- Calories: 233; Fats: 19.2g; Carbohydrates: 10.7g; Proteins: 0.7g

Mexican Chocolate Walnut Cake

Servings: 8
Cooking Time: 2 ½ Hours
Ingredients:

- Butter flavored cooking spray
- 1½ cups flour
- ½ cup cocoa powder, unsweetened
- 2 tsp baking powder
- 2 tsp ground cinnamon
- ¼ tsp cayenne pepper
- 1/8 tsp salt
- 1 cup sugar
- 3 eggs, beaten
- ¾ cup coconut oil melted
- 2 tsp vanilla
- 2 cups zucchini, grated
- ¾ cup walnuts, chopped, divided

Directions:

1. Spray the cooking pot with cooking spray and line the bottom with parchment paper.
2. In a medium bowl, combine dry ingredients and mix well.
3. In a large bowl, beat sugar and eggs until creamy.
4. Stir in oil, vanilla, zucchini, and ½ cup walnuts until combined. Fold in dry ingredients just until combined.
5. Pour batter into cooking pot and sprinkle remaining nuts over the top. Add the lid and set to slow cooking on high. Cook 2 ½ hours or until cake passes the toothpick test. Transfer cake to a wire rack to cool before serving.

Nutrition Info:

- Calories 452,Total Fat 28g,Total Carbs 48g,Protein 7g,Sodium 189mg.

Raspberry Cobbler

Servings: 8
Cooking Time: 2 Hours
Ingredients:

- 1 cup almond flour
- ¼ cup coconut flour
- ¾ cup Erythritol
- 1 teaspoon baking soda
- ¼ teaspoon ground cinnamon
- 1/8 teaspoon salt
- ¼ cup unsweetened coconut milk
- 2 tablespoons coconut oil
- 1 large egg, beaten lightly
- 4 cups fresh raspberries

Directions:

1. Grease the Ninja Foodi's insert.
2. In a large bowl, mix together flours, Erythritol, baking soda, cinnamon and salt.
3. In another bowl, stir in the coconut milk, coconut oil and egg and beat until well combined.
4. Add the prepared egg mixture into the flour mixture and mix until just combined.
5. In the pot of the prepared Ninja Foodi, add the mixture evenly and top with raspberries.
6. Close the Ninja Foodi's lid with a crisping lid and select "Slow Cooker".
7. Set on "Low" for 2 hours.
8. Press the "Start/Stop" button to initiate cooking.
9. Place the pan onto a wire rack to cool slightly.
10. Serve warm.

Nutrition Info:

- Calories: 164; Fats: 12.5g; Carbohydrates: 10.9g; Proteins: 4.7

Raspberry Lemon Cheesecake

Servings: 8
Cooking Time: 30 Minutes

Ingredients:

- Butter flavored cooking spray
- 8 oz. cream cheese, fat free, soft
- 1/3 cup sugar
- ½ tsp lemon juice
- 1 tsp lemon zest
- ½ tsp vanilla
- ½ cup plain Greek yogurt
- 2 eggs, room temperature
- 2 tbsp. white whole wheat flour
- Fresh raspberries for garnish

Directions:

1. Spray an 8-inch baking dish with cooking spray.
2. In a large bowl, beat cream cheese, sugar, lemon juice, zest, and vanilla until smooth.
3. Add yogurt, eggs, and flour and mix well. Spoon into prepared pan.
4. Place pan in the cooking pot and add the tender-crisp lid. Set to bake on 350°F. Bake 25-30 minutes or until cheesecake passes the toothpick test.
5. Transfer to a wire rack to cool. Cover with plastic wrap and refrigerate 2-3 hours. Serve garnished with fresh raspberries.

Nutrition Info:

- Calories 93,Total Fat 6g,Total Carbs 14g,Protein 5g,Sodium 127mg.

Egg Custard

Servings: 4
Cooking Time: 20 Min

Ingredients:

- 1 Egg plus 2 Egg yolks
- ½ cups Milk /125ml
- 2 cups Heavy Cream /500ml
- 2 cups Water /500ml
- ½ cup Sugar /65g
- ½ tsp pure rum extract /2.5ml

Directions:

1. Beat the egg and the egg yolks in a bowl. Gently add pure rum extract. Mix in the milk and heavy cream. Give it a good, and add the sugar. Pour this mixture into 4 ramekins.
2. Add 2 cups or 500ml of water, insert the reversible rack, and lay the ramekins on the reversible rack. Choose Pressure, set to High, and set the time to 10 minutes. Press Start. Do a quick pressure release. Wait a bit before removing from ramekins.

Apple Cider

Servings: 6
Cooking Time: 45 Min

Ingredients:

- 6 green apples, cored and chopped
- 1/4 cup orange juice /62.5ml
- 3 cups water /750ml
- 2 cinnamon sticks

Directions:

1. In a blender, add orange juice, apples, and water and blend until smooth; use a fine-mesh strainer to strain and press using a spoon. Get rid of the pulp. In the cooker, mix the strained apple puree, and cinnamon sticks.
2. Seal the pressure lid, choose Pressure, set to High, and set the timer to 10 minutes. Press Start. Release the pressure naturally for 15 minutes, then quick release the remaining pressure. Strain again and do away with the solids.

Hazelnut Cheesecake

Servings:8
Cooking Time: 25 Minutes

Ingredients:

- Unsalted butter, for greasing
- 1 store-bought premade graham cracker crust
- 2 packages cream cheese, at room temperature
- ¼ cup confectioners' sugar, sifted
- 2 eggs
- 1 jar hazelnut spread
- 1 cup water

Directions:

1. Grease the Ninja Multi-Purpose Pan with butter. Place the crust in the pan, crumbling as necessary to fit.
2. In a medium bowl, beat together the cream cheese, sugar, and eggs with a hand mixer until well incorporated. Add the hazelnut spread and beat until well combined. Add the cream cheese mixture over the crust.
3. Pour the water into the pot. Place Reversible Rack in pot, making sure it is in the lower position. Place pan on rack. Assemble pressure lid, making sure the pressure release valve is in the SEAL position.
4. Select PRESSURE and set to HI. Set time to 25 minutes. Select START/STOP to begin.
5. When pressure cooking is complete, allow pressure to naturally release for 10 minutes. After 10 minutes, quick release remaining pressure by moving the pressure release valve to the VENT position. Carefully remove lid when unit has finished releasing pressure.
6. Remove rack and pan from pot. Gently dab the top of the cheesecake with a paper towel to remove excess moisture. Refrigerate for at least 2 hours before serving.

Nutrition Info:

- Calories: 676,Total Fat: 47g,Sodium: 375mg,Carbohydrates: 57g,Protein: 9g.

Spiced Poached Pears

Servings: 4
Cooking Time: 4 Hours
Ingredients:

- 4 ripe pears, peeled
- 2 cups fresh orange juice
- ¼ cup maple syrup
- 5 cardamom pods
- 1 cinnamon stick, broke in 2
- 1-inch piece ginger, peeled & sliced

Directions:

1. Slice off the bottom of the pears so they stand upright. Carefully remove the core with a paring knife. Stand in the cooking pot.
2. In a small bowl, whisk together orange juice and syrup. Pour over pears and add the spices.
3. Add the lid and set to slow cooking on low. Cook 3-4 hours or until pears are soft. Baste the pears every hour or so.
4. Serve garnished with whipped cream and chopped walnuts if you like, or just serve them as they are sprinkled with a little cinnamon.

Nutrition Info:

- Calories 219,Total Fat 1g,Total Carbs 53g,Protein 2g,Sodium 6mg.

Almond Milk

Servings: 4
Cooking Time: 20 Min
Ingredients:

- 1 cup raw almonds; soaked overnight, rinsed and peeled /130g
- 2 dried apricots; chopped
- 1 cup cold water /250ml
- 4 cups water /1000ml
- 1 vanilla bean
- 2 tbsp honey /30ml

Directions:

1. In the pot, mix a cup of cold water with almonds and apricots. Seal the pressure lid, choose Pressure, set to High, and set the timer to 1 minute.
2. When ready, release the pressure quickly. Open the lid. The almonds should be soft and plump, and the water should be brown and murky. Use a strainer to drain almonds; rinse with cold water for 1 minute.
3. To a high-speed blender, add the rinsed almonds, vanilla bean, honey, and 4 cups or 1000ml water. Blend for 2 minutes until well combined and frothy. Line a cheesecloth to the strainer.
4. Place the strainer over a bowl and strain the milk. Use a wooden spoon to press milk through the cheesecloth and get rid of solids. Place almond milk in an airtight container and refrigerate.

Carrot Cake

Servings: 8
Cooking Time: 40 Minutes
Ingredients:

- Butter flavored cooking spray
- 3 eggs
- 1 cup almond flour, sifted
- 1/3 cup Stevia
- 1 tsp baking powder
- 1 tsp apple pie spice
- ¼ cup coconut oil, melted
- ½ cup + 1 tbsp. heavy cream
- 1 cup carrots, grated
- ½ cup walnuts, chopped
- 4 oz. cream cheese, soft
- ¼ cup butter, soft
- ½ tsp vanilla
- ½ - 1 cup powdered Stevia

Directions:

1. Lightly spray a 6x3-inch cake pan with cooking spray.
2. In a large bowl, beat eggs, flour, Stevia, baking powder, apple pie spice, oil, and ½ cup cream until fluffy.
3. Fold in carrots and nuts and pour into prepared pan.
4. Place in cooking pot and add tender-crisp lid. Set to bake on 350 °F. Bake 30-35 minutes or until cake passes the toothpick test. Transfer to wire rack and let cool 10 minutes in pan, then invert onto serving plate.
5. In a large bowl, beat cream cheese, butter, and remaining cream until smooth and creamy.
6. Stir in vanilla and enough powdered Stevia until frosting is thick enough to spread. Cut cake in half horizontally and spread with 1/3 of the frosting in the middle, then frost outside. Serve.

Nutrition Info:

- Calories 345,Total Fat 34g,Total Carbs 25g,Protein 8g,Sodium 137mg.

Strawberry And Lemon Ricotta Cheesecake

Servings: 6
Cooking Time: 35 Min
Ingredients:

- 10 strawberries, halved to decorate
- 10 oz. cream cheese /300g
- 1 ½ cups water /375ml
- ¼ cup sugar /32.5f
- ½ cup Ricotta cheese /65f
- One lemon, zested and juiced
- 2 eggs, cracked into a bowl
- 3 tbsp sour cream /45ml
- 1 tsp lemon extract /5g

Directions:

1. In the electric mixer, add the cream cheese, quarter cup of sugar, ricotta cheese, lemon zest, lemon juice, and lemon extract. Turn on the mixer and mix the ingredients until a smooth consistency is formed. Adjust the sweet taste to liking with more sugar.
2. Reduce the speed of the mixer and add the eggs. Fold it in at low speed until it is fully incorporated. Make sure not to fold the eggs in high speed to prevent a cracker crust. Grease the spring form pan with cooking spray and use a spatula to spoon the mixture into the pan. Level the top with the spatula and cover it with foil.
3. Open the Foodi, fit in the reversible rack, and pour in the water. Place the cake pan on the rack. Close the lid, secure the pressure valve, and select Pressure mode on High pressure for 15 minutes. Press Start/Stop.
4. Meanwhile, mix the sour cream and one tbsp of sugar. Set aside. Once the timer has gone off, do a natural pressure release for 10 minutes, then a quick pressure release to let out any extra steam, and open the lid.
5. Remove the rack with pan, place the spring form pan on a flat surface, and open it. Use a spatula to spread the sour cream mixture on the warm cake. Refrigerate the cake for 8 hours. Top with strawberries; slice it into 6 pieces and serve while firming.

Cherry Almond Bar Cookies

Servings: 9
Cooking Time: 15 Minutes

Ingredients:

- Butter flavored cooking spray
- ¼ cup dates
- 2 bananas
- 1 cup oats
- ½ cup cherries, dried, chopped
- ½ cup almond flour
- ½ cup almonds, chopped

Directions:

1. Place the rack in the cooking pot. Spray an 8x8-inch baking pan with cooking spray.
2. Place the dates in a food processor and pulse until they form a paste.
3. In a large bowl, mash the bananas with a fork.
4. Mix in remaining ingredients. Spread evenly in prepared pan.
5. Place the pan on the rack and add the tender-crisp lid. Set to bake on 325°F. Bake 15 minutes or until top is golden brown. Remove to wire rack to cool before cutting.

Nutrition Info:

- Calories 177,Total Fat 5g,Total Carbs 30g,Protein 5g,Sodium 2mg.

Delicious Almond And Apple

Servings: 4
Cooking Time: 14 Min

Ingredients:

- 3 Apples, peeled and diced
- ½ cup Milk /125ml
- ½ cup Almonds; chopped or slivered /65g
- ¼ tsp Cinnamon /1.25g

Directions:

1. Place all ingredients in the Foodi. Stir well to combine and seal the pressure lid. Cook on Pressure for 4 minutes at High. Release the pressure quickly. Divide the mixture among 4 serving bowls.

Sweet And Salty Bars

Servings:12
Cooking Time: 10 Minutes

Ingredients:

- 1 cup light corn syrup
- 1 cup granulated sugar
- 1 teaspoon vanilla extract
- 1 bag mini marshmallows
- 1 cup crunchy peanut butter
- 1 bag potato chips with ridges, slightly crushed
- 1 cup pretzels, slightly crushed
- 1 bag hard-shelled candy-coated chocolates

Directions:

1. Select SEAR/SAUTÉ and set temperature to MD:HI. Select START/STOP to begin. Let preheat for 5 minutes.
2. Add the corn syrup, sugar, and vanilla and stir until the sugar is melted.
3. Add the marshmallows and peanut butter and stir until the marshmallows are melted.
4. Add the potato chips and pretzels and stir until everything is evenly coated in the marshmallow mixture.
5. Pour the mixture into a 9-by-13-inch pan and place the chocolate candies on top, slightly pressing them in. Let cool, then cut into squares and serve.

Nutrition Info:

- Calories: 585,Total Fat: 21g,Sodium: 403mg,Carbohydrates: 96g,Protein: 9g.

Carrot Raisin Cookie Bars

Servings: 16
Cooking Time: 15 Minutes

Ingredients:

- Butter flavored cooking spray
- ½ cup brown sugar
- ½ cup sugar
- ½ cup coconut oil, melted
- ½ cup applesauce, unsweetened
- 2 eggs
- 1 tsp vanilla
- ½ cup almond flour
- 1 tsp baking soda
- 1 tsp baking powder

- ¼ tsp salt
- 1 tsp cinnamon
- ½ tsp nutmeg
- ½ tsp ginger
- 2 cups oats
- 1 ½ cups carrots, finely grated
- 1 cup raisins

Directions:

1. Place the rack in the cooking pot. Spray an 8x8-inch pan with cooking spray.
2. In a large bowl, combine sugars, oil, applesauce, eggs, and vanilla, mix well.
3. Stir in dry ingredients until combined. Fold in carrots and raisins. Press evenly in prepared pan.
4. Place the pan on the rack and add the tender-crisp lid. Set to bake on 350°F. Bake 12-15 minutes or until golden brown and cooked through.
5. Remove to wire rack to cool before cutting and serving.

Nutrition Info:

- Calories 115,Total Fat 7g,Total Carbs 19g,Protein 3g,Sodium 56mg.

Tres Leches Cake

Servings:8

Cooking Time: 38 Minutes

Ingredients:

- 1 box of yellow cake mix
- Cooking spray
- 1 can evaporated milk
- 1 can sweetened condensed milk
- 1 cup heavy (whipping) cream

Directions:

1. Close crisping lid. Select BAKE/ROAST, set temperature to 400°F, and set time to 43 minutes. Select START/STOP to begin. Let preheat for 5 minutes.
2. Prepare the cake batter according to the box instructions.
3. Grease a Ninja Multi-Purpose Pan or a 1½-quart round baking dish with cooking spray. Pour the batter into the pan. Place the pan on Reversible Rack, making sure rack is in the lower position.
4. Once unit has preheated, open lid and place rack with pan in pot. Close lid, and reduce temperature to 315°F. Cook for 38 minutes.
5. In a medium bowl whisk together the evaporated milk, condensed milk, and heavy cream.
6. When cooking is complete, remove rack with pan from pot and let cool for 10 minutes.
7. Remove pan from the rack. Using a long-pronged fork, poke holes every inch or so across the surface of the cake. Slowly pour the milk mixture over the cake. Refrigerate for 1 hour.
8. Once the cake has cooled and absorbed the milk mixture, slice and serve. If desired, top with whipped cream and strawberries.

Nutrition Info:

- Calories: 644,Total Fat: 28g,Sodium: 574mg,Carbohydrates: 89g,Protein: 12g.

Lemon Cheesecake

Servings: 12

Cooking Time: 4 Hours

Ingredients:

- For Crust:
- 1½ cups almond flour
- 4 tablespoons butter, melted
- 3 tablespoons sugar-free peanut butter
- 3 tablespoons Erythritol
- 1 large egg, beaten
- For Filling:
- 1 cup ricotta cheese
- 24 ounces cream cheese, softened
- 1½ cups Erythritol
- 2 teaspoons liquid stevia
- 1/3 cup heavy cream
- 2 large eggs
- 3 large egg yolks
- 1 tablespoon fresh lemon juice
- 1 tablespoon vanilla extract

Directions:

1. Grease the Ninja Foodi's insert.
2. For crust: in a suitable, add all the ingredients and mix until well combined.
3. In the pot of prepared of Ninja Foodi, place the crust mixture and press to smooth the top surface.
4. With a fork, prick the crust at many places.
5. For filling: in a food processor, stir in the ricotta cheese and pulse until smooth.
6. In a large bowl, add the ricotta, cream cheese, Erythritol and stevia and with an electric mixer, beat over medium speed until smooth.
7. In another bowl, stir in the heavy cream, eggs, egg yolks, lemon juice and vanilla extract and beat until well combined.
8. Stir in the egg mixture into cream cheese mixture and beat over medium speed until just combined.
9. Place the prepared filling mixture over the crust evenly.
10. Close the Ninja Foodi's lid with a crisping lid and select "Slow Cooker".
11. Set on "Low" for 3-4 hours.
12. Press the "Start/Stop" button to initiate cooking.
13. Place the pan onto a wire rack to cool.
14. Refrigerate to chill for at least 6-8 hours before serving.

Nutrition Info:

- Calories: 410; Fats: 37.9g; Carbohydrates: 6.9g; Proteins: 13g

Coconut Cream "custard" Bars

Servings:8
Cooking Time: 20 Minutes

Ingredients:

- 1¼ cups all-purpose flour
- 6 tablespoons unsalted butter, melted
- 2 tablespoons granulated sugar
- ½ cup unsweetened shredded coconut, divided
- ½ cup chopped almonds, divided
- Cooking spray
- 1 package instant vanilla pudding
- 1 cup milk
- 1 cup heavy (whipping) cream
- 4 tablespoons finely chopped dark chocolate, divided

Directions:

1. Select BAKE/ROAST, set temperature to 375°F, and set time to 15 minutes. Select START/STOP to begin. Let preheat for 5 minutes.
2. To make the crust, combine the flour, butter, sugar, ¼ cup of coconut, and ¼ cup of almonds in a large bowl and stir until a crumbly dough forms.
3. Grease the Ninja Multi-Purpose Pan or an 8-inch round baking dish with cooking spray. Place the dough in the pan and press it into an even layer covering the bottom.
4. Once unit has preheated, place pan on Reversible Rack, making sure the rack is in the lower position. Open lid and place rack in pot. Close crisping lid. Reduce temperature to 325°F.
5. Place remaining ¼ cup each of almonds and coconut in a Ninja Loaf Pan or any small loaf pan and set aside.
6. When cooking is complete, remove rack with pan and let cool for 10 minutes.
7. Quickly place the loaf pan with coconut and almonds in the bottom of the pot. Close crisping lid.
8. Select AIR CRISP, set temperature to 350°F, and set time to 10 minutes. Select START/STOP to begin.
9. While the nuts and coconut toast, whisk together the instant pudding with the milk, cream, and 3 tablespoons of chocolate.
10. After 5 minutes, open lid and stir the coconut and almonds. Close lid and continue cooking for another 5 minutes.
11. When cooking is complete, open lid and remove pan from pot. Add the almonds and coconut to the pudding. Stir until fully incorporated. Pour this in a smooth, even layer on top of the crust.
12. Refrigerate for about 10 minutes. Garnish with the remaining 1 tablespoon of chocolate, cut into wedges, and serve.

Nutrition Info:

- Calories: 476,Total Fat: 33g,Sodium: 215mg,Carbohydrates: 39g,Protein: 6g.

Cinnamon Apple Cake

Servings: 10
Cooking Time: 40 Minutes

Ingredients:

- Butter flavored cooking spray
- ½ cup coconut oil, soft
- ½ cup + 1 tbsp. honey, divided
- 1 egg
- 1 tsp vanilla
- 1¼ cups + 2 tbsp. whole wheat flour, divided
- 1 tsp baking powder
- ½ tsp baking soda
- 2 tsp cinnamon, divided
- ½ tsp salt
- 2 cups apple, chopped
- ¼ cup oats
- ½ cup pecans, chopped

Directions:

1. Spray an 8-inch cake pan with cooking spray.
2. In a large bowl, beat together oil, ½ cup honey, egg, and vanilla until smooth.
3. In a medium bowl, stir together 1 ¼ cups flour, baking powder, baking soda, 1 teaspoon cinnamon, and salt.
4. Add apples to dry ingredients and toss to combine. And mixture to wet ingredients and mix well. Pour into prepared pan.
5. In a small bowl, combine remaining flour, cinnamon, oats, pecans, and 1 tablespoon honey and mix well. Sprinkle over the top of the cake batter.
6. Add the cake to the cooking pot along with the tender-crisp lid. Set to bake on 325°F. Bake 35-40 minutes until edges begin to brown.
7. Transfer to a wire rack and let cool in the pan 10 minutes. Then invert onto serving plate and let cool completely before serving.

Nutrition Info:

- Calories 267,Total Fat 16g,Total Carbs 31g,Protein 3g,Sodium 111mg.

Brown Sugar And Butter Bars

Servings: 6
Cooking Time: 55 Min

Ingredients:

- 1 ½ cups Water /375ml
- 1 cup Oats /130g
- ½ cup Brown Sugar /65g
- ½ cup Sugar /65g
- 1 cup Flour /130g
- ½ cup Peanut Butter, softened /65g
- ½ cup Butter, softened /65g
- 1 Egg
- ½ tsp Baking Soda /2.5g

- ½ tsp Salt /2.5g

Directions:

1. Grease a springform pan and line it with parchment paper. Set aside. Beat together the eggs, peanut butter, butter, salt, white sugar, and brown sugar. Fold in the oats, flour, and baking soda.
2. Press the batter into the pan. Cover the pan with a paper towel and with a piece of foil. Pour the water into the Foodi and add a reversible rack. Lower the springform pan onto the rack.
3. Seal the pressure lid, choose Pressure, set to High, and set the time to 35 minutes. Press Start. When ready, do a quick release. Wait for 15 minutes before inverting onto a plate and cutting into bars.

Cranberry Pie

Servings: 8

Cooking Time: 35 Minutes

Ingredients:

- Nonstick cooking spray
- ¾ cup flour
- ½ cup sugar
- ¼ tsp salt
- 2 cups cranberries
- 1/3 cup walnuts, chopped
- ½ stick butter, melted
- ½ cup liquid egg substitute
- 1 tsp almond extract

Directions:

1. Place the rack in the cooking pot. Spray an 8-inch pie plate with cooking spray.
2. In a large bowl, stir together flour, sugar, and salt.
3. Add cranberries and walnuts and toss to coat.
4. Add butter, egg substitute, and almond extract and mix well. Spread in prepared pan and place on the rack.
5. Add the tender-crisp lid and set to bake on 350°F. Bake 30-35 minutes or until pie passes the toothpick test. Transfer to wire rack to cool.

Nutrition Info:

- Calories 145,Total Fat 9g,Total Carbs 27g,Protein 4g,Sodium 149mg.

Coconut Cream Dessert Bars

Servings: 10

Cooking Time: 2 Hour

Ingredients:

- Butter flavored cooking spray
- 1 cup heavy cream
- ¾ cup powdered Stevia
- 4 eggs
- ½ cup coconut milk, full fat
- ¼ cup butter, melted
- 1 cup coconut, unsweetened, grated
- 3 tbsp. coconut flour
- ½ tsp baking powder
- ½ tsp vanilla
- ½ tsp salt

Directions:

1. Spray cooking pot with cooking spray.
2. Place cream, Stevia, and coconut milk in a food processor or blender. Pulse until combined.
3. Add remaining ingredients and pulse until combined.
4. Pour mixture into cooking pot. Place two paper towels over the top. Add the lid and set to slow cooking on high. Cook 1-3 hours or until center is set.
5. Carefully remove lid so no moisture gets on the bars. Transfer cooking pot to a wire rack and let cool 30 minutes.
6. Refrigerate, uncovered at least 1 hour. Cut into 10 squares or bars and serve.

Nutrition Info:

- Calories 190,Total Fat 17g,Total Carbs 24g,Protein 4g,Sodium 236mg.

Cranberry Cheesecake

Servings: 8

Cooking Time: 1 Hr

Ingredients:

- 1/3 cup dried cranberries /44g
- 1 cup water /250ml
- ½ cup sugar /65g
- 1 cup coarsely crumbled cookies/ 130g
- 1 cup mascarpone cheese, room temperature /130g
- 2 eggs, room temperature
- 2 tbsp sour cream /30ml
- 2 tbsp butter, melted /30ml
- ½ tsp vanilla extract /2.5ml

Directions:

1. Fold a 20-inch piece of aluminum foil in half lengthwise twice and set on the pressure cooker. In a bowl, combine melted butter and crushed cookies; press firmly to the bottom and about 1/3 of the way up the sides of a 7-inch springform pan. Freeze the crust while the filling is being prepared.
2. In a separate bowl, beat together mascarpone cheese and sugar to obtain a smooth consistency; stir in vanilla extract and sour cream. Beat one egg and add into the cheese mixture to combine well; do the same with the second egg.
3. Stir cranberries into the filling. Transfer the filling into the crust. Into the pot, add water and set the reversible rack at the bottom. Center the springform pan onto the prepared foil sling. Use the sling to lower the pan onto the reversible rack.
4. Fold foil strips out of the way of the lid. Close the crisping lid and select Bake/Roast; adjust the temperature to 250°F or 122°C and the cook time to 40 minutes. Press Start.

5. When the time is up, open the lid and let to cool the cheesecake. When, transfer the cheesecake to a refrigerator for 2 hours or overnight.
6. Use a paring knife to run along the edges between the pan and cheesecake to remove the cheesecake and set to the plate.

Pineapple Cake

Servings: 4
Cooking Time: 50 Min

Ingredients:

- 2 oz. dark chocolate, grated /60g
- 4 oz. butter /120g
- 7 oz. pineapple chunks /210g
- 8 oz. self-rising flour /240g
- ½ cup sugar /65g
- 1 egg
- ½ cup pineapple juice /125ml
- 2 tbsp milk /30ml

Directions:

1. Preheat the Foodi to 390 °F or 199°C. Place the butter and flour into a bowl and rub the mixture with your fingers until crumbed. Stir in the pineapple, sugar, chocolate, and juice. Beat the eggs and milk separately, and then add them to the batter.
2. Transfer the batter to a previously prepared (greased or lined) cake pan, and cook for 40 minutes on Roast mode. Let cool for at least 10 minutes before serving.

Orange Banana Bread

Servings: 12
Cooking Time: 45 Min

Ingredients:

- 3 ripe Bananas, mashed
- 1 cup Milk /250ml
- 1 ¼ cups Sugar /162.5g
- 2 cups all-purpose Flour /260g
- 1 stick Butter, room temperature
- 1 tbsp Orange Juice /15ml
- 1 tsp Baking Soda /5g
- 1 tsp Baking Powder /5g
- ¼ tsp Cinnamon /1.25g
- ½ tsp Pure Vanilla Extract /2.5ml
- A pinch of Salt

Directions:

1. In a bowl, mix together the flour, baking powder, baking soda, sugar, vanilla, and salt. Add in the bananas, cinnamon, and orange juice. Slowly stir in the butter and milk. Give it a good stir until everything is well combined. Pour the batter into a medium-sized round pan.
2. Place the reversible rack at the bottom of the Foodi and fill with 2 cups of water. Place the pan on the reversible rack. Seal the pressure lid, select Pressure and and set the time to 40 minutes at High. Press Start. Do a quick pressure release.

Chocolate Chip Brownies

Servings: 16
Cooking Time: 20 Minutes

Ingredients:

- Butter flavored cooking spray
- 3 bananas, mashed
- 1 egg
- ½ tsp vanilla
- ¼ cup dark cocoa powder
- ¼ cup chocolate chips, sugar free

Directions:

1. Place the rack in the cooking pot. Spray an 8x8-inch baking pan with cooking spray.
2. In a large bowl, combine bananas, egg, vanilla, and cocoa powder, mix well. Fold in chocolate chips and spread evenly in prepared pan.
3. Place the pan on the rack and add tender-crisp lid. Set to bake on 350°F. Bake 15-20 minutes or until top is firm.
4. Transfer to wire rack and let cool completely. Cover and refrigerate at least one hour before cutting.

Nutrition Info:

- Calories 91,Total Fat 5g,Total Carbs 10g,Protein 2g,Sodium 7mg.

Sugar Cookie Pizza

Servings:6
Cooking Time: 35 Minutes

Ingredients:

- 22 ounces premade sugar cookie dough
- 5 tablespoons unsalted butter, at room temperature
- 1 package cream cheese, at room temperature
- 2 cups confectioners' sugar
- 1 teaspoon vanilla extract

Directions:

1. Select BAKE/ROAST, set temperature to 325°F, and set time to 40 minutes. Select START/STOP to begin. Let preheat for 5 minutes.
2. Press the cookie dough into the Ninja Multi-Purpose Pan in an even layer.
3. Once unit is preheated, place the pan on the Reversible Rack and place rack in the pot. Close crisping lid and cook for 35 minutes.
4. Once cooking is complete, remove the pan from the pot. Let cool in the refrigerator for 30 minutes.
5. In a large bowl, whisk together the butter, cream cheese, confectioners' sugar, and vanilla.
6. Once the cookie is chilled, carefully remove it from the pan. Using a spatula, spread the cream cheese mixture over cookie. Chill in the refrigerator for another 30 minutes.

7. Decorate with toppings of choice, such as sliced strawberries, raspberries, blueberries, blackberries, sliced kiwi, sliced mango, or sliced pineapple. Cut and serve.

Nutrition Info:

- Calories: 791,Total Fat: 44g,Sodium: 551mg,Carbohydrates: 92g,Protein: 7g.

Vanilla Hot Lava Cake

Servings: 8

Cooking Time: 40 Min

Ingredients:

- 1 ½ cups chocolate chips /195g
- 1 ½ cups sugar /195g
- 1 cup butter /130g
- 1 cup water /250ml
- 5 eggs
- 7 tbsp flour/105g
- 4 tbsp milk /60ml
- 4 tsp vanilla extract /20ml
- Powdered sugar to garnish

Directions:

1. Grease the cake pan with cooking spray and set aside. Open the Foodi, fit the reversible rack at the bottom of it, and pour in the water. In a medium heatproof bowl, add the butter and chocolate and melt them in the microwave for about 2 minutes. Remove it from the microwave.
2. Add sugar and use a spatula to stir it well. Add the eggs, milk, and vanilla extract and stir again. Finally, add the flour and stir it until even and smooth.
3. Pour the batter into the greased cake pan and use the spatula to level it. Place the pan on the trivet in the pot, close the lid, secure the pressure valve, and select Pressure on High for 15 minutes. Press Start/Stop.
4. Once the timer has gone off, do a natural pressure release for 10 minutes, then a quick pressure release, and open the lid.
5. Remove the rack with the pan on it and place the pan on a flat surface. Put a plate over the pan and flip the cake over into the plate. Pour the powdered sugar in a fine sieve and sift it over the cake. Use a knife to cut the cake into 8 slices and serve immediately (while warm).

Pumpkin Spice Bread Pudding

Servings: 8

Cooking Time: 5 Hours

Ingredients:

- Butter flavored cooking spray
- 1 ¼ cups almond milk, unsweetened
- ¾ cups pumpkin puree, sugar free
- ½ cup honey
- 1 egg
- 4 egg whites
- ½ tsp cinnamon
- ¼ tsp ginger
- 1/8 tsp allspice
- 1/8 tsp cloves
- 5 cups whole grain bread, cubed

Directions:

1. Lightly spray the cooking pot with cooking spray.
2. In a large bowl, whisk all ingredients, except bread, until smooth and combined.
3. Place the bread in the cooking pot and pour the liquid mixture over it, stir gently.
4. Add the lid and set to slow cooking on low. Cook 4-5 hours or until bread pudding passes the toothpick test. Let cool slightly before serving.

Nutrition Info:

- Calories 155,Total Fat 2g,Total Carbs 30g,Protein 6g,Sodium 162mg.

Rhubarb, Raspberry, And Peach Cobbler

Servings:6

Cooking Time: 40 Minutes

Ingredients:

- 1 cup all-purpose flour, divided
- ¾ cup granulated sugar
- ½ teaspoon kosher salt, divided
- 2½ cups diced fresh rhubarb
- 2½ cups fresh raspberries
- 2½ cups fresh peaches, peeled and sliced into ¾-inch pieces
- Cooking spray
- ¾ cup brown sugar
- ½ cup oat flakes (oatmeal)
- 1 teaspoon cinnamon
- Pinch ground nutmeg
- 6 tablespoons unsalted butter, sliced, at room temperature
- ½ cup chopped pecans or walnuts

Directions:

1. Select BAKE/ROAST, set temperature to 400°F, and set time to 30 minutes. Select START/STOP to begin. Let preheat for 5 minutes.
2. In a large bowl, whisk together ¼ cup of flour, granulated sugar, and ¼ teaspoon of salt. Add the rhubarb, raspberries, and peach and mix until evenly coated.
3. Grease a Ninja Multi-Purpose Pan or a 1½-quart round ceramic baking dish with cooking spray. Add the fruit mixture to the pan.
4. Place pan on Reversible Rack, making sure the rack is in the lower position. Cover pan with aluminum foil.
5. Once unit has preheated, place rack in pot. Close crisping lid and adjust temperature to 375°F. Cook for 25 minutes.

6. In a medium bowl, combine the remaining ¾ cup of flour, brown sugar, oat flakes, cinnamon, remaining ¼ teaspoon of salt, nutmeg, butter, and pecans. Mix well.
7. When cooking is complete, open lid. Remove the foil and stir the fruit. Spread the topping evenly over the fruit. Close crisping lid.
8. Select BAKE/ROAST, set temperature to 400°F, and set time to 15 minutes. Select START/STOP to begin. Cook until the topping is browned and the fruit is bubbling.
9. When cooking is complete, remove rack with pan from pot and serve.

Nutrition Info:

- Calories: 476,Total Fat: 19g,Sodium: 204mg,Carbohydrates: 76g,Protein: 6g.

Apple Vanilla Hand Pies

Servings: 8
Cooking Time: 40 Min

Ingredients:

- 2 apples, peeled, cored, and diced
- 1 package refrigerated piecrusts, at room temperature
- 1 lemon, juiced
- 3 tbsps sugar /45g
- ¼ tsp salt /1.25g
- 1 tsp vanilla extract /5ml
- 1 tsp corn-starch /5g
- Cooking spray

Directions:

1. In a large mixing bowl, combine the apples, sugar, lemon juice, salt, and vanilla. Allow the mixture to stand for 10 minutes, then drain, and reserve 1 tbsp of the liquid. In a small bowl, whisk the corn-starch into the reserved liquid and then, mix with the apple mixture. Put the crisping basket in the pot and close the crisping lid. Choose Air Crisp, set the temperature to 350°F or 177°C, and the time to 5 minutes. Press Start/Stop to preheat.
2. Put the piecrusts on a lightly floured surface and cut into 8 circles. Spoon a tbsp of apple mixture in the center of the circle, with ½ an inch's border around the dough. Brush the edges with water and fold the dough over the filling. Press the edges with a fork to seal.
3. Cut 3 small slits on top of each pie and oil with cooking spray. Arrange the pies in a single layer in the preheated basket. Close the crisping lid. Choose Air Crisp, set the temperature to 350°F or 177°C, and set the time to 12 minutes. Press Start/Stop to begin baking. Once done baking, remove, and place the pies on a wire rack to cool. Repeat with the remaining hand pies.

Irish Cream Flan

Servings: 3
Cooking Time: 10 Minutes

Ingredients:

- ¼ cup + 2 tbsp. sugar, divided
- 1 tbsp. water
- 1 cup half and half
- ¼ cup Irish cream flavored coffee creamer
- ¼ cup Irish cream liqueur
- 2 eggs

Directions:

1. In a small saucepan over medium heat, heat ¼ cup sugar until melted and a deep amber color. Swirl the pan occasionally to distribute the heat.
2. When the sugar reaches the right color remove from heat and carefully stir in the water until combined. Drizzle over the bottoms of 3 ramekins.
3. In a small oven-safe bowl, whisk the eggs.
4. In a small saucepan over medium heat, stir together half and half, creamer, Irish cream, and remaining sugar. Heat to simmering.
5. Gradually whisk the warm liquids into the eggs 2 tablespoons at a time, whisking constantly. After a 1/3 of the cream mixture has been added, slowly pour the remaining mixture into the eggs, whisking constantly until combined.
6. Pour 1 cup water into the cooking pot and add the trivet.
7. Pour the egg mixture into the ramekins and cover tightly with foil. Place them on the trivet.
8. Secure the lid and set to pressure cooking on high. Set the timer for 5 minutes. When the timer goes off, use natural release to remove the lid. Transfer custards to a wire rack and uncover to cool.
9. Cover with plastic wrap and refrigerate at least 4 hours before serving. To serve, use a small knife to loosen the custards from the sides of the ramekin and invert onto serving plate.

Nutrition Info:

- Calories 215,Total Fat 9g,Total Carbs 25g,Protein 7g,Sodium 134mg.

Pecan Apple Crisp

Servings: 6
Cooking Time: 35 Minutes

Ingredients:

- Butter flavored cooking spray
- 3 apples, peeled & diced
- 1 tbsp. sugar
- 1 3/8 tsp cinnamon, divided
- ¼ cup + ½ tbsp. almond flour, divided
- ½ cup oats
- ¼ cup pecans, chopped
- 1/8 tsp salt
- 1/8 cup coconut oil, melted
- 1/8 cup honey

Directions:

1. Place the rack in the cooking pot. Spray an 8x8-inch baking pan with cooking spray.

2. In a large bowl, combine apples, sugar, 1 teaspoon cinnamon, and ½ tablespoon almond flour, toss to coat the apples. Pour into prepared pan.
3. In a medium bowl, combine oats, remaining flour, pecans, remaining cinnamon, salt, oil, and honey. Use a fork to mix until mixture resembles fine crumbs. Pour over apples.
4. Place on the rack and add the tender-crisp lid. Set to bake on 350°F. Bake 30-35 minutes, or until apples are tender and topping is golden brown.
5. Transfer to a wire rack to cool slightly before serving.

Nutrition Info:

- Calories 293,Total Fat 18g,Total Carbs 30g,Protein 7g,Sodium 62mg.

Tiramisu Cheesecake

Servings: 12
Cooking Time: 1 Hour + Chilling Time

Ingredients:

- 16 ounces Cream Cheese, softened /480g
- 8 ounces Mascarpone Cheese, softened /240g
- 2 Eggs
- ½ cup White Sugar /65g
- 1 ½ cups Ladyfingers, crushed /195g
- 1 tbsp Cocoa Powder /15g
- 2 tbsp Powdered Sugar /30g
- 1 tbsp Kahlua Liquor /15ml
- 1 tbsp Granulated Espresso /15g
- 1 tbsp Butter, melted /15ml
- 1 tsp Vanilla Extract 5ml

Directions:

1. In a bowl beat the cream cheese, mascarpone, and white sugar. Gradually beat in the eggs, the powdered sugar and vanilla. Combine the first 4 ingredients, in another bowl. Spray a springform pan with cooking spray. Press the ladyfinger crust at the bottom. Pour the filling over. Cover the pan with a paper towel and then close it with aluminum foil.
2. Pour 1 cup or 250ml of water in your Foodi and lower the reversible rack. Place the pan inside and seal the pressure lid. Select Pressure and set time to 35 minutes at High pressure. Press Start. Press Start.
3. Wait for about 10 minutes before releasing the pressure quickly. Allow to cool completely before refrigerating the cheesecake for 4 hours.

Crispy Coconut Pie

Servings: 8
Cooking Time: 1 Hour

Ingredients:

- 3 eggs
- 1 ½ cup Stevia
- 1 cup coconut, grated
- ½ cup butter, melted
- 1 tbsp. vinegar
- 1 tsp vanilla
- 1/8 tsp salt
- 1 9" pie crust, raw

Directions:

1. In a large bowl, beat the eggs.
2. Add remaining ingredients and mix well. Pour into pie crust.
3. Use a foil sling to carefully place the pie in the cooking pot. Add the tender-crisp lid and set to bake on 350°F. Bake 1 hour or until top is nicely browned and crisp.
4. Transfer to a wire rack to cool before serving.

Nutrition Info:

- Calories 427,Total Fat 22g,Total Carbs 45g,Protein 3g,Sodium 304mg.

Chocolate Cake

Servings: 16
Cooking Time: 30 Minutes

Ingredients:

- Butter flavored cooking spray
- 8 Eggs
- 1 lb. semi-sweet chocolate chips
- 1 cup butter

Directions:

1. Place the rack in the cooking pot. Line the bottom of an 8-inch springform pan with parchment paper. Spray with cooking spray and wrap foil around the outside of the pan.
2. In a large bowl, beat eggs until double in size, about 6-8 minutes.
3. Place the chocolate chips and butter in a microwave safe bowl. Microwave at 30 second intervals until melted and smooth.
4. Fold 1/3 of the eggs into chocolate, folding gently just until eggs are incorporated. Repeat two more times.
5. Pour the batter into the prepared pan. Pour 1 ½ cups water into the cooking pot. Place the cake on the rack.
6. Add the tender-crisp lid and set to air fry on 325°F. Bake 25-30 minutes or until center is set.
7. Transfer to wire rack to cool. When cool, invert onto serving plate, top with fresh berries if desired. Slice and serve.

Nutrition Info:

- Calories 302,Total Fat 25g,Total Carbs 15g,Protein 5g,Sodium 130mg.

Mocha Cake

Servings: 6
Cooking Time: 3 Hours 37 Minutes
Ingredients:

- 2 ounces 70% dark chocolate, chopped
- ¾ cup butter, chopped
- ½ cup heavy cream
- 2 tablespoons instant coffee crystals
- 1 teaspoon vanilla extract
- 1/3 cup almond flour
- ¼ cup unsweetened cacao powder
- 1/8 teaspoon salt
- 5 large eggs
- 2/3 cup Erythritol

Directions:

1. Grease the Ninja Foodi's insert.
2. In a microwave-safe bowl, stir in the chocolate and butter and microwave on High for about 2 minutes or until melted completely, stirring after every 30 seconds.
3. Remove from the microwave and stir well.
4. Set aside to cool.
5. In a small bowl, stir in the heavy cream, coffee crystals, and vanilla extract and beat until well combined.
6. In a suitable bowl, mix the flour, cacao powder and salt.
7. In a large bowl, stir in the eggs and with an electric mixer, beat on high speed until slightly thickened.
8. Slowly, stir in the Erythritol and beat on high speed until thick and pale yellow.
9. Stir in the chocolate mixture and beat on low speed until well combined.
10. Stir in the dry flour mixture and mix until just combined.
11. Slowly stir in the cream mixture and beat on medium speed until well combined.
12. In the prepared Ninja Foodi's insert, add the mixture.
13. Close the Ninja Foodi's lid with a crisping lid and select "Slow Cooker".
14. Set on "Low" for 2½-3½ hours.
15. Press the "Start/Stop" button to initiate cooking.
16. Transfer the pan onto a wire rack for about 10 minutes.
17. Flip the baked and cooled cake onto the wire rack to cool completely.
18. Cut into desired-sized slices and serve.

Nutrition Info:

- Calories: 407; Fats: 39.7g; Carbohydrates: 6.2g; Proteins: 9g

Chocolate Soufflé

Servings: 2
Cooking Time: 25 Min
Ingredients:

- 2 eggs, whites and yolks separated
- 3 oz. chocolate, melted /90ml
- ¼ cup butter, melted /32.5ml
- 2 tbsp flour /30g
- 3 tbsp sugar /45g
- ½ tsp vanilla extract /2.5ml

Directions:

1. Beat the yolks along with the sugar and vanilla extract. Stir in butter, chocolate, and flour. Whisk the whites until a stiff peak forms.
2. Working in batches, gently combine the egg whites with the chocolate mixture. Divide the batter between two greased ramekins. Close the crisping lid and cook for 14 minutes on Roast at 330 °F or 166°C.

Portuguese Honey Cake

Servings: 8
Cooking Time: 15 Minutes
Ingredients:

- Butter flavored cooking spray
- 3 egg yolks, room temperature
- 2 eggs, room temperature
- 2 tbsp. powdered sugar
- ¼ cup honey
- 4 ½ tbsp. cake flour

Directions:

1. Place the rack in the cooking pot. Spray an 8-inch round baking dish with cooking spray and lightly coat with flour.
2. In a large bowl, beat egg yolks, eggs, and powdered sugar until combined.
3. In a small saucepan over medium heat, heat honey until it starts to simmer. Let simmer 2 minutes.
4. With mixer running, slowly beat in the hot honey. Beat mixture 8-10 minutes until pale and thick and doubled in size. Gently tap the bowl on the counter to remove any air bubbles.
5. Sift flour into mixture and gently fold in to combine. Pour the batter into the pan and tap again to remove air bubbles. Place the cake on the rack.
6. Add the tender-crisp lid and set to bake on 350°F. Bake the cake 15 minutes, center should still be soft.
7. Transfer to a wire rack and let cool in pan 30 minutes. Invert onto serving plate and serve.

Nutrition Info:

- Calories 97,Total Fat 3g,Total Carbs14 g,Protein 3g,Sodium 23mg.

Blueberry Lemon Pound Cake

Servings: 12

Cooking Time: 1 Hour 5 Minutes

Ingredients:

- Butter flavored cooking spray
- 1 ¾ cups + 2 tsp flour, divided
- 2 tsp baking powder
- ½ tsp salt
- 1 ½ cups blueberries
- ¾ cup butter, unsalted, soft
- 1 cup ricotta cheese, room temperature
- 1 ½ cups sugar
- 3 eggs, room temperature
- 1 tsp vanilla
- 1 tbsp. lemon zest

Directions:

1. Spray a loaf pan with cooking spray
2. In a medium bowl, combine flour, baking powder, and salt, mix well.
3. Add the blueberries to a bowl and sprinkle 2 tsp flour over them, toss to coat.
4. In a large bowl, beat together butter, ricotta, and sugar on high speed, until pale and fluffy.
5. Reduce speed to medium and beat in eggs, one at a time. Beat in zest and vanilla.
6. Stir in dry ingredients, a fourth at a time, until combined. Fold in blueberries and pour into prepared pan.
7. Add the rack to the cooking pot and place the pan on it. Add the tender-crisp lid and set to bake on 325°F. Bake 1 hour 10 minutes or until cake passes the toothpick test. After 40 minutes, cover the cake with foil.
8. Transfer to wire rack and let cool in pan 15 minutes. Then invert and let cool completely before serving.

Nutrition Info:

- Calories 303,Total Fat 17g,Total Carbs 32g,Protein 6g,Sodium 147mg.

Lime Blueberry Cheesecake

Servings: 6

Cooking Time: 30 Minutes

Ingredients:

- ¼ cup 1 teaspoon Erythritol
- 8 ounces cream cheese, softened
- 1/3 cup Ricotta cheese
- 1 teaspoon fresh lime zest, grated
- 2 tablespoons fresh lime juice
- ½ teaspoon vanilla extract
- 1 cup blueberries
- 2 eggs
- 2 tablespoons sour cream

Directions:

1. In a suitable, stir in ¼ cup of Erythritol and remaining ingredients except for eggs and sour cream and with a hand mixer, beat on high speed until smooth.
2. Stir in the eggs and beat on low speed until well combined, then fold in blueberries.
3. Transfer the mixture into a 6-inch greased springform pan evenly.
4. With a piece of foil, cover the pan.
5. In the Ninja Foodi's insert, place 2 cups of water.
6. Set a "Reversible Rack" in the Ninja Foodi's insert.
7. Place the springform pan over the "Reversible Rack".
8. Close the Ninja Foodi's lid with a pressure lid and place the pressure valve in the "Seal" position.
9. Select "Pressure" mode and set it to "High" for 30 minutes.
10. Press the "Start/Stop" button to initiate cooking.
11. Switch the pressure valve to "Vent" and do a "Natural" release.
12. Place the pan onto a wire rack to cool slightly.
13. Meanwhile, in a small bowl, stir in the sour cream and remaining erythritol and beat until well combined.
14. Spread the cream mixture on the warm cake evenly.
15. Refrigerate for about 6-8 hours before serving.

Nutrition Info:

- Calories: 182; Fats: 16.6g; Carbohydrates: 2.1g; Proteins: 6.4g

Raspberry Cheesecake

Servings: 6

Cooking Time: 30 Min

Ingredients:

- 1 ½ cups Graham Cracker Crust /195g
- ¾ cup Sugar /98g
- 1 cup Raspberries /130g
- 1 ½ cups Water /375ml
- 3 cups Cream Cheese /390g
- 3 Eggs
- ½ stick Butter, melted
- 1 tbsp fresh Orange Juice /15ml
- 1 tsp Vanilla Paste /5g
- 1 tsp finely grated Orange Zest /5g

Directions:

1. Insert the reversible rack into the Foodi, and add 1 ½ cups or 375ml of water. Grease a spring form. Mix in graham cracker crust with sugar and butter, in a bowl. Press the mixture to form a crust at the bottom.
2. Blend the raspberries and cream cheese with an electric mixer. Crack in the eggs and keep mixing until well combined. Mix in the remaining ingredients, and give it a good stir.
3. Pour this mixture into the pan, and cover the pan with aluminium foil. Lay the spring form on the tray. Select Pressure and set the time to 20 minutes at High pressure. Press Start. Once the cooking is complete, do a quick

pressure release. Refrigerate the cheesecake for at least 2 hours.

Chocolate Fondue

Servings: 12
Cooking Time: 5 Min
Ingredients:

- 10 ounces Milk Chocolate; chopped into small pieces /300g
- 1 ½ cups Lukewarm Water /375ml
- 8 ounces Heavy Whipping Cream /240ml
- 2 tsp Coconut Liqueur /60ml
- ¼ tsp Cinnamon Powder /1.25g
- A pinch of Salt

Directions:

1. Melt the chocolate in a heat-proof recipient. Add the remaining ingredients, except for the liqueur. Transfer this recipient to the metal reversible rack. Pour 1 ½ cups or 375ml of water into the cooker, and place a reversible rack inside.
2. Seal the pressure lid, choose Pressure, set to High, and set the time to 5 minutes. Press Start. Once the cooking is complete, do a quick pressure release. Pull out the container with tongs. Mix in the coconut liqueur and serve right now. Enjoy!

Baked Apples With Pecan Stuffing

Servings: 4
Cooking Time: 45 Minutes
Ingredients:

- 4 Fuji apples
- ½ cup pecans, chopped
- ¼ cup Stevia
- 2 tbsp. coconut oil, melted
- 1 tbsp. molasses
- ½ tsp cinnamon
- ½ cup water

Directions:

1. Hollow out the apples by carefully removing the core and seeds. Place in the cooking pot.
2. In a medium bowl, combine nuts, Stevia, oil, molasses, and cinnamon, mix well. Spoon into the apples, stuffing them fully.
3. Pour the water around the apples. Add the tender-crisp lid and set to bake on 350 °F. Bake 40-45 minutes. Let cool slightly before serving.

Nutrition Info:

- Calories 329,Total Fat 17g,Total Carbs 49g,Protein 2g,Sodium 11mg.

Cranberry Almond Rice Pudding

Servings: 6
Cooking Time: 40 Minutes
Ingredients:

- 1 tbsp. almonds
- 1 cup brown rice, short grain
- 2 ½ cups almond milk, unsweetened
- 1 tbsp. Stevia
- 2 tsp vanilla
- ½ tsp cinnamon
- ¼ cup dried cranberries, chopped

Directions:

1. Set cooker to sauté on low heat. Add almonds and toast 3-5 minutes. Transfer to cutting board and chop.
2. Increase heat to med-high. Add the rice, milk, Stevia, and vanilla and stir to mix. Bring to a boil stirring frequently.
3. Reduce heat to low and simmer, 35-40 minutes or until rice is cooked through.
4. To serve, ladle into bowls or dessert dishes. Sprinkle with cinnamon and top with almonds and cranberries.

Nutrition Info:

- Calories 200,Total Fat 4g,Total Carbs 36g,Protein 6g,Sodium 49mg.

Pumpkin Crème Brulee

Servings: 4
Cooking Time: 3:00 Hours
Ingredients:

- 1 egg yolk
- 1 egg, lightly beaten
- ¾ cup heavy cream
- 4 tbsp. pumpkin puree
- 1 tsp vanilla
- 4 tbsp. sugar, divided
- ¾ tsp pumpkin pie spice

Directions:

1. In a medium bowl, whisk together egg yolk and beaten egg, mix well.
2. Whisk in cream, slowly until combined.
3. Stir in pumpkin and vanilla and mix until combined.
4. In a small bowl, stir together 2 tablespoons sugar and pie spice. Add to pumpkin mixture and stir to blend.
5. Fill 4 small ramekins with mixture and place in the cooking pot. Carefully pour water around the ramekins, it should reach halfway up the sides.
6. Add the lid and set to slow cooking on low. Cook 2-3 hours or until custard is set.
7. Sprinkle remaining 2 tablespoons over the top of the custards. Add the tender-crisp lid and set to broil on 450°F. Cook another 2-3 minutes or until sugar caramelizes, be careful not to let it burn. Transfer ramekins to wire rack to cool before serving.

Nutrition Info:

- Calories 334,Total Fat 21g,Total Carbs 30g,Protein 6g,Sodium 59mg.

INDEX

C

Q

R

S

T

V

W

Z

Printed in Great Britain
by Amazon